A GRIP
on the
MANE of LIFE

An Authorized Biography of
Earl V. Shaffer
1918–2002

The story of the first man to hike the entire
Appalachian Trail in one continuous trek

From notes, interviews, and research compiled by
DAVID DONALDSON

Organized and written by
MAURICE J. FORRESTER

Appalachian
Trail Museum™

To Marge and Earle Towne,
a.k.a. Honey & Bear,
of The Cabin in Maine,
whose largeness of heart
and kindness
has been known to many

Published by
Appalachian Trail Museum
1120 Pine Grove Road
Gardners, PA 17324
www.atmuseum.org

Printed in the United States

10 9 8 7 6 5 4 3 2 1

First Edition

Cover design by Sanne Larsen Bagby
Cover photo by ArtoftheTrail.com; cover portrait of Earl Shaffer courtesy of the Earl Shaffer Foundation

Unless otherwise indicated, all photos are courtesy of the Shaffer family and the Earl Shaffer Foundation, and may not be reproduced without written consent.

ISBN-13: 978-0-9912215-2-3

Contents

List of Illustrations

Preface

The reputation of Earl Shaffer, although well established within the hiking community, has only infrequently crossed paths with the larger world. One of those rare intersections occurred in 1998 when, at the age of 79, he walked for the third time the entire length of the Appalachian Trail in a single trip—a distance of more than 2,000 miles. On that most recent occasion, as he moved north from Georgia toward his destination at Mount Katahdin in Maine, he was bedeviled by representatives of the media who became increasingly persistent and numerous as he neared his goal. Earl himself was alternately flattered and annoyed by this unwonted attention.

In 1948 he had become the first person known to have hiked the entire Appalachian Trail in a single trip, a journey undertaken as a way of ridding himself of the malaise that had resulted from his Army experiences. Fifty years later he became the oldest person to have performed this feat. In 1965, between those two hikes, he made the hike from north to south.

In the pantheon of noteworthy trail people, Earl Shaffer's position is secure. He ranks with those other legendary trail personages: Benton MacKaye and Myron Avery. MacKaye gave birth to the concept; Avery took the concept and built a trail from it; and Shaffer demonstrated the potential of the finished product.

Between hikes Earl built trails and trail shelters (sometimes single-handedly), and he helped found a hiking club and establish a statewide hiking federation. On behalf of the Appalachian Trail Conference, he responded to requests for advice from novice hikers.

Primarily though, he thought of himself as a writer. Although his best known book is *Walking With Spring*, a prose hiking memoir, his preferred medium was verse. As a poet he believed himself unappreciated, a belief that has some merit. His poetic output was immense but uneven, the published portion being only a small fraction of the whole. A selection of the best of his poetry would make a volume of respectable size and quality. Such a book has yet to be published.

Early in June 1948, shortly after passing the midpoint of his walk from Georgia to Maine, Earl Shaffer paused at a trail register to read what previous hikers had written. He was particularly struck by some lines of verse that an enthusiastic hiker had quoted from the poem "The Outland Trails," by the American poet Henry Herbert Knibbs:

> Sun and wind and the sound of rain!
> Hunger and thirst and strife!
> God! To be out on the trails again
> with a grip on the mane of life!

It is easy to see why Earl was attracted to these lines, both as poetry and philosophy. From beginning to end he had a firm grip on life's mane even when the ride was rougher than he might have wished.

—M.J.F.

Foreword

Most readers picking up this biography will think of his thru-hiking and backpacking history as the most important thing in Earl's life. This was just a small accomplishment during his lifetime. He considered his Army service during World War II and his poetry to be his most satisfying achievements of all. He was born the "middle" child on what is known as "False Armistice Day" of World War I. He was born in the city of York, but the family moved to a small rural farm known for its food growing ability in the village of Shiloh, northwest of the city of York, when Earl was five.

This set the tone for Earl's future: fur trapping, farm work, and outdoor activities in general. He met a neighboring farm boy soon after moving to Shiloh. They would grow up together hiking, trapping and working as farm hands. Walter Winemiller was a true woodsman and he and Earl got along fine together until Walter's death at Iwo Jima during World War II. Earl never fully recovered from the shock of Walter's death.

Earl had strong principles and followed through on anything he started.

Although slight of build he was an excellent farm hand during his teen years. He first worked as a carpenter before volunteering for one year of Army service. Of course during that first year Pearl Harbor happened, and everyone was in for the duration. He served in the Pacific theatre of operations, many times on dangerous assignments installing RADAR and communications equipment in forward areas. His idle time was spent writing poetry and on his hobby of photography.

Returning from the war, Earl initially did carpenter work. Later his work was primarily buying, refinishing and selling antiques. He clerked at a local auction for many years. In 1948 while still recovering from Army duty he decided to attempt what was considered impossible: Hike the entire Appalachian Trail in one season. He endured many hardships as covered in his first book *Walking With Spring*. He was stubborn and tenacious, and completed the journey much to the amazement of the Appalachian Trail Conference. Earl was never quite satisfied with his writings. He edited and finally self-published in 1981 his first book *Walking With Spring*. Later it was picked up by the A.T. Conference and is still in print today. His poetry was typed, arranged and edited but he was never quite satisfied with the result.

It wasn't until 1998 after meeting photographer Bart Smith on his anniversary hike that Earl produced another book. Westcliffe Publishers in conjunction with Bart Smith asked Earl for a submission. Earl was under the impression it would be published as *Ode to the Appalachian Trail*. The publisher Westcliffe turned Earl's *Ode* into a narrative calling it *Calling Me Back to the Hills* after a poem that Earl wrote while in the Army in the South Pacific. Earl was furious and I finally convinced him they were following the trend of outdoor books. I promised him it would be published in *Ode* format at a later date. Earl was concerned about getting his writings into print. We formed the Earl Shaffer Foundation for that purpose.

Earl did not want to earn any money from his writings but preferred to have the proceeds given to some of his favorite charities. The results of the writings so far may be found at www.earlshaffer.org.

He was the family member that we all took for granted. He was popular with people regardless of age or livelihood. Dedicated in his views of personal rights of all persons. Always had opinions on current events. A friend of the Quakers. He was an environmentalist with sympathy for the American Indian.

He was my brother. All of his brothers and sister admired him even if we didn't all approve of his life style.

—John Shaffer

Introduction

"Nothing lives long, only the earth and mountains."
—White Antelope, Southern Cheyenne

In 1948 a loaf of bread cost fourteen cents. Citation won the Triple Crown. Truman defeated Dewey. Mahatma Gandhi was assassinated and the Republic of Israel was born. Laurence Olivier won the Academy Award for best actor while Dinah Shore ruled the American pop charts. The 33⅓ rpm vinyl record replaced the 78 rpm to become the latest innovation in recording technology. The ENIAC computer, the world's first super-computer, had been operational for barely a year. The Berlin Airlift and Marshall Plan helped a war-torn Europe back onto its feet. And on August 5 of that year, a young man from York, Pennsylvania, accomplished something many believed impossible: a hike along the entire length of the Appalachian Trail.

Fast forward fifty years: Late May, 1998, just outside Erwin, Tennessee, I first met Earl Shaffer as he was crossing the Nolichucky River along the wonderfully named Chestoa Pike. The first thing I noticed about Earl were his eyes; they had a steely intensity which seemed to shine forth, like the look of a hawk sizing up its prey. Quite noticeable also was Earl's astonishingly youthful appearance. In fact, his entire demeanor belied his seventy-nine years. He was lean and obviously fit, having covered the 330 miles from trail's start in a little over three weeks, whereas it had taken me five weeks to cover the same distance—and I was less than half his age! Barely two years after reading Earl's seminal hiking book, *Walking With Spring*, in my adopted hometown of San Diego, I wondered to myself, could this really be happening?

Indeed, it was happening. And now here was the proclaimed living legend, standing before a rag-tag collection of would-be long distance hikers, casually munching a hamburger and swapping stories, just another hiker. Hardly. As with so many others who were awestruck when meeting this man for the first time, I felt a little smaller. Perhaps, in my case, because at the outset of my hike I'd chosen as my trail name, Spirit of '48, inspired entirely by the man with whom I was now sharing a meal. Only in my wildest dreams did I imagine meeting Earl Shaffer. Introducing myself, I told Earl my name was David, forgoing the ritual of explaining to him my trail moniker.

Our respective paths along the trail would cross on and off for the next several months. As fate would have it, just north of Andover, Maine, we teamed up to complete the last 260 miles of trail together. Local as well as national media, including The Associated Press and NBC News, descended upon Abol Bridge in Maine and were on hand to record the last day's hike on October 21, 1998. Two weeks earlier Harry Smith and a CBS news crew had tramped along the trail with us, producing a very complimentary piece on Earl that aired within days of the finish. For myself, who six months earlier was wondering if I had what it takes to complete a 2,000-mile hike through the rugged, mountainous terrain, this was a truly storybook ending.

With his third and final thru-hike finished, Earl returned to the six partially wooded acres in Pennsylvania he called home, where he grew vegetables and raised goats. I relocated to Northern Virginia, where I'd grown up and had family. Earl was barely a ninety-minute drive away. Our friendship, forged on the trail, flourished in the following years. Against this backdrop, I came up with the idea of writing about the stories Earl had shared with me. During our time spent together, Earl regaled me with stories of his life: growing up poor during the Depression on a rural farm in Pennsylvania; working as a farmhand; his deep friendship with Walter Winemiller and their plans, including panning for gold in the Klondike and hiking the Appalachian Trail; clerking at auctions; buying and selling antiques; protesting the building of Kinzua Dam; four and a half years of service during World War Two; yodeling; writing poetry; his time spent hiking; and, of course, his beloved Appalachian Trail. As anyone who has ever read *Walking With Spring* knows, Earl was a writer of natural, gifted talent. Therefore, it was with a certain sense of awe and apprehension that I broached the subject with Earl of writing a biography. After some minor hemming and hawing, and to my great surprise, Earl agreed.

In the spring following his final hike, Earl was honored at Appalachian Trail Days, celebrated annually in Damascus, Virginia, and attended that year by over ten thousand people. Earl and I drove there together through a driving rainstorm and spent the hours on the road catching up and reliving our life on the trail. With Earl's celebrity status among the hiking community firmly established, large crowds appeared wherever he went. Just walking to breakfast one morning took over an hour due to all the well-wishers wanting to stop and talk to Earl. Earl always made time to talk trail, and it seemed in those instances he felt most comfortable, happiest to be amongst his tribe. To top that, in June the Smithsonian Institution American History Museum in Washington, D.C., adopted into its collection gear used by Earl on his historic 1948 hike, including his well-worn Russell Birdshooter boots. Many other awards and trips to hiker get-togethers filled the remaining years of Earl's life, cementing his status as an American Outdoor Icon.

In the beginning stages of the biography, I spent several hours interviewing and recording Earl and others who knew Earl. I spent an entire winter in Millinocket, Maine, transcribing cassette tapes into computer files. Later, there were trips to the Library of Congress and Smithsonian Archives Center for further research. Yet, after several years I was no closer to having written the book than when I started. I struggled with how best to capture in words the essence of another human being. Intuitively my mind informed me this must be the challenge of all would-be writers. For, it was only in person one could hear Earl's distinct pronunciation of the word "App-uh-latch-in"; only in person when he sang his hauntingly sublime "Timberline Song," one felt his passion for solitude; only in person when telling his stories in that mesmerizing baritone voice one could relive his trailblazing hike of 1948. Those stories, *his* stories, the stories of someone whose memory spanned a good deal of the twentieth century, of a vanishing way of life, the stories of someone who himself has made a bit of history, are all we now have left.

Serendipitously, I eventually moved to York, Pennsylvania, along with a wife and two children, buying a house owned by Earl's brother John which overlooks the seven-acre property called by Earl's family, "The Old Place." It was here Earl grew up, lived for forty years of his life, and was a place he loved dearly. My children play in the same creek Earl did. During the winter I can see through the trees to the back of the upper meadow, across to where Earl's friend Walter grew up. I can scarcely imagine the emptiness Earl must have felt upon returning home at war's end, only to look across that same field and know he would never see his best friend again.

Near the end of his life, I would go to visit Earl at the Veterans Hospice. Sometimes I would wheel him around the outskirts of the property and we would reminisce about hiking together or some other topic, to help pass the time. The last time I saw Earl, the day he died, we were alone in his room together. By then Earl was beyond communicating with words. His breathing was labored and his eyes were roving the ceiling as if in search of something. It was apparent he was very near death. I admired Earl so much then, just as I did watching him ascend Mt. Katahdin in 1998: fearless and undaunted, fighting and clawing his way to the end. Just before Earl passed, I placed my hand across his forehead and said, "Imagine what it would be like to sleep on Mt. Katahdin tonight." Shortly thereafter, he was gone.

Ah, the plans of life, how they can change. My son's middle name is Earl. Sometimes, I like to dream that one day we too will hike the trail together, sharing camaraderie and swapping stories like in the days of old, with my Trail Partner. But knowing the way of life only time will tell if this dream will come to pass. As I have walked the trail of family and career, the biography seemed to be falling more and more to a side-trail. Fortunately for me I was introduced to Maurice Forrester, who wrote the introduction to *Walking With Spring*. In my stead, Maurice hoisted virtual pen to paper and has breathed life into Earl's incredible stories, for it is in those stories that one comes closest to discovering just who this remarkable man was.

—David Donaldson
June 2013
York, Pennsylvania

THE SOMEWHERE TRAIL

There's a footloose pathway filing
out across the future years,
Its impartial lure beguiling
unto laughter, dearth or tears,
Branching widely onto somewhere
east or west or south or north
For the faithful who will find there
that for which they venture forth.

There are unfound treasures waiting
in some yet untrespassed land
For which fate is contemplating
an adventure still unplanned.
Take the somewhere trail to nowhere;
take the high roads wild and free
And perhaps I'll meet you out there
if the fates should so decree.

There's a trail out through the darkness
to a land of dawning hope,
To the widening horizons
of a broader clearer scope,
Out across the petty wrangling
to a truer, closer bond
Of the long reluctant changeling
with the waiting host beyond.

There are havens free from conflict,
there is right to live and grow
Where is found the peace intrinsic
such as men by right should know.
Take the somewhere trail of learning
through the corridor of dawn
Where the flame of truth is burning
beckoning forever on.

—Earl V. Shaffer

PART ONE

BETWEEN THE WARS

CHAPTER 1

PARENTS

E arly in November of 1918 it became apparent that the First World War was quickly approaching its end. The American public waited in a fever of excitement for the final victory. Although the actual signing of the armistice did not occur until November 11, there were a number of earlier anticipatory rumors. One of the "false armistice" reports circulated on November 8, the day that in Pennsylvania's York County witnessed the birth of Earl Shaffer. In honor of the great victory that was believed to have just been won, the new infant was given the middle name Victor.

Earl Victor Shaffer was born in York, Pennsylvania, to Daniel Shaffer and Frances Attitia Gallagher, parents who blended German (Pennsylvania Dutch) on his father's side with Irish and a little Welsh—and possibly a bit of Native American—on his mother's. His mother's grandfather on her father's side fled Ireland during the potato famine of the mid-19th century. It is part of the Shaffer family's oral tradition that, once arrived in America, this ancestor married a woman who was half American Indian. (Earl later assigned great significance to this reported Indian connection, believing that it accounted for much of his adaptability to the woods and trails in which he wandered.) Frances herself was said to have skills more likely to be found in an American Indian than an Irish colleen. For example, she was able to skin animals Indian fashion and make fish hooks from bones. Both of these skills she passed on to her sons.

Frances's mother's heritage was also largely Irish, although she was known to have had a grandmother who was Welsh. Frances's father was

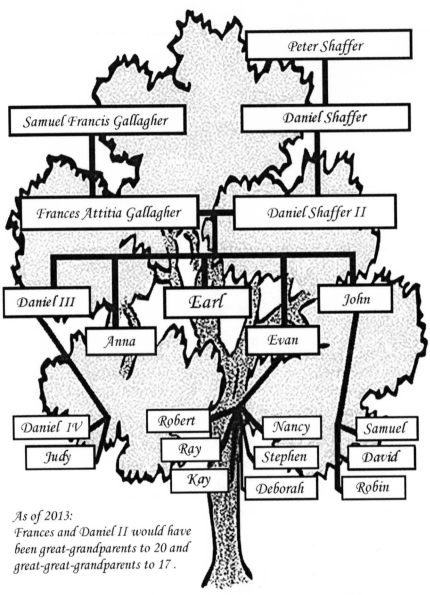

Peter Shaffer

Samuel Francis Gallagher

Daniel Shaffer

Frances Attitia Gallagher

Daniel Shaffer II

Daniel III

Earl

John

Anna

Evan

Daniel IV

Robert

Nancy

Samuel

Judy

Ray

Stephen

David

Kay

Deborah

Robin

As of 2013:
Frances and Daniel II would have
been great-grandparents to 20 and
great-great-grandparents to 17 .

Earl Shaffer Family Tree

a farmer, described by Earl as being "black Irish,"[1] and tall, standing about six foot two. Although her father was born into an Irish Catholic family, he left the Church; her mother was Irish Protestant.

Frances's father—Grandfather Gallagher—stayed for a time with the Shaffers in their Shiloh home following the death of his second wife. He was, it seems, a restless man, and one morning after only six months or so, just as the children were leaving for school, he came downstairs carrying two suitcases. Earl's sister Anna recalls her mother saying, "Oh dad, don't, don't, don't."

His reply was, "Frances, my feet are itching." He loved to travel; from Chambersburg, a town about fifty miles to the west, he wrote Frances a letter saying, "I'm going to head west. As soon as I'm settled, I'll let you know where I am." The family never heard from him again.

Earl's father, on the other hand, came from undiluted Pennsylvania Dutch stock. The Dutch and Irish mixture did not always blend well, but their common commitment to the family they had created kept them together.

MOTHER

The new victory child, the third born to Frances and Daniel, was the middle one of five, of whom only the second, Anna, was a girl. Earl seemed to attach great significance to the fact that he was the middle child of five. Throughout his life he often referred to himself as the middle son. "The middle son," he would say, "was born in the middle of Scorpio in the middle of the night" while the rest of the country was celebrating the supposed end of the Great War. The regular family doctor was in France, so the attending physician was an elderly man who happened to be asleep on a couch downstairs at the time of the birth and was awakened by the sound of the new infant hitting the floor, "probably on my head," Earl would add. The future iconic hiker's youthful propensity for falling was further confirmed when, as a toddler, he fell down the cellar stairs. "They claim I almost broke my back," he observed a bit skeptically. He did, however, have a lifelong scar on his back that resulted from the mishap on the cellar stairs.

The first four children were born within a period of less than six years, with the youngest, John, coming along seven years later. Frances

---

[1]The meaning of the term Black Irish is variable and its origin obscure. Most commonly it is used to describe persons of Irish ancestry whose appearance does not conform to the standard Irish stereotype of blue or green eyes, reddish hair, and pale skin, but rather have brown eyes, dark hair and dark complexions.

would comment in later years to Anna that John was the only baby she could really enjoy since the others appeared so close together. In the early years, more often than not, she had two in diapers at the same time—diapers that had to be washed by hand on a washing board.

Frances was a sickly woman in the best of circumstances, and each pregnancy brought nine months of illness. Indeed, the time of Earl's birth may have been the very worst, coming as it did during the Spanish influenza pandemic. Frances contracted the disease, and although she survived, Earl attributes his own survival during his first few weeks to the care he received from his paternal grandmother. It may have been his contemplation years later of this threat to his own and his mother's survival that caused him to believe that the flu pandemic was the world's first instance of germ warfare, introduced by Germany in a frantic effort to stave off its impending defeat.

Earl's first recollection of his mother goes back to when he was only two years old—an unusually early age for a first remembrance, as he readily admitted. But he insisted that the memories associated with a visit to the hospital to have his tonsils and adenoids removed were quite vivid. He remembered his mother coaxing him through the hospital door because, he said, it was not in her nature to use force and drag him inside. Other memories connected with that youthful hospital visit were equally vivid. He remembered his mother helping a nurse tuck him into a bed. Then he recalled a ride down the hall to the operating room, and a voice in his ear saying, "go to sleep." Remembered too was the return home where the other children teased him because he had left a part of himself behind at the hospital, which for some reason infuriated him.

Frances Shaffer was a small, pretty woman, about five foot two, who carried herself with erect pride. Her skin was very light and subject to sunburn; she never tanned. She had a lush growth of straight black hair and bluish eyes that her children variously described as blue, green, lavender, or purplish blue. (Earl described her as being typical "black Irish.")

Frances was a powerful influence in the lives of all her children, perhaps most notably in that of Earl who inherited her green thumb and her way with animals. They lived on a small farm where Frances raised vegetables and chickens and kept a cow. She would take her eggs, butter, and vegetables in a buggy to York, the family's former place of residence, where she would sell them to her erstwhile neighbors. Before he was old enough to go to school Earl would accompany her on these trips. After a few years the horse and buggy was replaced with a Ford Model T.

Earl felt that he was his mother's favorite, a belief he supported by noting that she went to more effort with him than she did with any of the others. Although she herself never went beyond the fifth grade, she taught Earl to read and write even before he started school, imparting to him her own beautiful handwriting. When he was only in the first grade Earl's handwriting was already so good that teachers from higher grades brought their students to Earl's classroom to observe his writing.

Although the Shaffer family had moved to Shiloh from York, in part because the parents thought the more rural environment would be good for the children, country living was not without its own

Frances Gallagher Shaffer, age eighteen, Earl's mother

perils—real and imaginary. Hobos passing by on the road on their way from one railroad line to another were one cause for alarm. Even more so from the mother's perspective were the gypsies who occasionally set up camp in the neighborhood. Frances lived in great fear of these people, believing—as did many in that era—that gypsies commonly stole children. To protect herself and her family from this threat she insisted on acquiring a .25 caliber pistol, which she herself learned to use, becoming an expert with the weapon. At their mother's insistence the children were all taught how to use it. Earl, however, readily acknowledged that he could never hit anything with it.

Son John tells of an incident when Frances was home alone, and the dog started barking outside. Suspecting the possibility of a prowler lurking about, she went out with a flashlight and her rifle. Shining the light around, she spotted something up in a tree that she thought was a man. "Come down or I'll shoot," she shouted. There was no response so she took aim and fired. Down fell a screech owl, shot right between the eyes. There is some sibling disagreement on this point, however. Sister Anna always insisted that the owl was shot with a pistol, to which John's response was that if so, at that range the result was pure luck.

When they moved to the small farm near Shiloh, they acquired a horse that came with the property. The horse had apparently been subjected to abuse by a man (or men), since whenever Earl's father approached the animal, it began kicking and biting. Frances, on the other hand, could harness the horse, hitch it to the buggy, and drive into York with no objection at all from the animal. "She got along with animals," Earl would say, "and so do I."

Along with her many other talents Frances was also an accomplished seamstress who made most of her family's clothes. Anna recalls the "big, long flannel nightgowns" her mother made, and also notes that she did a lot of crocheting and embroidering.

Frances was also the primary disciplinarian when it came to keeping the children in line. Earl tells of an incident when he was about ten, and decided to run away. He went to the far edge of the farm and waited there until dark, having apparently forgotten that he was afraid of the dark. It was therefore not long after sunset when he decided to return home. After giving the errant boy his supper, the mother then brought out the dreaded razor strop. First she explained carefully why she was using this instrument, and then applied it judiciously. The strop was used, according to Earl, because it would sting and hurt, but not do any serious damage. This was the last time he ever tried to run away.

It was Frances's aim in life to raise perfect children, and her greatest disappointments came when any of her children fell short of that perfection. Anna remembered that when she was about nine she told her mother a lie for the first time. Initially the trusting mother believed her daughter, but later apparently she discovered the truth. That night Anna woke up to hear her mother crying, and heard her say to Anna's father, "But Dan, we've never lied to our children, how could we have a liar in the family? Dan, how could this be?"

When Anna was seventeen and a junior in high school, she was obliged to drop out of school to take care of her mother during the latter's final illness. Then when her mother died Anna continued to stay home to care for the younger children. Before her death the mother once asked Anna if she minded dropping out of school. Anna's answer was "No," although she had long dreamed of going to college.

Shortly before her fortieth birthday Frances entered the hospital with what had been diagnosed as jaundice; there she underwent gall bladder surgery—a much more serious procedure in those days. Although she came through the surgery well and appeared to be recovering, she suddenly died for reasons that remain unclear. Her oldest son, Dan, commented that it was one of those cases where "the operation was successful but the patient died."

Anna, Earl, and Evan went to see her just a few days before she died, and she seemed to be doing fine. She was talking to the other women on the ward about them, and they expected her to be coming home soon. John was too young to be allowed in the hospital as a visitor; he waited in the car in the parking lot, and his mother stood at the window to wave to him.

The Shaffers lived a distance of about half a mile from a telephone, and Evan recalls that one morning, about five o'clock, somebody knocked on the door. "My dad went down and talked to the visitor who then left. Very, very slowly, my dad came up the stairs. At the top of the stairs he called to all of us, to make sure that we were awake. And then he told us that our mother had died. That's one of those things indelibly imprinted in my mind."

Earl's last memory of his mother while she was alive was of her waving to him from the hospital window. The viewing was at home and the burial from the church. She died in 1933, just two days after Christmas.

FATHER

Earl Shaffer's great-great-grandfather (on his father's side) was one Johannes Shaffer who was born in 1759 to a family, of German origin, already settled in British North America, and living at that time probably in what would later become New York State. At some point between 1770 and 1800 he moved to York County in Pennsylvania where he settled in Windsor Township. In due course Johannes fathered twelve children, one of whom was named Peter. This Peter had a son named Daniel, who in turn had a son also named Daniel. The second Daniel was Earl's father, who was born June 20, 1889. Earl's oldest brother was the third in line to bear the name Daniel.

Daniel Shaffer, Earl's father, grew up on a farm where he worked as a teenager, developing the kind of strength and sturdiness that resulted from farm work in that era. His son Dan describes him as being tough and rugged, even though relatively small in stature. At five foot six he was shorter than all four of his sons. Although Daniel's formal education did not extend beyond the fourth or fifth grade, he read extensively, being especially fond of Shakespeare and poetry in general. The Shaffer family spoke Pennsylvania Dutch at home, and the young Daniel did not learn English until he started school at about the age of five. By the time he reached adulthood, however, in addition to Pennsylvania Dutch he

Daniel Shaffer II, Earl's father

spoke and read fluently both English and standard German.

Daniel worked at various jobs and trades as they became available, including silk weaving and cabinet making. He also worked for a time in a brick yard. He learned blacksmithing as a very young man. This led to his first job in York with a manufacturer of wagons where Daniel's job involved the fabrication of the various metal parts that were used in these conveyances.

After the wagon works burned, Daniel took a job with a chain manufacturer, where he did hand welding over an open fire. In time he was offered the position of supervisor, which he declined since he did not want the responsibility that went with a supervisory position. Thereafter he found the attitude at the wagon works increasingly unpleasant, and eventually left to take a job with a competitor. In his new job he organized the company's first union, and later became the union president, serving in that capacity for many years. He had a lifelong interest in the labor movement in which he played an active role.

While he was working at the chain works, those of the Shaffer children who were attending high school in York would ride in to school with their father at seven o'clock, an hour and a half before school started. This was necessary because of the lack of school bus service and the family's inability to afford public transportation which, in any case, was so inconvenient as to be a less than desirable option. Fortunately such problems were apparently so common that the school opened the auditorium well before school started, and early arrivals were able to study while they waited for classes to begin.

Not long after moving to Shiloh, Daniel bought a Model T Ford, and learned how to take the vehicle apart and put it back together again. Evan reports that every time his father took the Model T apart it ran a whole lot better when he reassembled it. What seemed puzzling, however, was the fact that on each of these occasions he finished with a cigar box full of leftover parts.

Although Daniel "could not carry a tune" according to his eldest son, he was very fond of music and built and repaired violins. Earl notes that his father's woodworking skills were limited and specialized, observing that he could make a violin but could not build a building. He learned to play by ear the violins he made, although he never learned to read a note of music.

He was a man of many interests. In addition to his love of music, both classical and semi-classical, and his voracious reading, he also did water-color painting. When Frances accepted his marriage proposal, he went outside and picked a handful of violets from which he made a watercolor painting. Other watercolors created by Daniel which are still in existence include woodland scenes and a painting of a horse. Regrettably a painting that he did of his wife was later destroyed in a fire.

His children remembered Daniel as an affectionate parent who tended to be easy going and mild mannered. He never remarried after his wife's untimely death in 1933 even though he was himself only in his early forties. Some of his children attributed this decision to the stories he had heard of "evil stepmothers" who abused their stepchildren. At bedtime he would sit down, position the younger children on each knee, and sing to them (presumably off-key) before putting them to bed. Like his wife, Daniel had a strong sense of personal integrity. If anything, he was too lax with his children, without any of the instincts of the born disciplinarian.

In matters of discipline he much preferred to leave this responsibility to the children's mother, to whom he deferred in most matters. But not always, or at least not entirely. Frances was adamantly opposed to both drinking and smoking. Daniel did not drink and generally he did not smoke either. When it came to smoking, however, he did not share his wife's mission-ary zeal. At election time, when the local politicians handed out

"Violets," painting by Earl's father

cigars, Daniel would take one, smoke it for perhaps ten minutes or so, and then put it out. The half smoked cigar would then be placed on the mantlepiece where it would remain for months. Earl claimed his father performed this ritual only to show that he was not henpecked.

When it came to dealing with problems involving his children, Daniel tended to have a very light touch. Unfortunately his solutions were sometimes less than fully successful. Earl and Evan as children shared a bed, with one cover between them. Invariably disputes arose between the two regarding a fair allocation of the bed covering. The result would be a noisy tug of war between the boys. Daniel's solution was to install two slabs of wood at the head of the bed and two at the foot forming a groove at each end. In this groove he fastened a long board with the blanket underneath. Earl and Evan, however, quickly discovered that by bracing themselves they could still pull the cover under the board. The simpler solution of getting two separate covers was evidently not tried. Perhaps this too was a function of the family's limited financial resources.

Older brother Dan reports that Earl and Evan both tended to talk in their sleep. Sometimes they would do so simultaneously, but with each one holding forth on a different subject. This resulted in some highly amusing unintended conversations causing frequent chuckles on the part of Dan who slept in the same bedroom with the other two.

Life was not easy for the Shaffers during the Great Depression. At times Daniel was working only three days a week at a weekly salary of $2.50. This was precious little to support a family of seven. Shoes for the entire family at that time would cost $1.98, a cost, however small, that they could not afford. Daniel's response was to buy a big piece of leather, cut out the soles for each one, and nail them on the still usable uppers.

Daniel had a curious connection with Henry E. Lanius, who served in the Pennsylvania State House of Representatives from 1912 until 1920 when a heart attack incapacitated him for a couple of years. Lanius returned to politics in 1922 and served in the State Senate until 1942. As a young man he had been blinded at the age of twenty-one in an industrial accident while working as a machinist. This event led to his becoming a vigorous advocate of the blind throughout his legislative career. It is known that Daniel Shaffer lived with Lanius for a time while working on the senator's farm. While there, Daniel would often read to the older man. Throughout his life Lanius remained a close friend and mentor to Daniel. Earl's youngest brother, John, remembers family trips to visit the senator.

According to Earl, his mother cooked to please his father, whose Pennsylvania Dutch dietary preferences ran to the heavy, greasy meals typical of that day. Bean soup, one of his favorite dishes, always gave him violent headaches—what Daniel called "sick headaches." But he refused to change his diet. Earl reports that his father used to raise pigs "because he liked pig meat."

Henry E. Lanius

He died at the relatively early age of fifty-nine from a sudden heart attack. Although he reportedly had medical support within minutes, nothing could be done to save him. He had just had a physical examination only a few weeks before he was stricken. At that time the doctor gave him a clean bill of health and commented on his excellent physical condition. It seems likely that the food he loved most while he lived contributed to his sudden demise.

CHAPTER 2

BROTHERS AND SISTER

DANIEL

Earl's oldest brother, Daniel, was the third in successive generations to bear that name. (There is now one in the fourth generation.) Daniel III was born March 31, 1915, in York, Pennsylvania. In time he grew to become, at six-foot-three, the tallest member of the family. With blue eyes and dark hair, Dan looked like his mother's side of the family. According to Anna he was his mother's "pride and joy" from whom she expected more perhaps than she should have. This led to intermittent friction between the two.

Anna reports that when she was growing up she went to Dan with any problems, and only if he was unable to offer a solution would she turn to her parents. "I really looked up to him until our late teens; then I found out he didn't know absolutely everything." Anna also observes that Dan was very honest and would not tell a lie.

After spending some time in the Army, Dan settled into working in a machine shop while simultaneously taking college courses connected to shop practice and design. He stayed in that field for the rest of his working life, the final twenty-seven years of which were with Cole Steel in York. About half of that time was spent as a tool and die specialist, making sheet metal equipment, and the other half designing the tooling to make office furniture.

ANNA

Anna Mary Shaffer was born November 26, 1916, on the 1900 block of West King Street in York. She lived in York and Shiloh for eighty years

Daniel III, Earl's oldest brother,
in 1932

Anna, Earl's only sister

before moving with her husband, Frederick Miller, to South Carolina. Four years later they returned to Pennsylvania. The couple never had any children.

When Anna was seven years old the family moved from the city to a small farm near Shiloh, a few miles northwest of York. In the Shaffer family no one was born in a hospital. They were all born at home, with the doctor coming to the house and their father's mother coming to assist. Dan, Anna, and Earl were born at the same house, and Evan at a different York house. Only John was born at the country home to which they had by then moved.

Anna lived at the farm—"The Old Place"—until her father died. Then her oldest brother, Dan, and his wife, Betty, moved there from Philadelphia and took over the farm for a while. Betty, however, soon decided that she did not particularly like farm life, and the property subsequently was purchased by Anna.

EVAN

Evan Shaffer was born November 17, 1920, making him almost exactly two years younger than Earl. Of the four Shaffer boys, Earl and Evan are the two closest to each other in age. This inevitably brought them into more contact with each other than with any other of their siblings. Evan's

Evan, Earl's younger brother, in 1938   *John, Earl's youngest brother, in 1946*

recollection of their youthful relationship is somewhat warmer than Earl's.

Being so close in age, much of what the two did as boys was done in tandem. Before they were even in their teens both boys began working seasonally for neighboring farmers. The two Shaffer boys along with the neighboring Winemiller boys became so good at farm work—threshing, cutting, shocking, and husking corn—that they were always assured of jobs until the changing season brought an end to the work.

Evan enlisted in what was then the U.S. Army Air Corps on December 8, 1941, the day after the Japanese attack on Pearl Harbor. Following his final training at the officer candidate school at Roswell, New Mexico, he was commissioned as a B-29 flight engineer. To his regret, he never got any time overseas, the war having come to an end the same month he completed his officer training.

When the war was over he felt a call to preach in the Evangelical Christian faith, and went back to school, finishing seminary at the age of thirty-one. In 1977 he went to Haiti and set up a seminary to train national pastors. The school was located in the country's interior at an elevation of 1,600 feet, where the temperature and humidity are more pleasant than at the lower elevations near the coast. Eventually free schools for children were started in the same towns and villages where churches had been established by the new national pastors.

JOHN

The youngest of the Shaffer brood, John, was born on November 5, 1927, at the farm in Shiloh, the only one to be born at The Old Place. He attended the Shiloh school through the eighth grade, and York's William Penn Senior High School, from which he graduated in 1946.

During the war, there was a shortage of radio repairmen, so he learned to repair radios in a business called Jim's Radio Shop, which later became known as JRS Distributors. Following high school he opened his own radio repair shop in a two-car garage in Shiloh. During that time he also did occasional broadcast work for several local radio stations.

Although, by the time John finished high school, World War II had come to an end, he was nevertheless among the first group in York County to be drafted for the Korean War. He married a former high school classmate in July of 1952, about a year before he got out of the Army. They now have three children and five grandchildren.

During Earl's Fiftieth Anniversary Hike in 1998, John was a key factor in ensuring the success of that endeavor. He kept track of Earl's whereabouts and welfare, made numerous trips to meet with Earl and bring him equipment and supplies as needed, and helped to fend off the representatives of the media who became increasingly persistent and annoying as the hike neared its dramatic end.

John was a good bit younger than the rest, coming along as he did seven years after Evan. Perhaps it is for that reason that he seems to have been exempt from the inter-sibling frictions that broke out periodically among the others. Of John, Dan says, "He was a kind of family pet. Everybody loved him." From Anna: "He was our sweetheart. We all loved him." Even Earl said, "I get along pretty good with John." And from temperamental Earl this counts as high praise.

CHAPTER 3

THE OLD PLACE

When Earl was born there in 1918, the city of York was a thriving metropolis, renowned for its skilled mechanics and other industrial workers. The oldest Shaffer boy, Dan, recalls that when he went to Philadelphia to school, everyone there generally assumed that he would succeed at whatever he undertook because he was a "Yorker."

When Earl lived on King Street, this area of the city was often referred to as Bullfrog Alley, so named for a local gang of kids that called themselves the "Bullfroggers." Earl was familiar with the "Bullfroggers" name but he himself had never been connected with the gang, having been only four when the family left that part of the city.

York then had four covered market houses, one of which was the Carlisle Market—sometimes called the Western Market. It was here that Earl's mother later would bring her produce to be sold. Earl often accompanied her on these trips.

Notwithstanding all the city's attractions, Earl's mother grew increasingly apprehensive for her children's safety. Her special concern focused on automobiles which were becoming more and more common on the neighborhood streets. Finally the Shaffers determined to seek a quieter, safer place to live.

In the spring of 1924 when the Shaffer family decided to move out of the City of York, they bought a small seven-acre truck farm near Shiloh in West Manchester Township. Depending on where in York the measurement was taken, Shiloh was somewhere between three and four miles

Shaffer home, early 1940s

away—either one a daunting distance in a day when most people traveled by horse and wagon.

The purchase price of the new property was $2,850, a substantial amount for those days. It took many years to pay off the mortgage with a family income that was as modest as the cost of the property was dear—and with a still growing family.

When they moved into the farmhouse, they discovered that it was infested with bedbugs, whereupon Earl's father decided that drastic action was called for. The family all left the house for a weekend and went to stay with relatives. In their absence cyanide was applied throughout the building, and the infestation was ended.

Although John was the only one of the children actually born there, they all spent most of their growing-up years on this property, and all developed a deep affection for it. To all of them it came eventually to be known as The Old Place. Flowing through the rear of the farm is Derry Creek, a tributary of the Little Conewago Creek, which empties into the Big Conewago Creek, which in its turn empties into the Susquehanna River.

The house standing on this farm is very old, with a somewhat uncertain history. The structure itself is of a most unusual design. Earl said that he had never seen another like it anywhere. There are three levels to the building, the bottom one of which is a full-size stone house, built into a hillside of native sandstone. This base level had windows on three sides, and a door on the lower side toward the meadow. Built into the wall abutting the hillside is a large stone fireplace. The level above consists of a log cabin built on top of the stone house, with a third level, about two-thirds the height of the level below.

At the time it was purchased by the Shaffers, the lowest (basement) level had two sections; one part, which adjoined the rear door, had a wooden floor and was partitioned off from the other part which had a dirt floor. The latter section contained a stone fireplace, and butchering was done there. The next (main) level of the house consisted of a large kitchen with a substantial brick fireplace, a parlor, and a third small room to the rear. At this time the house had no indoor bathroom; the residents made use of an outhouse. Later when Dan and his wife moved in, the small room in the rear was turned into a bathroom. The top level contained three rooms, in addition to an open area at the top of the stairs.

By the time Anna sold the house many years later, she describes it as having "two beautiful curved stairways." The basement had been modified, and contained the kitchen and dining room; the next level had the living room, a small sitting room, and a bathroom. The bedrooms were on the topmost level. In Anna's view the main inconvenience was the single bathroom which necessitated a good bit of stair climbing.

The early history of the building and property, as well as the trail of ownership are at best tangled, with a good bit necessarily at the level of informed speculation. At the time of his final illness, Earl was still hoping to live long enough to write a book called "The Old Place," which would tell the story of the property, including his own conjectures about its history. It was Earl's belief that the building was deserving of some type of historical recognition.

As for the structure itself, both John and Earl believed that the building dated back to the mid-1700s. Earl was fairly certain that originally there was an Indian village in that area, and that someone came along and put up the building to serve as a trading post. It is not clear whether this individual had formally purchased the property or was merely a squatter. Earl believed that the latter was more likely. He thought also that the builder was most likely a Swede, his reason being that of the various immigrant nationalities found in this area at the time, the Swedes were the only ones from a country where log building was common. Earl believed this to be one of the oldest houses west of the Susquehanna River.

William Penn's original agreement with the Indians allowed land purchases only as far west as the Susquehanna, and not until 1749 was this

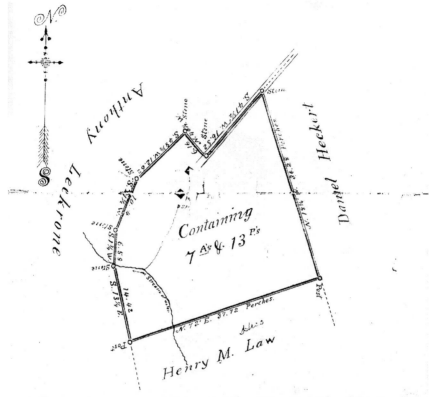

Situate in West Manchester Township, York
County, Pennsylvania. Containing as above
set forth Seven Acres and Thirteen Perches,
Neat Measure. Surveyed at the request of
Daniel Heckert for the use of Samuel Naylor
December 10th A. D. 1892

S. S. Aldinger,
Surveyor.

1892 survey of the Shaffer property in Shiloh, Pa. ("The Old Place")

extended farther west beyond the river. The original deeds for properties in the vicinity of The Old Place are dated 1776. However, a building
believed to be The Old Place was noted on a deed of 1805 as already
being in place. This strongly suggests that the house was there before
1776, and it could well have been there before 1749. A later deed dated

October 12, 1810, records a sale of the property for $748.80 by John Penn, one of William Penn's sons. The buyer was Dietrich Rupert of West Manchester Township, York. The deed notes that this property was part of a larger tract surveyed in 1767. There was apparently some question as to the boundary and any "improvement" (buildings). This deed specifies no improvements were on the property, but a neighboring property, perhaps owned by Peter Weigle, did have a mentioned improvement already in existence. So it is entirely possible that the Old Place is this building, but not mentioned in the deed due to a survey error.

Whatever its past history may have been, The Old Place came into the possession of the Shaffer family in 1924. At that time the property was a truck farm, well known in the area as the Rudy Place, named after the farmer who had previously lived there and worked the land, selling his produce at a farmers market in York. When the Shaffer father died in 1949, Anna moved out and got an apartment nearby, but John and Earl continued to live there. The oldest son, Dan, decided to move back from Philadelphia where he and his wife had been living to take up residence again at The Old Place. Dan's wife soon decided that she did not particularly enjoy farm life. John's wife, however, whom he had married while in the service, fell in love with The Old Place.

There was almost unanimous agreement among the family that the property should be kept intact and not broken up. The one exception was Dan who wanted to divide the property and build a house on part of it. Only Anna and John expressed interest in buying The Old Place, and there ensued a family discussion as to how to resolve the issue. Eventually it was suggested that names be put in a hat, with one to be drawn by Dan's daughter Judy, who reached in and pulled out Anna's name. John's wife was heartbroken.

Anna purchased the property in 1952 and lived there with her husband until the mid-1990s when she finally sold it. John eventually purchased another property adjoining The Old Place, where he lived for a time as its neighbor.

THE THREE-CORNERED PATCH

One day after Earl had returned from his Fiftieth Anniversary Hike, he and his brother John visited The Old Place to reminisce. By then the property was no longer in the family, having been sold by Anna. The two brothers paid particular attention to a small triangular piece of land that in their youth was planted with raspberries and blackberries, as well as some pear trees they called "honey pears." This patch was bounded by the creek and two property lines that met at a point beyond the stream.

Indicating an area on the side of the stream toward the house, Earl commented, "This was the most fertile ground I ever saw." The area was a meadow when they first moved in, and Earl called attention to a certain tree, one of three pin oaks that he had planted there. John observed that the watermelons and cantaloupes that used to be grown there were particularly good. Pumpkins were also grown in that area. Of the trees John said that "the squirrels planted" most of them. One exception was an old hickory tree which he remembered from his boyhood. He also recalled an occasion when he went down there and found the ground covered with seventeen-year locusts. "You couldn't walk without stepping on locusts," he said.

An adjacent patch on higher ground was used for potatoes, sweet potatoes and other assorted vegetables. Earl remembered that in his boyhood there was no lawn here; everything was vegetables. "Mom had me working in that little garden when I was five years old. That's why I grow gardens now, I guess; it got into me." Beside the house on the north and east sides was an area used for the rest of the gardening. A strawberry patch was next to Church road, and the rest of the farm contained fruit trees and fields for hay or corn.

John then pointed up to the springhouse which stands about fifty feet beyond the house. "It was an open spring when we first moved here. This is the shed we built over the spring," he observed. His father with help from his boys had built the springhouse in the late '30s. John comments wistfully that the spring probably does not even run anymore because of the falling water table. The spring had a concrete trough, he remembered, in which the family would float watermelons to chill them. The family had a water pump that was used to pump water up to the house. There used to be two big trees there, one on each side of the spring, Earl recalls. One of the trees was a willow, "The biggest willow I ever saw anywhere," Earl comments. The other tree was a giant maple.

The spring house

*The old barn
and the new barn*

The barn that stood on the farm when the Shaffers acquired the property was of the classic Pennsylvania forebay design. Although that original barn no longer exists, much of the timber survives in a barn that Earl built shortly after returning home from the War. He used timber that had been saved from the original barn.

CHAPTER 4

GROWING UP POOR

Earl is remembered by his sister Anna as a beautiful baby, and as a good baby who didn't cry. "He had big eyes and nice skin," she says. "And he was the quietest—he would sit and think." At that time they had big baby shows in York, and once when Earl was entered in a show he was judged the prettiest baby of all. In time, this beautiful blue-eyed baby grew up to become a young man who was strikingly, movie-star handsome.

It was an early spring day in April of 1924 when the Shaffer family first took up residence in The Old Place. At the time Earl was not yet six years old, but long afterward he still remembered clearly that there was snow on the ground with bright green patches of grass poking through. The moving man was an acquaintance from York who had a coal truck that he was using for the move. In approaching the house on the muddy dirt road, he slid into the ditch at the side. As it happened, a neighboring farmer, Clay Bott, who was plowing his field with a horse-drawn plow observed what had happened. He stopped the team, unhitched them and took them to his barn; then returning with a wagon onto which all the household furnishings were loaded, he hauled everything the rest of the way to the new home. Finally, as a crowning touch he used his team to pull the truck out of the ditch. Earl's father then asked the neighbor, "What do we owe you?"

"Nothing," Bott replied. " Just be a good neighbor." Over time the two families became good friends, exchanging regular visits. The Botts

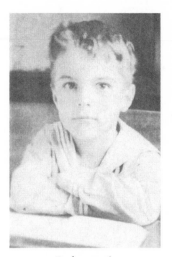

Earl, age six

were the only neighbors with whom the Shaffers developed such close relations.

DERRY CREEK

The Shaffer boys—being boys—quite naturally made endless use of Derry Creek, which flowed through the back of the property to which they had moved. At that time the creek had a small dam, and the water was deep enough to allow the boys to swim in it. They could also paddle around in a canoe that Earl built. The creek was home to a variety of creatures: fish, muskrats, crayfish, pollywogs, frogs, and even an occasional snapping turtle or two. There were also a lot of eels in the early years. Although the Shaffers did not harvest them, other people did, working at night and using flashlights and a harpoon-like device described by John as being "like a long fork."

Although they were abundant back when the Shaffer boys were young, there have been no muskrats in the creek for many years. Back then, the boys would capture them, using steel traps which they would set near the animal's hole or near a slide or at a place where it was apparent that they went to feed on vegetation. Then the boys skinned the animal and sold the fur to a fur dealer who would come around periodically. Later when the dealer's son was about fourteen or fifteen and had begun to drive a car, his father would send him out to buy the furs. The price fluctuated from a low of thirty cents per hide up to a high of $1.25. Usually the price was in the lower range. Earl remembered that he got forty-five cents for his very first muskrat pelt. After skinning the animal, the skin was stretched but not tanned since the purchaser generally wanted to do the tanning his way.

Occasionally the muskrat's dark red meat was eaten. This once provided the setting for a practical joke on Aunt Minnie, a relative who would come to visit once or twice a year. They served her muskrat for a meal during one visit, but without telling her what it was. She assumed that she was eating rabbit, and proclaimed it the best rabbit she had ever eaten. The Shaffer boys were convinced that if she were told what she was actually eating, she would have had a heart attack and died on the spot.

A farmer whose land was adjacent to the Shaffer property had to ford Derry Creek to reach some of his fields to the east side of the stream. The water level today is even lower than it was back then. John attributes this to the general lowering of the water table in the area. Occasionally floods would come along and wash quantities of soil downstream to form a kind of natural dam.

It was believed by some that there had been an Indian village near the Big and Little Conewago Creeks, essentially adjacent to the tract on which The Old Place would later stand. Over the years

Brother John paddling Earl's canoe

many arrowheads and tomahawks had been found in this area by artifact hunters. Although the Shaffer boys did a lot of searching, they found few, the land having been by then pretty well picked over. John Shaffer, however, did once find a tomahawk in the middle of Church Road, the road leading back into The Old Place. As recently as 1995 John found an arrowhead at a site where the Township drilled a water well.

Certainly, however, this fertile valley would be an attractive place for the local Indians. The two creeks would have been traversable by canoe back then.

———————

Looking back on his boyhood Earl perceives himself as "kind of the black sheep of the family." Following the death of his mother when he was fourteen, he became a loner with a powerful stubborn streak. Toward the end of his life he commented, "I have things I started sixty years ago and I'm still trying to complete them because I'm too stubborn to give them up." Tempering this bleak view of himself with a hint of optimism, he adds, "And maybe I'll live long enough to get some of them done."

Earl's mother taught him to read and write when he was only five years old, before he had even started school. As part of this informal "home schooling" she had him copy poems. It is to this precocious education that Earl attributes his later literary proclivities.

Earl in 1935

When the family moved from York City to the country Earl was only five years old. One day his older brother, Dan, wanting to explore the new surroundings, asked his mother for permission to take some time off from his farm work to do so. She agreed to the request but only on the condition that Dan take Earl with him. Dan objected that Earl was so little and had such short legs that he would not be able to keep up. His mother was adamant and told him, "It's take Earl or stay home."

So Dan took Earl with him. To Dan's amazement Earl kept right up with his big brother. Dan even tried intentionally to wear his little brother out, but found Earl determined to keep up, which he did. "He had very sturdy little legs," Dan commented years later.

As time passed there developed a family tradition of hiking. On a Sunday afternoon the older Shaffer boys along with the neighboring Winemiller boys would take off on a hike of eight or ten miles. One of the most ambitious walks they took was from The Old Place to the Susquehanna River and back. In the fall of the year when apples were ripening they would walk from orchard to orchard, sampling the fallen apples as they went along. They never picked apples from the trees, limiting themselves to the fallen ones which were much more likely to be ripe. Eventually they came to know every orchard between home and the river, a distance of about eight miles each way. They always took the dog along on these males-only excursions.

Still later the family took various motorized excursions as well; in these the female members of the family also participated. On one spring occasion in the late 1930s they all set off in the Model T Ford, which by then had been acquired, to visit Washington, D.C. The purpose of the trip was a combination visit to Earl's Aunt Alice, and an opportunity to see the famous cherry blossoms in the nation's capitol. Apparently the most memorable part of the trip was the traffic jam between Baltimore and Washington.

In the country school to which they transferred after the move to The Old Place they found themselves ostracized from many activities. Their new country classmates referred to them as "city geeks." Although Earl thought that he had a generous share of natural athletic ability, he rarely got to participate in games in grade school. When sides were chosen up for a game, he would be picked last or not at all. If he was needed to complete a side, he got to play. Otherwise, he would stand and watch. Another problem was his size: Until he was about sixteen he remained quite small. Then he had a growth spurt when he gained about six inches in height and thirty pounds in weight.

Once, on a cold Saturday the Shaffer boys were out exploring along the creek in an area where there were many bramble bushes. Ice had been forming along the edge of the creek, and Earl noticed a bird that was caught in the water and struggling to get free. In an effort to rescue the trapped bird Earl crawled down through the brambles to try to reach it. While doing this a bramble thorn scratched his eyeball across the pupil. He was eleven or twelve at the time and did not think the injury was particularly serious. By Monday, however, the condition had worsened and it was clear that there was a serious problem that needed professional attention. His mother took him into York to an eye, ear, nose, and throat specialist—the same doctor who had operated on his tonsils when he was two.

The doctor examined the eye and without comment used one of his tools to remove a film from the eye. At first the doctor believed that Earl would wind up losing that eye. After applying some drops to dilate the eye, he gave the liquid to Earl's mother with instructions to apply more at intervals throughout the day, and to keep hot compresses on the eye. This she did faithfully for five days, after which they returned to the doctor who examined the eye again and decided that it would not have to be removed.

Dan described all of the Shaffer children as being introverts. When they moved to the country they encountered "a bunch of tough kids." They all had to find their place, and Dan found his first. His response was to change from a backward kid to a fighter. Seeing that everyone was picking on Earl, Dan realized that what his brother needed was to have his self-confidence built up. So the older brother took Earl aside and taught him everything he knew about boxing: how to avoid punches, how to hit, and other boxing tactics. The result was that Earl became a good boxer, a skill that served him well throughout his later military career.

Growing up as he did in the midst of the Great Depression, Earl turned to hunting and trapping largely as a response to financial necessity. "I never liked to kill anything," he said. "It was always for the meat or the pelt; it was always for a purpose." He shot deer for the meat and the hide, which he sometimes tanned himself. He even made a buckskin shirt once which, he claims, John and his friends wore out while he was in the Army. Another time he made a rabbit skin robe which, he said, was warm enough to allow sleeping outside in the dead of winter with only the robe as covering.

Reminiscing years later, Earl said that he grew up as a poor boy and in spite of all the fame he later achieved, he was still poor at the end.

CHAPTER 5

JOBS AND
THE GREAT DEPRESSION

After helping his mother with the garden work for a number of years, Earl finally started working for pay in his early teens. He and Evan generally worked together for neighboring farmers, which earned them each a dollar a day. Depending on the season, the kind of work they did varied greatly. One of the major tasks came with the threshing season. Since only very large individual farmers could afford their own threshing machine, the modest-size farms near the Shaffers had to make do with one rig for the whole community. Along with its crew of about thirty, the machine went from farm to farm until everyone's threshing got done.

Threshing was dangerous, demanding work that required a substantial amount of skill. This skill the two Shaffer boys quickly acquired, thereby assuring that their services were always in demand. The main trick came in stacking the hay properly so that it would stay on the wagon and not slide off—as happened once when a load of hay was crossing a ford through Derry Creek. No one ever said who stacked that load.

There were, of course, many other farm jobs the boys did. Sometimes they would work at night and sleep in the haymows. After a bounteous breakfast prepared by the farmers' wives, the boys would work all morning before sitting down to another generous meal at noon. Again at evening another abundant meal would appear. It was these meals that seemed to be most remembered. "We couldn't have done it without the food. It was like a banquet; every meal was like a banquet," Earl once said. Even at breakfast there would be cake and pie. And the cook would be offended if the workers declined anything. There would be perhaps half a dozen cooks making food in tremendous amounts, because they had to feed thirty guys who had been working like crazy for hours. And the food was acclaimed by all. The women, in turn, were very proud of their handiwork.

"You start in the morning, and by noon you were starving almost. You'd eat until you couldn't eat any more, and by evening you were starving again. And you just ate and ate and ate," in Earl's words.

In that era most farm work was still being done with mules and horses. For plowing, the old-style walking plow was used, and Earl often did that even when he was still a kid. When he was not yet out of his early teens Earl was "feeding the thresher," one of the most dangerous jobs in farming at that time, farming itself being an inherently dangerous occupation.

Other times they would milk the cows and drive the cows in and out. Milking was done by hand then, of course, and had to be done twice a day. It was surprisingly hard work; after milking only about eight cows, the boys would be tired out.

For several years Earl worked about six weeks each fall cutting and husking corn. When cutting, he got paid by the shock and usually made about two dollars a day. In those days the corn was cut by hand using a machete-like knife, after which it was gathered into shocks in the field. When husking by the day—at $1.50 per day—the husked corn was left in piles beside each shock. In the evening after supper and after the milking was done, a high-sided wagon would be brought into the field to collect the piles of corn, which was then transported to the corn cribs into which it was shoveled.

Cutting corn was not an assignment that Earl much enjoyed. Half a dozen stalks would be cut and held in one circled arm to form a sheaf. Then the sheaves were grouped together to form a shock—usually twelve sheaves to a shock. The shocks were secured either by using a corn stalk or with the use of tar rope. (Tar rope, which is still available commercially—although with increasing rarity—is Manila hemp with a light soaking of tar. Usually about one-sixteenth inch in diameter, it is brown in color, and was used for both corn shocks and wheat shocks. It was rough on the hands, and left a residue of tar on them.)

By the end of the day Earl's left arm was tired out; his clothing would wear through and his skin would become chafed—a condition which would be especially aggravating on a frosty morning. Generally about six workers—men and boys—would form a team, each contributing his sheaves toward the creation of a single shock. Some days Earl and the other boys worked as much as fifteen hours.

THE GREAT DEPRESSION

After high school, from 1935 to 1941 Earl started at first working on the neighboring farms. Then he switched to carpentry and also some warehouse work. "That's the way it was in the depression, you worked for whatever you could find," Earl said. He also did some concrete and stone work, which he particularly enjoyed. Actually he wound up doing almost any kind of construction work.

By 1936 Earl had saved enough money to be able to spend thirty-five dollars to buy a Model A Ford.

All of this time the nation was in the depths of the Great Depression. The boys' father was working three days every other week at a salary of $2.50 per week. Money obviously was extremely scarce. The boys were left with the need to provide their own clothing and whatever else they needed or wanted. They learned as kids to do men's work. In addition to whatever outside work they could find, they turned to hunting and trapping as additional sources of income.

Happily, they were surrounded by a number of farms on which they were welcome to pursue such activities. As a result of the good reputations the Shaffer boys had acquired by working for the various farmers in the neighborhood, they had no difficulty getting permission to hunt and trap on the farms. The farmers were confident the boys would not leave gates open or break down fences, and that they would take good care of everything.

The father made all the family's shoes; the mother made most of their clothing. On their little farm the mother also raised vegetables which she sold in town. She was especially good with strawberries and asparagus. She also made and sold butter with milk from the family's cows. In addition she canned vast quantities of food for the family's own use throughout the winter. Anna referred to "hundreds and hundreds" of jars of food preserved this way. Knowing, as they did, what acquaintances in York were suffering as they tried to survive sometimes on only one bowl of soup a day procured from the soup line offered by a community charity, the Shaffers felt fortunate to have what little they did.

When the depression hit, the Shaffers' financial position was made especially difficult by the fact that they had purchased their little farm at a time when real estate prices were high just after the First World War. For a while this seemed like a good investment. The property had a vari-

ety of fruit trees along with an abundance of rich soil. They started raising chickens for eggs to sell to hatcheries. Even though the bottom fell
out of the real estate market, the family was still burdened with a mortgage to be paid. The people who had loaned them the money to buy the
farm had decided they would like to have this prize farm themselves and
hoped for an opportunity to foreclose on the mortgage. Unless they were
to be left homeless, the Shaffers had to produce the monthly payment
right on time. That they managed to do this seems a kind of miracle.

CHAPTER 6

EDUCATION AND RELIGION

EDUCATION

The two oldest Shaffer children started school while the family was still living in the city of York. When Dan was in the fourth grade they moved to The Old Place, and he and his sister suddenly found themselves in a country school where their educational environment was dramatically different. Dan recalled the York school as being very modern, and using the latest teaching techniques. Their new school, located in nearby Shetters Grove, was an old-fashioned, two-room country school that had to accommodate eight grades—four in each room. The students, moreover, were considerably more unruly than was the case back in York.

It was the policy in the country school for boys to sit on one side of the classroom and girls on the other. If a boy spent too much time talking or otherwise acting up, he would be moved to the girls' side. Dan remembered one occasion when he was talking to those near him and found himself moved over to the girls' side. He was not over there long before he began conversing with some of the girls, whereupon he was promptly moved back to the boys' side.

Dan seems to have done well in school; once he was third in the county spelling contest, for which he received a $2.50 gold piece, a coin smaller than a penny but worth today at least a hundred times its face value. Since Shiloh was too small a community to support its own high school, he attended high school in York where, among other subjects, he took three years of Spanish and three years of Latin.

When Earl was in the first grade in the Shetters Grove school he had a teacher that in retrospect he considered incompetent. He had one bad eye which caused him to squint and the teacher thought he was winking at her. "And she beat on me for six months," Earl said. "She was a flapper, she ran around at night. She'd fall asleep right in the room; they fired her." The next teacher he had was the opposite of the first one, and the boy's behavior and attitude improved dramatically. Thereafter he missed school on only two occasions: once when he was riding a sled and ran into a fence injuring his face, and the other time when he injured his eye.

The first school Earl attended was about a mile from home; later in life he was fond of telling people that his hiking career began when he was five and had to hike two miles every day going to school and back. When Earl was in the fifth grade they built a new four-room school which he attended through the seventh grade, when he was rewarded for good performance by being allowed to take the test for high school. He passed the test, skipped eighth grade, and finished high school at the age of sixteen.

Following elementary school Earl was bounced around somewhat. First he went to the Hannah Penn School (named for the second wife of William Penn), then in the middle of his first year there, he was moved to the Edgar Fahs Smith school. From there he went to the Lincoln school. Finally for eleventh and twelfth grade he went to William Penn High School which pleased him since it had a prestigious reputation.

As a result of the extremely solid foundation he obtained in elementary school, Earl did very well in high school. This was not an unmixed blessing, however. He found that he was able to coast through high school in all of his classes except Latin, which was the only one in which his grades fell. Apparently because he did not have to work in his other classes, he did not think he should have to work hard in Latin either.

Earl and Evan both became avid readers. Every day they would go to the school library where they would each take out a book. In the evening they would both read both books. The following day they would return the books and take out two more.

E. B. NEWMAN

A powerful influence on the education of every one of the Shaffer children was a man whose name usually appears as E. B. Newman; at other times he is referred to as Ed or "Pappy" Newman. Although no one seems sure of the source of the Pappy title, Earl's brother John suggests that it may simply have been because most of his students viewed him as a father figure. E. B. Newman taught seventh and eighth grades in the Shiloh four-room schoolhouse, where he also served as principal. The four oldest Shaffer children had him as a teacher. John just missed that experience because of Newman's retirement, but even John knew him as principal of the school.

E. B Newman

He is described as a forceful teacher who put great emphasis on English and mathematics. In those subjects, according to Earl, he gave his students a better grounding than most students got in high school. Earl's brother Evan calls Newman "one of the most effective teachers I've ever known."

E. B. Newman is said to have been a blacksmith until he was about twenty-two, when he decided to enroll in Normal School (a two-year state teacher's college of the day). Although not a very tall man, he was brawny and a strict disciplinarian who had little difficulty controlling his class. He was also a very religious man who every Friday afternoon would teach the week's Sunday School lesson—a practice less frowned upon in that era than would be the case today. He also had his students sing hymns during the Friday afternoon sessions. Earl laughingly commented that Newman would "be kicked out of school these days."

His religiosity carried over into his teaching, where his search for sentences for his students to diagram typically led him to the Bible.

Evan recalled an occasion when the county School Superintendent visited the Newman classroom. Delighted at this opportunity to show off his students' skill at diagramming sentences, Pappy Newman put his charges at the blackboard along the walls of the room and invited the superintendent to give them a sentence to diagram. Evan thought the sentence was from the Bible although he did not remember which book. What Evan remembered was, "Memory, a pensive rue, when gleaning the fields of childhood." Although this is clearly derived from the Book of Ruth, it is not literally from the Bible—nor, as it stands, is it a complete sentence. A trail of research, however, suggests that this is most likely a misremembering of at least a portion of the following sentence from George William Curtis's 1852 work, *The Howadji in Syria*: "In that calm Syrian afternoon, Memory, a pensive Ruth, went gleaning the silent fields of childhood and found the scattered grain still golden, the morning sunlight yet fresh and fair." In any case, we may probably safely assume that the students went dutifully about the task of justifying their teacher's faith in them.

In summarizing his feelings about this powerful teacher, Earl said, "We'd have a much better educated group of young people if we had more Pappy Newmans."

Earl attributed his own intense interest in the correct use of English to two main factors, one of which was his exposure to the teaching of E. B. Newman. The other was a book, *The Working Principles of Rhetoric* by John Franklin Genung, a professor of rhetoric at Amherst College. This 676-page work was published in 1900 and was, in turn, a revision of an earlier book, *Practical Elements of Rhetoric* by the same author. Earl said that he studied Professor Genung's book as intensely as one would a series of college lecture notes.

One wonders how such a book, surely not a best seller even back then, fell into the hands of a York County farm boy. We can probably never know.

RELIGION

Earl's great grandfather on his mother's side served in the Union Army during the Civil War, winding up in the Confederacy's infamous Libby Prison at Richmond, Virginia. Libby was probably second in notoriety only to Georgia's Andersonville. While there, Great Grandfather Gallagher nearly starved to death along with many others. He survived, however, and in due course fathered three children, one of whom was Samuel Francis (Frank) Gallagher, Earl's grandfather. The family at this time was Roman Catholic.

When the tough old Civil War veteran finally died, candles were placed on his coffin in accordance with common Catholic practice of the day. Francis later told his daughter, Earl's mother, how as a boy he watched the candles burning lower and lower and began to worry that they would burn his father. Finally he went and blew them out, whereupon the priest slapped him in the face so hard that Francis was nearly knocked down.

Earl's great grandmother, the wife of the Civil War veteran, had previously died while still quite young, leaving her husband completely devastated. The three small children, were turned over to a sister, Molly Gallagher, to raise. Molly was a devout Protestant as it happened, who took her new charges with her to church every Sunday. It was just a matter of time until Frances and her two siblings themselves embraced Protestantism.

The family in which Earl grew up appears to have been a kind of generic Protestant that was readily adaptable to changing circumstances. When they were living in York they attended an Evangelical church. After moving to Shiloh, however, they found that getting to York every Sunday was difficult so they switched to the only church available there. This was a combined Lutheran and Reformed church where the two denominations used the same building, alternating every week. Sunday School was a "union" activity with both Lutheran and Reform congregants attending. Dan and Anna sang in the choir for both churches.

At the family level the Shaffers were also very dedicated to their faith. They had a family altar, with prayer and Bible readings every evening.

CHAPTER 7

LEISURE ACTIVITIES

When Earl was a teenager he sometimes played a variety of sandlot football that was exceptionally rough. Although the boys had no protective equipment whatsoever, they played real tackle football. Earl's recollection was that he was very good at it. Unfortunately it got to the point that almost every game saw some boy breaking one thing or another, so they finally had to quit it. Earl never had the opportunity to participate in school sports, partly because of his small size that persisted well into his senior year, and partly because of depending on his father for transportation; he never had the after-school time demanded by such activities.

Later in life Earl always believed that he could have excelled at a number of sports if he had only had a chance to develop his native skills. He was convinced that the lack of opportunity in more conventional sports was what caused his natural athletic ability to be channeled into hiking.

His boyhood sports heroes were Babe Ruth and Jack Dempsey, although he disapproved of the Babe's private life. At school when the teacher took a pre-fight poll of the students, about ninety percent of the class favored Tunney but Earl was for Dempsey. Boxing was a favorite leisure activity among the Shaffer boys—a sport in which they engaged on a concrete floor.

It was during his teens that Earl's interest began to turn to hiking and camping as favored leisure activities. His first experience with sleeping outdoors came one October when he was sixteen or seventeen. He rode his bicycle about forty miles to a spot near Pine Grove Furnace. It turned out to be an unusually cold night and at that time he had no sleeping bag. The moon was full, he recalled, and he slept in a cemetery. The next day he rode home, having decided that he did not want to spend another night in the cold.

He was also in his teens when he and Evan decided to undertake a week long hike on the Appalachian Trail.The plan was for Dan to take them—in a Model A Ford with a rumble seat—to the Snowy Mountain Fire Tower, which was on the Appalachian Trail near Caledonia and U.S. Route 30. They would then walk north toward Dillsburg, Pa. It was very hot that summer with water hard to come by. The first day they walked through Caledonia State Park until they decided to stop for the night. After making a fire and eating their supper, they suddenly heard a scream nearby which was probably a bobcat or some other wild cat. This unsettled both of the boys.

Later they left the trail to look for water and found a promising area with abundant fern growth. As they were searching for a spring Earl suddenly saw a large copperhead near his leg and apparently poised to strike. He slowly pulled out the H&R .22 revolver he was carrying and pointed it toward the snake, which meant that he was also pointing it very near his leg. He was reluctant to pull the trigger because he knew that if he missed, the snake would strike him. Meanwhile, Evan had found a long hickory pole with which, after carefully positioning himself, he killed the snake with one blow.

Another night they slept near a cabin where a group of people stopped just at dusk. In order to avoid any confrontation they got up early the next morning and went on their way without taking time to eat. Just when they thought they were clear of the cabin and any problems it might bring, the trail suddenly entered a meadow and widened. Here, to their surprise, they found themselves in the midst of a great many tents, the sides of which were rolled up, revealing inside each tent young girls sleeping on cots. They soon realized they were in a Girl Scout camp through which the trail passed. Quickening their pace to nearly a run in an effort to avoid detection, they managed to get to the edge of the camp where the trail crossed a small stream and started up a slope. As they began the climb away from the camp, they heard the loud call of a bugle followed by the squeals of the girls as they jumped from their cots. It was a close call for two very shy country boys.

Earl and Evan covered so many miles so quickly that they arrived in Dillsburg days before Dan was scheduled to pick them up. After hiding their packs in some bushes, they walked into town where they went to a restaurant for a meal. The Shaffer males tended to develop facial hair early, and this of course was unshaved. With their scraggly beards and shabby clothes, the waitress at the restaurant assumed they were part of the timber crews who were at that time cutting trees in the area. The record does not reveal if she was ever disabused of her erroneous assumption. They sent a postcard to Dan to arrange a new pick-up; the Shaffers at that time had no telephone at home so that mode of communication was not an option.

The members of the Shaffer family all tended to have some musical aptitude. Earl and Dan played guitar, Evan played banjo, and Anna played ukulele. Consequently family recreation often took the form of of a group sing-along. Earl credits Dan with being the best guitar player in the family. Dan and Anna were also accomplished singers.

Radio shows were also popular sources of entertainment. "Fibber McGee and Molly" was one of Earl's favorites as was "Amos 'n Andy."

PART TWO

WALTER WINEMILLER

CHAPTER 8

WALTER AT HOME

The small farm of the Shaffer family near Shiloh in Pennsylvania's York County was bordered by a number of larger properties, one of which was the ten-acre farm owned by the Winemillers. The father and head of the household was William Winemiller, known locally as "Billy," who was something of a legend throughout the area. He was both a master basket-weaver and an uncommonly successful gardener.

Derry Creek ran through the middle of the Winemiller property. On one side of the creek the land was fertile and tillable but not so on the other side because of shale and a hillside. The tillable portion was devoted to raising fruits and vegetables. Across the creek the land eventually was planted in pine trees. Along the creek itself grew willows which were used by Billy in his basket-weaving.

Billy once told Earl that he could make sixty different basket styles, mostly market baskets and wash baskets, the latter being his specialty. These often had distinctive characteristics, such as handles on the sides instead of the ends because many women preferred them that way.

In addition to his farming and basket-weaving activities, Billy worked part-time as a laborer for the State Department of Transportation and operated a Sunday newspaper route.

Billy and Tilley produced six children, four boys first, followed by two girls. According to Earl's sister Anna, the Winemillers "were all very light blondes: the father, the mother and all six children." The oldest of the four Winemiller boys was Walter.

Winemiller-Shaffer property boundary, where Earl and Walter met

Not long after the Shaffers first moved into the house near that of the Winemillers, the two families met down along Derry Creek. Billy was cutting willows and Tilley was carrying the baby. Earl and Walter were both five years old. The two quickly formed a powerful bond. Earl and Walter played together, adventured together, and worked together on various farms in the area. Often joining Earl and Walter in their activities was the next oldest Winemiller son, William Jr., who was most often called by his nickname, Gord, which derived from "Flash Gordon," a popular comic strip of that era. Whatever income the Winemiller boys derived from trapping or working at the local farms was contributed to the family expenses.

Walter could handle a walking plow and a team of horses by the time he was ten years old. Earl described him as being "burly and strong but small of waist and quick as a pouncing cat."

When servicing his Sunday newspaper route, Billy would drive the car while one of his sons acted as delivery boy. This duty often fell to the oldest son Walter. One of the customers on Billy's route was the novelist, Katharine Haviland-Taylor, who took an interest in Walter and lent him books from her personal library of more than ten thousand volumes.

Earl writes that although Walter, at his father's insistence, quit school after the eighth grade, the boy was better read and much brighter than would be expected from his limited education.

The daily routine of the two boys was dauntingly strenuous. They did a lot of trapping together which got them out of bed around four o'clock in the morning to check their traplines. Then they would work about ten hours, often together on the same farm. Walter was only three months older than Earl, and from the very beginning the two exchanged few spoken words, seeming to communicate silently. According to Earl, even though Walter might be working on a hill a quarter of a mile away, Earl would only need to stare at his friend for a second or two before Walter would turn his head to return the look.

Their busiest time of the farming year was the harvest season, when they worked with the thirty-man threshing team that followed the community's only thresher from farm to farm until everyone's threshing was completed. It was at this season that each year Earl and Walter would build a kind of ceremonial bonfire to celebrate the bounty of the harvest time. This ritual was celebrated by Earl long afterward in one of his poems to Walter called "Trail Pardner." (The original title had been "Trail Buddy" but "Buddy" was crossed out by hand, and "Pardner" written in, perhaps because "Buddy" failed to reflect the closeness between the two.)

Walter's favorite hunting weapon was the bow and arrows, both of which he made himself and used with uncanny accuracy. As he gradually grew older, larger, and stronger, he progressively made larger and more powerful bows. By the time he reached his late teens the bows he made required a pull of nearly one hundred pounds.

Gord, Walter, Evan, and Earl on a raccoon hunt

The outdoor adventures of the two often included walks along stream banks as they watched for water-loving wildlife of various kinds. From time to time Walter would suddenly leap down a ten-foot bank and seize by the neck some snake, woodchuck, or other small animal that he spotted. Poisonous snakes were as likely as any other kind to be the target of his attacks.

Sometimes on moonlit nights in the autumn the two would go out looking for skunks which they would (carefully) pursue around the fields. They would try to pick the animals up by the tail without getting "stunk up." Usually these efforts failed and the two got sprayed. Occasionally their eyes received a dose of the pungent liquid which "burned like fire," but apparently did no permanent harm. Actually, Earl claims, it sometimes seemed they could see even better afterward.

Years later Earl recalled that once during the war when he and Walter were stationed in different parts of the Pacific, he received a letter from his friend in which Walter wrote, "Remember the shadows we cast on water 'twixt sunset and sunrise, like panning for gold or something lost?"

Walter seems to have had a certain aura that impressed all who knew him. He could climb any tree (often barefoot) however smooth and apparently unclimbable its bark might appear. When he reached the branching level, he would cavort about like a monkey, leaping from tree to tree in a manner that terrified the onlookers below. The Winemillers' farm had a large barn, across the top of which Walter once stretched a rope, and walked barefoot from one end of the barn to the other. Earl's sister Anna describes watching this happen. She also states that Walter had the ability to hypnotize animals—snakes and toads, among others. He would stroke them a certain way and they would become immobile and apparently unconscious.

Very often at the end of their long working day, which generally concluded with their helping with the milking, they would relax by boxing, a pastime of which they were both inordinately fond. These sparring matches would begin very playfully, with a lot of dancing about, feinting and pulling of punches. Gradually they would become more spirited and physical, until at some point one or the other would be staggered and the bout would end with apologies.

Although Walter was only three months older than Earl, he was—by Earl's own admission—stronger and quicker and the better woodsman. Over a five year period the two went hiking every Sunday afternoon, often accompanied by Walter's brother Gord and one or more of Earl's brothers. Their walking routes would vary: one day perhaps east to the

Susquehanna River, another time west to the Pidgeon Hills, some fifteen miles beyond Shiloh.

Once they made a cave in the woods near the Little Conewago Creek where there were some old stumps left over from a logging operation. They tilted one of the stumps over and dug a shaft straight down and off to the side where they made a little room. This space was used by the boys as a hideout. Earl's oldest brother, Dan, knew they were hiding someplace but never figured out exactly where. As a result, Dan often wound up being stuck with chores that had been assigned to Earl. After the cave was abandoned, the younger Winemiller boys discovered it and showed it to Earl's brother John.

Walter and Earl were great admirers of the Indians, and tried to copy various activities that they believed were typical of those early inhabitants of the land. Among other exploits they went barefoot in the snow, even though the instructions of Earl's father were that they should not go barefoot until the first bluebird of the season was seen. They shot crows which they then cooked and ate, and they mastered the art of catching fish with their bare hands. Once, instead of a fish, they brought up a snake. Many of these assorted delicacies were later carried home for Earl's sister Anna to prepare.

This admiration of the Indians likely had a bearing on the nicknames they chose for each other when they separated to go into different military branches. The opening lines of Earl's poem "Lone Brave's Return" read "You gave me the name of Lone Brave/When the trails led out to war." Presumably it was Earl who assigned Walter his nickname, "Big Ears." Exactly why these particular names were chosen no one seems to know.

On their woodland excursions the two boys always carried slingshots, pocket knives, and matches. If they got hungry, they had all they needed to kill a rabbit, skin it and cook it. In their later teens the boys headed to the mountains for their hiking. In these more rugged settings, Walter demonstrated his physical skills in climbing over rocky ledges and leading the way through dense woods even on the darkest of nights

On one of their overnight camping excursions, accompanied by Earl's brother Evan, the three boys built a campfire. While they sat around the flickering flames they began hearing a "weird wailing sound" which Earl described as being like a primitive violin or a wildcat caught in a trap. The sound persisted, seeming to come from the top of the ridge, and after a time the boys decided to investigate. After climbing for at least a mile they determined the noise was the result of two trees being slowly rubbed together by the breeze that was blowing.

It was seated at this campfire that Earl composed the first poetry he ever committed to paper. Previously he had fashioned lines in his head but never wrote them down, and they were presumably forgotten. On this occasion as he sat looking at Walter on the opposite side of the fire, he saw the flames reflected on his friend's face and was inspired to compose three lines:

> I hear the sighing of the pines beside a mountain stream
> A lit face that dimly shines as if by the firelight's gleam
> And then across the borderlines awaken from my dream.

He never gave this fragment a name, although he later confirmed that it referred to Walter without specifically mentioning him.

There exists a four-page reminiscence of Walter that Earl meticulously typed, with the addition of some handwritten editorial changes. At the end of this document, however, has been added a final handwritten paragraph that Earl apparently felt was too important to be omitted. In it Earl describes one February day when the two boys decided to go muskrat trapping in a stream ten miles away. With a heavy load of traps and equipment, they set off cross country and eventually reached the stream where they set up camp. During the night a sleet storm came up and blew down the tiny tent they had brought along. The result of this disaster was that they huddled together in "freezing discomfort" for the rest of the night. When day came, they gathered up their heavy load once again and trudged home through sleet and rain, arriving in a state of near semiconsciousness.

CHAPTER 9

WALTER AT WAR

In 1940, with the nation increasingly moving to a state of wartime preparedness, Earl found himself saddled with a draft number low enough that for six months it kept him from getting a job. Potential employers all declined to hire someone likely to be lost to the Army within a few months. Finally, tired of waiting, Earl volunteered for the one-year draft. Although coaxed by Earl to accompany him in joining the Army, Walter chose instead to enlist in the Marines along with his brother Gord. Earl had a low regard for the Marines, considering them "too gung-ho," always seeking glory and martyrdom, with newsmen and photographers on hand to document the mayhem. In any case, Earl and Walter saw each other only once more when they both happened to be home at the same time on a three-day pass.

Walter was an excellent swimmer, so much so that at an advance training camp, he was made a swimming instructor. His swimming skill was demonstrated in a typically flamboyant fashion during preparations for the amphibious assault on Iwo Jima. Walter and his brother Gord were both part of the force that had been assembled for the imminent assault, but they were on different ships. The mail for the personnel in the assault force was delivered by seaplane. One day a letter addressed to Gord was mistakenly delivered to Walter. Rather than return the letter to the mail personnel, which would have delayed it perhaps for days or even weeks in view of the fast approaching attack, Walter put the letter in a waterproof gun case and swam the half mile to Gord's ship, where he delivered the letter and then swam back again.

Walter holding muskrats while home on leave

Although Walter and Gord served in the same battalion, their differing assignments did not always send them into battle together. Walter was a "scout sniper," one of those who were likely to wind up with the more dangerous jobs, while Gord was "only" an expert marksman. In addition, Walter seemed to be blessed with exceptionally strong senses and instincts. At Iwo Jima, Gord was seriously wounded but survived and was able to bring back with him many stories about Walter's close calls and charmed life.

Well before the storming of Iwo Jima, Walter was made a staff sergeant and put in charge of a platoon of scout snipers. At times in these early engagements, in particularly dangerous situations he would go out by himself into enemy territory without asking any of his men to accompany him. On one such occasion he was out alone between the opposing lines when his men began hearing shooting and yelling coming from the area where they knew Walter was. After half an hour went by with no sign of Walter and with his men assuming the worst, he suddenly appeared approaching at a dead run without his rifle or any of his equipment except for the knife he always carried. He never told anyone what had happened, leaving them only with the image of himself running toward them at top speed.

Another time Walter's platoon was at the most forward part of the line. Men would alternate going to the front, taking turns every hour or so. Once when Walter had come back for a breather he was sitting with his back to the front line. Suddenly a Japanese soldier appeared running at full speed toward Walter with his bayonet fixed. Walter did not see him at first until one of the others called out. Walter fell to one side and managed to kill the soldier just before the enemy reached him.

Walter carried with him a big machete which he had somehow acquired. Once in a similar situation a Japanese soldier approached him and at the last moment Walter was again alerted, and he spun around and took the enemy's head completely off with the machete.

The acuteness of Walter's senses was demonstrated on another occasion when he was out on patrol. He had been gone a long time; his brother became worried and went looking for him in what was essentially a no-man's land. Eventually Gord came upon a building in a village and began sliding up along the side, staying close to the wall until he came to a window, and carefully looked to see what was inside. And there was Walter sitting in the building with a bin full of canned Japanese fish which he was opening with his trench knife and eating with chopsticks, his feet comfortably propped up. When his brother got close to the window, but before he even looked inside, Walter called out, "Hi, Gord. Come on in." He knew just by the sound of his brother's movements who it was.

Eventually Walter acquired a reputation with the enemy and they began looking for him personally, sending men on "kamikaze" assignments to get him. Before Iwo Jima all those efforts failed, but a mortar shell on the beach at that fateful landing finally ended Walter's run of luck.

During the assault on Iwo Jima, the craters formed by mortar shells provided some of the few places of shelter on the exposed beach. The attacking Americans often used these giant pits for protection. One of the tactics used by the Japanese defenders during the storming of the island was to drop a large mortar shell on the beach. Then without changing the mortar's target settings they would wait until a number of Americans were huddled within the crater. Then the Japanese would drop another shell in precisely the same spot, killing whoever was inside. Walter's platoon fell victim to this deadly strategy.

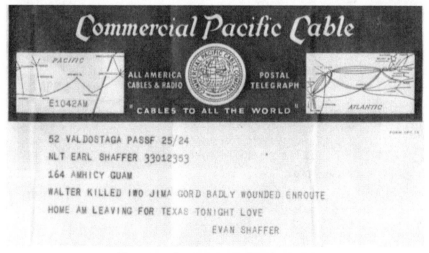

Cablegram informing Earl of Walter's death

Walter in "dress blues"

While Walter was headed for Iwo Jima, Earl was a thousand miles away on Angaur in the Palaus, where he received his last letter from Walter. Its tone was ominous and heavy with foreboding, reflecting the premonition that Walter clearly felt. He closed the letter by promising to write again "if still afloat after the noise."

On the morning of the Iwo Jima landing Earl awoke to a feeling of desolation, his mind overwhelmed with a heavy sense of despair. When word came later that the Iwo Jima landing was under way, Earl knew "that Walter had come to the end of the trail." A few days later he received from home a radiogram, the contents of which he knew without opening it. Years later, after coming home from the war, Earl told his brother John that at the time of his friend's death, Earl had the distinct impression that something was wrong, that something had happened to Walter.

CHAPTER 10

WALTER ON THE TRAIL

By 1940 Earl and Walter had already taken a short trip on the Appalachian Trail, which they had discovered thanks to a neighbor, another outdoorsman, who spent much of his spare time searching for arrowheads and who somehow had acquired literature and maps about the Appalachian Trail.

Shortly after the war, Earl read in an outdoor magazine an article about the Appalachian Trail. The article noted that no one had ever hiked the entire Trail in one season, and indeed that such a feat was generally considered impossible. This was the kind of challenge that Earl found irresistible. Walter and Earl had talked about one day hiking the entire Appalachian Trail together. But when Earl came home and Walter did not, Earl was by his own admission "disgusted," and at first abandoned the idea of hiking the Trail. He got a job working as a carpenter for eighty-five cents an hour, work that before the war had paid him only twenty cents an hour. By the time the long delayed three-hundred-dollar Army bonus finally reached him, the earlier feelings had dissipated enough to let him see the extra money as an opportunity. "Now here's your chance," he thought, and in 1948 he set off (alone) on his history-making hike.

Years later, when asked if he thought at all about Walter during his hike, Earl answered that he was mostly too busy thinking about the hike itself and its immediate concerns. The one exception was a time hiking along the Smokies at night when he did think about Walter. Earl may have been remembering by moonlight the face that he had once watched by firelight.

Occasionally Earl would dream about his friend. Always the dreams were of Walter coming back from the war alive; he never dreamed of his dying. Surely a friend living, if only in a dream, is better than one completely lost.

PART THREE

WORLD WAR II

CHAPTER 11

MR. AMERICA

In 1940, with the war in Europe steadily intensifying, it became obvious to most people that the United States was bound to become involved sooner or later. We were already supplying more and more assistance to Britain, and American ships had come under attack by German submarines. The sense of imminent involvement grew even stronger when in September of 1940 Congress enacted the first peacetime draft in the nation's history. The law authorized the enrollment of up to nine hundred thousand men and provided that all men between the ages of twenty-one and forty-five had to register for one year of service. A national lottery was set up to determine the order of selection.

As noted earlier, Earl drew a number that was in the mid-range, leaving his likelihood of being chosen uncertain. At twenty-two years old and looking for work, Earl found himself essentially unemployable because of the uncertainty of his draft status. After waiting six months without being called into the service, he finally decided to volunteer for the draft to get it over with. Once in the Army, however, he discovered that being a volunteer made no difference; he was treated the same as any draftee.

So it was that on Tuesday, April 15, 1941, Earl Shaffer was part of a trainload of draftees who left York at 6:00 A.M., bound for the Army Center at New Cumberland near Harrisburg, Pa. There the men underwent a physical examination to determine their fitness to serve. Those who passed were forthwith sworn in, after which they were marched to the dispensary where they were given two shots and a vaccination simultaneously. Such was their introduction to the Army way of doing things.

After being fed an unappetizing breakfast, the York contingent were put on another train along with other men from all over Pennsylvania, their destination this time being New York City. After a gloomy start, the atmosphere on the train brightened somewhat when one of nature's born comedians made his presence known and entertained his fellow yard-birds with a line of amusing banter that featured tales about his home in "Pleasant Valley." It turned out that this piece of heaven was actually a coal mining town that one suspects was a long way from "pleasant." Nevertheless, the storyteller continued his outrageous bragging which he clearly expected no one to believe. The train ride proved much more relaxing than might have been expected.

Upon arrival in Grand Central Station, the draftees were transferred to another train for the relatively short trip to the Signal Corps training camp at Fort Monmouth, New Jersey. Following IQ and various aptitude tests, Earl found himself assigned to the radio repair school, along with men from a wide range of backgrounds, including one man who had been a judge in civilian life. Most of Earl's fellow apprentice repairmen were bachelors in their early thirties, with no dependents. The average IQ was high and many later became officers. Although Earl's own IQ was above average, his distaste for the officers he had so far encountered had left him with no desire to become an officer himself.

There followed a dreary daily routine of rising at 5:30 in the morning, eating a barely edible breakfast prepared by student cooks with little interest in that trade, and marching a mile each way to the site of the classrooms where the day was passed in a tiresome combination of tradi-tional military drill and classroom schooling.

Probably as a result of being Signal Corps personnel, they had little firearms training, and what they did have was somewhat haphazard, involving the Springfield rifle and .45 caliber revolver. In their rifle train-ing they were taught how to hold a rifle and how to squeeze the trigger gently. On the rifle range Earl forgot the new training he had just received and reverted to the firing style he had used at home. When he realized what he was doing, he turned to the man coaching him and started to apologize. The coach told him to continue what he was doing since he seemed to be hitting mostly bullseyes anyway.

The firing practice with the revolver became somewhat hectic, not to mention dangerous. One sergeant was alarmingly careless, waving his weapon here and there in a random fashion. He was quickly hustled off the range. The man who brought the sergeant's weapon back was little better, and he too was led away for safety's sake. Later on, Earl also had familiarization training with the Thompson submachine gun, the Eddystone rifle, and the M16. He never had occasion to use any of these weapons in combat, although much of his work in the South Pacific was under combat conditions, and occasionally he did come under enemy fire.

When a boxing tournament was announced, Earl promptly signed up. He and Walter had spent many hours boxing together at home, and Earl considered himself reasonably competent in the ring. Although the common practice was to withhold passes until the men had completed basic training, the winner of the boxing tournament was promised a three-day pass. Earl won and got his pass. His first stop was in Philadelphia to visit his oldest brother, Dan, who lived in the Germantown section of the city.

Throughout his military career, which lasted four and one-half years, he found that the regard his uniform brought him was frequently less than favorable. While walking down the street near his brother's home he passed a little boy playing on the sidewalk. The boy looked up and noticing the uniform said, "You're a bum; all soldiers are bums." Earl just kept on going. Several years later in Hawaii, Earl recalled passing a boy of about eight who looked up at him and said, "Mr. America."

"So I guess I'm somewhere in between," Earl observed, "but that was the extremes that I've been called in my lifetime."

Except for the extraordinary three-day pass that he managed to get, there were limited opportunities for individual excursions off base. As partial compensation, however, the Army authorities did, on occasion, assemble groups which were taken on a tour of New York City at night. As part of the tour they were taken by boat up the coast past Staten Island and the Statue of Liberty, after which they walked for several hours in Manhattan before heading back to camp. Unexciting as this experience may sound, it did provide the men with a break from routine and some time away from camp.

After basic training Earl spent some time at Camp Claiborne in Louisiana before participating in the famous "Carolina Maneuvers." The latter was a massive military exercise conducted late in 1941 over a vast area of the two Carolinas. It involved half a million men, nearly a third of the U.S. Army at that time. A similar exercise was conducted over much of Louisiana. The two events were intended to prepare the U.S. Military establishment for eventual involvement in the war then raging in Europe. Earl later described the Carolina Maneuvers as "one of the most rugged experiences of my life."

On one occasion most of the trucks in Earl's outfit got mired in the mud of a pasture following a heavy overnight rain. The next day the trucks were hauled out by teams of fifty men and one very heavy rope.

It was during the Maneuvers, still fairly early in his military career, that Earl experienced an example of the uncertainties that could derail hopes for Army advancement. Earl's outfit had the best record by far of all the sections, but for some reason the Commanding Officer did not like the Section Sergeant. As a consequence, Earl's group never got any recognition or ratings. The Sergeant said that since they were always behind the eight ball, they might as well call themselves the Eight Ball Section. Taking the Sergeant at his word, one of the section members painted an eight ball on a board, which the men then bolted on their truck's grill guard.

"People stared at it when we passed by," Earl wrote, "and we laughed, and they laughed too, but didn't know the reason."

They returned to Camp Claiborne early in December, about a week before the bombing of Pearl Harbor. After that momentous event there followed, at first, little noticeable change in their routines. On the night before Christmas, however, at about bedtime, the whistle blew and the men were told to prepare to leave in six hours. They frantically loaded all the trucks with the many tons of equipment needed for the battle zone communications depot they were intended to be. At about dawn on Christmas day, the men were once again assembled and told that there had been a change of plans. The trucks that had been hastily packed had to be unpacked and then repacked in a more orderly fashion. While this work was being done, they had their hurried Christmas dinner in relays. The loaded trucks were then taken to a railroad siding where they were cabled on flatcars. At this point the orders were changed again, and the men had to move the gear from the trucks into railroad boxcars. By the time this work was finished, it was midnight of the day after Christmas and the men had still had no rest. Then they were rushed to the dispensary for yellow fever shots. After turning in everything except the personal items in their barracks bags, they were assembled in tents and told to await the orders to move. The exhausted men sat on the ground, back to back, and promptly fell asleep.

The following day they set off on their long, tedious train trip to the west coast. The new year arrived someplace in west Texas; they never knew exactly where. A few of the bored, weary men decided that a celebration was called for if there was any way one could be arranged. When the train stopped at a siding to refuel, they spotted a rough-looking man nearby. After catching his attention, he was given a five-dollar bill and asked to get them "a bottle." The man took the money and headed off, disappearing around a corner. A scoffer in the group assured all within hearing that the man and money would never be seen again. The cynic seemed to be right when the train started to pull away from the siding. At the last moment, however, the man appeared and, running up to the train handed them not only a bottle of whisky but a handful of change as well. It wasn't much liquor for the number of men involved, but a modest celebration did take place.

They passed through Los Angeles at night, arriving at a San Francisco dock in the rain the following morning. The men all assumed they were about to ship off to war. Instead, they were loaded on a harbor vessel that took them to a transit camp on Angel Island not far from Alcatraz. They stayed there for three weeks where their principal occupation was speculating about what would happen next. Then they were put back on the same harbor vessel to sail back to the dock they had started from three weeks earlier, and where it was once again raining. There they found their trucks parked, but with their canvas tops removed and the contents gone. They never saw their equipment again. After putting the tops back on the trucks, they climbed aboard and headed down the coast to Fort Ord.

Earl and his team passed about three months at Fort Ord where they did nothing but routine duty—KP and guard duty principally. They were seemingly lost in some bureaucratic military shuffle. Next they were moved—again in the rain—to the Cow Palace, a large farm show arena on the south side of San Francisco. This facility at that time was surrounded by high fences with guards at all entrances. The men were assigned quarters in box stalls with dirt floors under the grandstand, four men per stall. The area had not been cleaned very well, and still gave off the aroma of former bovine inhabitants. Other men were quartered in every conceivable place where a bunk could be inserted. Meals were served outdoors; when it rained, the troops simply donned rain gear and ate in the rain.

One night while at the Cow Palace the men were "entertained" by a makeshift USO show. A stage was fabricated and set up, and a section of seats cleared. The show itself left much to be desired. First there was a dancing class of young girls who performed one of their beginner routines. Next, a young woman offered a reading from Shakespeare in which she herself took all of the parts. Finally, a more mature woman, who had outgrown whatever youthful talent she may once have had, sang some songs. At about this stage in the evening's proceedings Earl noticed that

Cow Palace at time of Earl's residence

men had begun to leave, and he decided to do the same. Alas, he had waited too long, and guards were now stationed at all the doors to prevent a total exodus. This was the first of only three USO shows that Earl saw during his four and a half years in the service.

From the Cow Palace the men were shuttled back through San Francisco and up along the Sacramento River to the city of Sacramento where they were housed for a few weeks in buildings at the State Fairground. In due course they left the California capitol to return to San Francisco, this time to the Presidio where in 1776 the Spanish established their military center in North America. At the time of Earl's stay there, the Presidio was one of the premier Army posts in the U.S. Here, at last, Earl and his team were on the brink of embarkation.

The evening before their departure Earl took a stroll along the shore for a last look at the bay. As he walked along he happened to glance toward the incoming surf where he saw a dead soldier who had been washed in, having drowned the week before. Earl located a patrolling guard whom he informed about his find. Earl himself then left the area as quickly as he could, not wanting to be detained as a witness and possibly separated from the rest of his outfit.

A ROUGH PASSAGE

They left San Francisco the next day headed for Hawaii, a voyage that would normally take three or four days. The vessel on which they sailed was an old one. Built in 1903 as a luxury liner, it had been converted during World War I into a troop ship, which is what it had been ever since. It had declined considerably since its luxury days. Earl described it as "a dirty, rough old thing." The toilet facilities for the troops had been built on the deck from slab lumber, and were flushed every five minutes by a surge of sea water that washed the waste overboard. "The food was terrible," Earl said. "We almost starved."

The ship had been out on the water at the time of the Pearl Harbor bombing. When a submarine was sighted ahead of the convoy the ship was part of, they turned back and speeded up. In the process they burned out the engine which later took six months to repair. Consequently Earl was on the maiden voyage of a rebuilt engine that could cruise at only six knots. Top speed was nine knots. The troop ship was the slowest one in the convoy, and all the others were obliged to accommodate the laggard. It took them nine days to reach Hawaii.

A partial compensation for the mostly unpleasant voyage was provided at the start by two girls high above them on the Golden Gate Bridge, waving colorful scarves. Later on, Earl resolved to write a book about the war after he got home; the book he contemplated would start with these lines:

> They waved from Golden Gate bridge,
> as the big troop ship passed under,
> two girls with colorful scarves,
> who were they I wonder?

Earl had never been more than 100 miles away from home before he entered the Army. He had even turned down a chance to go to the New York Worlds Fair which was only 150 miles away. His life was clearly changing.

CHAPTER 12

ARMY LIFE

ARMY FOOD

Army food was "generally terrible." The best food, strangely enough, was usually provided by the Navy. On one occasion they were in a situation where the Air Corps was supposed to feed them but would not do so. Earl's unit acquired some Navy dungarees and other apparel that allowed them to go through the Navy food line and "get half decent food." As a bonus, the Navy had ice cream mix and refrigeration on their ships, so they got ice cream, which otherwise for two years they only got when they happened to get back to Hawaii.

During the early months of Earl's Army career the cooks that he generally encountered were student cooks who did not really want to be cooks. The Army's philosophy at that time seemed to be not to let a new recruit do what he wanted to do. Anyway, according to Earl, "There would be ten guys at a table, and once a week they would bring out a great big platter and on the platter was half cooked macaroni in long strips that had never been broken, with canned tomatoes dumped on top. And it wasn't cooked." Some of the men would just skip the meal and eat candy bars from the PX.

For breakfast sometimes the men were served the old Army standard: SOS (shit on a shingle), which was a military approximation of creamed dried beef on toast. Actually this was the first meal he got in the Army. That uninspiring breakfast was followed up by shots in both arms, one for typhoid and one for tetanus. Earl blamed this combination—food and shots—for a problem he had at reveille. "They kick you out of bed at 5:15, yelling and hollering." After hastily pulling on his clothes and rushing outside to stand in formation, he just passed out. This happened twice. After the first instance, the sergeant told him if he felt this coming on, he should just break ranks and leave. So the next time he felt this condition developing, he started to leave and even as he was continuing to walk he started to sag and was about to fall on his face when one big, strong individual who saw what was happening jumped out and grabbed him before he fell.

Eventually he got to sick call and, after waiting three or four hours, the doctor took one look at him and said he had enteritis (inflammation of the intestine). When he went to the dispensary to get the pills the doctor ordered, he was told that they "didn't make any this week and you'll have to come back next week. "In the meantime I could have died!" Earl said. " That's the Army. They don't care about the individual in the Army. They can always replace you. It's pretty hard to replace guns and tanks and stuff, but they can replace a man."

DENTAL PROBLEMS

Earl's teeth went bad while he was in the Army because of the lack of dental care. For more than two years he was stationed on various islands where there was no dentist for months at a time; no chance of even getting a tooth pulled. The pain that inevitably developed simply had to be suffered. This problem was further aggravated once when the monthly supply ship was sunk and the troops had to survive for a time on what could be flown in. In these airborne deliveries was included a supply of hard candy which, out of sheer hunger, Earl and others chewed up instead of letting the sugar dissolve. The result was even more dental damage.

He did manage to get some dental work done once when he was back in Hawaii, but he was never there long enough for a comprehensive dental program to be implemented. Throughout much of his later life Earl claimed that he avoided toothache by taking bonemeal tablets, and he never went to dentists because he did not want the dentures that he was sure they would recommend.

SIGNAL CORPS

Earl's unit was frequently moving from place to place and island to island, essentially living in a foxhole or slit trench. "On those Godforsaken little places," as Earl put it. Often they were so near sea level they couldn't use a foxhole "or we'd have drowned," as Earl put it. If the tide were extra high, then a slit trench forced the occupants to lie in water.

When bombs hit the palm trees, they would explode and scatter shrapnel everywhere. For protection they cut the fallen palm trees into shorter sections with which they covered the slit trenches, leaving just enough room to crawl into the trench.

Their barracks bags were from World War I, as were the guns they were provided. They had the old-style mess kits without partitions so that everything got dumped in one pile. In addition to everything else, they were often half-starving.

FIREARMS

As a country boy growing up in rural Pennsylvania, Earl had been shooting guns most of his life—mostly .22 calibers. At Fort Monmouth he was issued a .45-caliber revolver from World War I cavalry. When he got to Hawaii, however, they gave him a "Tommy" gun (Thompson submachine gun). Before leaving, they took the Tommy gun back because, according to Earl, they didn't want it to get out of their control. He was then sent to the South Pacific with a British World War I machine gun that had been chambered for American ammunition.

Although Earl was not in Hawaii during the Japanese bombing of Pearl Harbor, he heard all the stories that have since become part of World War II folklore. Many of the service men had been given weekend passes, and their weapons and ammunition had been locked up. When the attack started about eight o'clock on Sunday morning, many thought it was American planes practicing. Once they realized what was really happening, they began breaking down doors to get to their locked-up weapons. The result was, among other things of course, that a great many pistols were taken and never returned. Earl worked with a man who had stolen a .45 automatic in this way.

Once down in the islands Earl found himself on a sailing schooner with a New Zealand captain, an Australian mate, and a Micronesian crew. The machine gun available had been ruined by sea water and was inoperable. The ammunition for it, moreover, was heavily corroded but they found that it did fit the old beat-up rifles they had. The captain gave them the ammunition from which they scraped the corrosion before putting it in their rifles. Mostly they used it to shoot at gulls and other handy targets. "It's a wonder we didn't kill each other," Earl later observed.

ADDING INSULT TO INJURY

After Germany surrendered, the military authorities created a movie *Two Down and One to Go*. All service men were required to see the movie, and it went on their service record. The movie's main message was that now that everything was resolved in Europe the men would have to go to the Pacific and finish the job. Earl took personal offense at this since he had already been in the Pacific for three years.

WAR'S END

Earl was back in Hawaii when the war ended; they were up on a plateau in the pineapple fields. The night the war ended they could look down on Pearl Harbor ten miles away where a multitude of anti-aircraft guns were being fired in celebration. Earl took his little old camera and put it on time exposure, and then let it sit for about five minutes. When the film was developed, all he got was a band of light right across the picture.

By this time Earl was so sick of the war that he didn't feel much of anything at its end. He was emotionally numb. In retrospect he attributed his survival to a guardian angel. Or "maybe it was for the sake of my poetry, I don't know."

CHAPTER 13

MILITARY MISADVENTURES

NOTE: When this writer was in the Army (as an enlisted man) in the mid-1950s, there was a common saying: "There's a right way, a wrong way, and the Army way." Earl offers a multitude of examples that serve to justify that aphorism.

—M.J.F.

Throughout the war Earl often believed that he was unfairly treated and taken advantage of. It all began during his first stint in Hawaii. Based on his experience and skill, he had been selected to be part of an engineering inspection crew where he found himself the lowest ranked man on the team even though he was more knowledgeable than most of the others. This in itself would not have bothered him much if he had been allowed to express his ideas and suggestions, but he was rarely allowed even this much freedom. "I was always the lowest ranking guy on the crew, yet I was the most knowledgeable," he said. "That was the story of my life."

In spite of the often dismal living conditions, Earl's team became skilled and efficient in doing their jobs. This proficiency did not always work to their advantage. On occasion, a local commanding officer, having in the past endured sub-par service from other teams, would insist on keeping Earl's group longer than they would have preferred.

One time they couldn't get away from an island because the Navy commander there was unhappy about the lack of progress being made by other crews. At the same time, Earl's crew was doing the same type of work and getting finished much faster. Finally the officer had Earl's group take over the other team's work and finish it up. At this point the officer decided to put in a power system for the whole (rather small) island. This would involve high-tension work which Earl's team was not equipped to do. They expected to get themselves electrocuted. Earl described the proposed high-tension project as "stupid."

In seeking a solution to their dilemma they found that they were blocked from getting a radio message through to Headquarters in Hawaii. With the help of a sympathetic master sergeant they finally succeeded in communicating with headquarters. After explaining the situation, an order soon came through countermanding the orders of the local commander.

By the time he got back to the States, Earl was thoroughly embittered by the Army bureaucracy. Although he believed that he often knew better ways of doing the work at hand, he was not allowed to do it his way. Those who outranked him feared that if Earl's suggestions were used he would get a higher ranking than they had. Many times his anger nearly got away from him, but he was always outranked and forced to back off. "I did the most important work that we did and never got the credit for it," he said.

When Earl first started doing Signal Corps work in the islands, his small crew of from two to eight people would do any necessary work for whatever service branch needed it—sometimes Air Force, sometimes Navy. Later a joint-communications approach was instituted. The other branches were less than fully cooperative, however. Instead of full participation in a coordinated effort, the others would send a single representative and then claim that they participated. Then the other branch would go back and put in their own installation at a substantial increase in cost. The cost was further inflated by the limiting of each man's work to his own particular specialty. The end result was that it took perhaps twenty-four men to replicate what Earl's small team had been doing.

OFFICERS

With few exceptions, Earl had little but contempt for the officers he came in contact with during his Army career. For example, when the war finally ended and he was brought back to Hawaii, he wound up spending three months there waiting for the military mills to grind him through. At one time "this little shavetail that probably was in about nine months" spent some time telling the waiting men how lucky they were to be going back so soon. (*Shavetail* is military slang for a newly commissioned second lieutenant.) This particular officer was very demanding about being saluted.

The officer in command of the service company to which Earl's unit was attached started with a company of about two hundred men. Some of the men had been over there nearly six years when they were caught in the war about the time they were scheduled to go back home. Pearl Harbor was bombed and they were frozen with their units. Later replacements were supposedly sent so the long-timers could at least have a furlough. The officer in charge, however, simply kept them all, old and new, and gradually built up the numbers in his command until he had the equivalent of a battalion. When he complained about this "inequity" he was given a promotion.

Marine Corps officers, including their non-coms, were, in Earl's opinion, the worst of all. Many were threatened by the men under them, and took a demotion rather than to sail into combat with the men. They feared being thrown overboard at night. "That's one reason I didn't like the Marine Corps;" Earl said, "because of their attitude and that they killed my buddy needlessly."

One of the rare exceptions was an officer who had come up through the ranks and gone to Officer Candidate School. He was friendly with the enlisted men and even shared his liquor ration with them. This made the other officers so angry that they took his jeep away. He happened to be the island communications officer but without any means of transportation.

LENDING MONEY

Earl had some bad experiences with lending money to fellow soldiers. This began while he was still at Fort Monmouth where a tech-sergeant from Texas who had a cold asked Earl to lend him five dollars to get cough medicine. Earl complied and never saw his money again. The cough medicine turned out to be whiskey.

The story about how this same tech-sergeant got his promotion was that while still a buck private he was part of a group that decided to go into town to get drunk. To expedite this adventure he took a jeep without permission, which he later wrecked. Regulations required that he pay for the cost of the jeep, so in order to pay off his debt sooner he was given a promotion to provide higher pay.

PLAYING FOOTBALL

While waiting for the Carolina maneuvers to get started. Earl was playing football one day when he was hit by a very large opposing player.

They had no padding or any other protection, and Earl's shoulder was badly hurt. It quickly became numb and he could feel nothing in it. He went to a medic who raised his arm and asked, "Does this hurt?"

Earl replied, "Of course not; it's numb." The doctor then rubbed some wintergreen on the shoulder, and sent Earl on his way. Earl had guard duty that night, by which time the shoulder had begun to hurt fiercely. "I walked guard in the middle of the night with a shoulder that was almost unbearable," Earl commented later.

CHAPTER 14

UNDER THE SOUTHERN CROSS

E arl calculated that during his time in the South Pacific he visited twenty-two different islands, some as many as four times. In many cases the visit was merely a refueling stop en route to another island. A list of these exotic names reads like a travel brochure designed to entice a tourist on a South Sea cruise: Fiji, Palau, Noumea (The Paris of the Pacific), Belep, Christmas Island, Tongareva, Bora Bora, Pago Pago, Samoa, Funafuti, Nanumea, and many others. And over most of them at night hung the Southern Cross, concerning which Earl wrote one of his more haunting poems.[2]

OAHU
First Assignment
Once arrived in Hawaii, Earl was made part of a detachment assigned to Fort Shafter in Honolulu. This was the oldest Army post in the islands and home to a major Signal Corps center. They landed in Honolulu in the midst of a Kona storm, a type of cyclone that generally strikes Hawaii two or three times a year, usually in the winter. They last about a week during which life is made unpleasant. "The rest of the time Hawaii is nice," Earl noted. "It never gets more than maybe eighty and never below about seventy." In any case Earl and his buddies found themselves crowded into tents through which the mud flowed from uphill.

---

[2]"The Southern Cross" is included with the poems collected in *Before I Walked With Spring*. See Appendix.

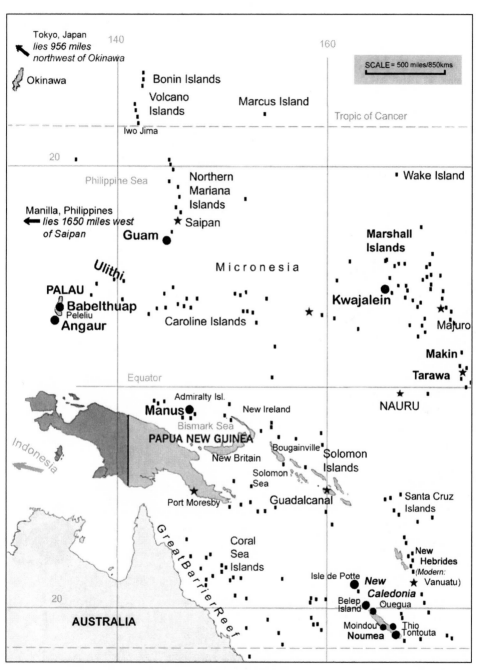

Western Pacific map

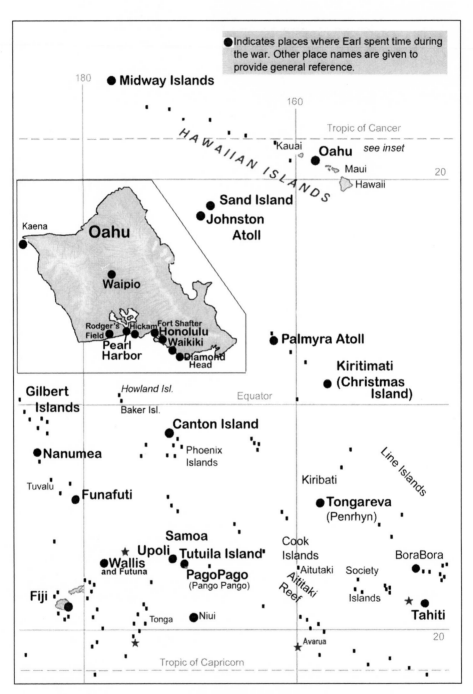

● Indicates places where Earl spent time during the war. Other place names are given to provide general reference.

Midway Islands

180

160

Tropic of Cancer

Kauai   **Oahu**   *see inset*

Maui

20

Hawaii

HAWAIIAN ISLANDS

Sand Island

Johnston Atoll

Kaena

Oahu

Waipio

Rodger's Field   Hickam   Fort Shafter
Honolulu
Waikiki
Pearl Harbor
Diamond Head

● **Palmyra Atoll**

Kiritimati (Christmas Island)

Gilbert Islands

Howland Isl.

Equator

Baker Isl.

Canton Island

Phoenix Islands

● **Nanumea**

Kiribati

Line Islands

Tuvalu

Funafuti

● **Tongareva** (Penrhyn)

Samoa
Upoli   **Tutuila Island**

Cook Islands

BoraBora

● **Wallis** and Futuna

PagoPago (Pango Pango)

Aitutaki

Society Islands

Aitutaki Reef

Fiji

Tonga   Niui

Avarua

Tahiti

20

Tropic of Capricorn

Eastern Pacific map

From this vantage point they could look down to Pearl Harbor where they could see the bottoms of overturned battleships sticking out of the water along with other wreckage. Nothing had yet been moved.

The Radar Crew

Earl was assigned to a seven-man radar crew which was dispatched to wherever they were most urgently needed for radar installations or other radar work. Everett Sturdy was a civilian in charge of the crew. Tex Davis was responsible for installing the diesels that provided the power. Of Davis, Sturdy commented years later, "He had a gun he carried with him; I guess all Texans carried a gun." The five remaining members were GIs who made up the "working crew." Somewhere in the South Pacific during a break from radar work, Earl—known to his crew mates as Shafe (rhymes with safe)—composed a lively poem describing the crew and its activities:

RADAR RACONTEURS

There's Tex and Sherman and Bobby
And Lyle and Eddie and me
Who travel with Mr Sturdy
To work in the Southern sea.

Our job is installing radar
And getting it "on the air."
We build what they plan on paper
In a planning room somewhere.

Sturdy's the boss and promoter
And Radio Engineer.
Tex Davis installs the diesels
For power to "fire the gear."

The rest of us guys are GI's
Who serve as the working crew:
Uncrating, installing, wiring,
Whatever there is to do.

We work from dawn to sunset
And after when we have light.

When Tex has given us power,
We work in the dead of night.

The deadline is never distant,
We always must race with time
Way out at some lonely outpost
Not far from the battle line.

Also according to Sturdy, Lyle was a "large fellow" and a good worker. Bobby, on the other hand, was given to drink. "I had to get him out of the stockade several times." Of Sherman, Sturdy says that he was a "good man. He was Jewish. One time we were eating ham and I said, 'Hey rabbi, you can't eat this, can you?' and he said 'I'll put some salt on it to keep it kosher.'"

Eddie Urbany and Earl were both Pennsylvanians, Eddie from Masontown (a small coal-mining town near Pittsburgh) and Earl from York. They both went through basic training at the same time at Fort Monmouth, New Jersey; they were both participants in the Carolina Maneuvers; and both were stationed at Camp Claiborne, Louisiana, at the same time. After they were both assigned to the Signal Corps at Fort Shafter in

Earl's radar crew on New Caledonia
(Back row: Prindle, Davis, Shaffer and Sturdy;
Front row: Robinson, Sherman and Urbany.)

Hawaii, they finally actually met on a flight to New Caledonia in 1942. As time passed Eddie came to be closer to Earl than anyone else on the crew.

Eddie remembered that Earl at times became depressed. It was during one of his depression episodes that Earl once said to Eddie, "If it wasn't against the Bible, I'd commit suicide."

As for Sturdy himself, he grew up in Los Angeles, and from an early age was attracted to the outdoors. He remembers going hunting for mule deer in the Santa Monica mountains as a boy. Sturdy arrived at Fort Shafter in January 1942. Because he had only one kidney, he did not serve in the military, but rather as a civilian radar engineer.

He recalled that Earl was very quiet and kept mostly to himself. "He was very mad about being in the Signal Corps. He wanted to be in the Rangers or Snipers or something." Although Sturdy knew nothing about Walter, it seems likely that Earl was envious of Walter's more exciting service as a Scout Sniper. Sturdy said that Earl "was always writing, I don't know what." As a worker Earl was "pretty good," Sturdy said, "but when there was a job to be done, Earl was always someplace else (hiking)."

Earl's unit worked for about six months setting up a radar installation on the north shore of the island facing the direction from which the Japanese planes had come. They labored in constant fear of a Japanese return to land and occupy Hawaii, which, Earl says, they could easily have done, but "they were too darn stupid to realize it."

Foraging on Oahu

When Earl and his crew rode around Oahu to their various work assignments, their transportation was in a lineman's truck, which had compartments for tools on both sides, and a space between where most of the crew rode. When passing a pineapple field, they sometimes stopped the truck long enough to grab some fruit, which they would then peel and chew on as they went on down the road, with the juice running down their chins. It was Earl's opinion that "pines" tasted infinitely better this way than out of a can. Of course this appropriation was illegal, and theoretically carried a twenty-five dollar fine. The potential punishment was routinely ignored and no fines were ever levied. At Waipio old pineapple fields were being used by the military, and the fruit had gone wild. Earl found these half wild pineapples even more tasty than the cultivated ones. At other times the men would grab a bunch of bananas which were then hidden in a tunnel while the fruit ripened. A somewhat more legal wild delicacy was the fruit of a cactus that grew on the Wai'anae Coast near Kaena Point.

Still another delicious fruit that the men knew only as a "mountain apple" was found on a sapling size tree that grew on the Koolau Range. The crew had been introduced to this fruit by a group of boys who regularly walked uphill along a flume that passed near the camp. The flume was used to carry water from higher up down to plantations in the plain below. Curiously, the men never saw the boys come back down again, and wondered why. Many years later Earl met a man who had lived for a time on Oahu and mentioned this puzzling pattern. The man laughed and replied that the answer was very simple: the boys floated back down in the plume and passed the camp unnoticed by the men.

Jake

On one occasion during his time in Hawaii, Earl and four others of his unit were summoned to the orderly room where they were informed that they were being assigned to a radar installation crew. In charge of the job was a civilian who had been employed by the Army for this task. Two other enlisted men had previously been assigned, making a total of seven enlisted men. The team was rounded out with one more individual, another civilian, but in this case a man who until recently had been serving in the Army before being discharged "for the convenience of the government." This former private first class (PFC) was named Jake.

The reason for Jake's change of status borders on the mysterious. He was barely twenty-one years old and had been serving in the Signal Corps in Hawaii during the Pearl Harbor bombing. He was on duty at the time of the attack, when he was operating an SCR-270 radar unit which was classified as portable, although it required three large trucks to transport it.

This massive equipment was operating on the north shore of Oahu, and was said to have a maximum range of 150 miles. Jake, however, had been able to extend the range to 400 miles. As a consequence, he detected the approaching Japanese planes two hours before they reached Pearl Harbor. Unfortunately his report of the "blips" to the north was discounted by his superiors because they simply refused to believe him, and no action was taken to prepare for an attack.

Jake was generally considered to be the best radar technician in the military. Because of the importance of the permanent radar installation being undertaken by Earl and his team, Jake was designated as chief consultant on the job. The new installation was on a cliff, and was completed very quickly under difficult conditions. Nonetheless, it worked perfectly the first time it was turned on. Earl attributes this success primarily to Jake's skill.

Twice during the months spent on installing the permanent radar, Jake was called back to Ft. Shafter to deal with problems that had developed in the radar rigs there—problems that no one on site had been able to correct. Earl was later told by Jake's coworkers at Shafter that in both cases Jake turned the unit on, scanned the scope several times, then turned it off, told the others what the problem was, and how to correct it. He was immediately brought back by truck in spite of the blackout. After sleeping in the truck during the return trip, Jake joined the rest of the crew on the job in the morning.

About six months later, Jake was sent to Guadalcanal where all of the radar rigs were operating either poorly or not at all. The spare parts for the radar units could not be found, so Jake made do with scavenged radio parts and managed to get all the units working properly. About the time Jake was preparing to leave, the missing radar parts turned up. They had been misdelivered to a Marine camp where they had simply been ignored.

Earl reports that after the Guadalcanal episode he never saw Jake again.

Ukulele and Guitar
Before leaving California on the troop ship bound for Hawaii, Earl had bought a guitar in Sacramento for five dollars. Although the men had been told not to take with them anything other than what was officially authorized, Earl, after fourteen months in the Army, was wise enough in military ways to know that the worst that could happen was that he would be ordered to throw it overboard. So he walked up the gangplank with a guitar in one hand and a barracks bag in the other, and nothing was said. In the end there were hundreds of men on the ship who played guitar, but only two guitars. Earl claimed that in nine days on the troop ship he never got to play his own guitar; it was just passed around among the other players. Some of those, it turned out, were accomplished professionals, including one man who had played in Roy Acuff's band.

Once after they got to Hawaii, Earl and a group of players got together and a man walked in carrying an antique ukulele made of coralwood. Earl described the wood as being a beautiful combination of alternating red and green colors. Apparently this particular ukulele was extremely old. The owner offered it to Earl for Earl's guitar and three dollars. To his later regret, Earl declined the offer only to have his guitar stolen from the supply room where he left it when he was sent to the South Pacific War Theater.

Later when he was getting ready for his return home, Earl bought a new ukulele like the one he had previously rejected. The new one cost him twenty-five dollars, although he believed it to be one of the last ever made.

Leaving Oahu

When their work on the Oahu radar installation was finished, and after idling around for a few weeks, Earl's group was summoned into head-quarters and offered an assignment "down under." This was to be a strictly volunteer job, since it was considered too important to put up with anyone who did not really want to be there. It would involve, they were told, working on radar installations in an active war zone. They were not given copies of their orders or even told the destination; only that they would fly to get there. This caused Earl some very brief hesitation, since he had never flown before and had always been uneasy about height. The temptation to see the South Sea islands was too great, however, and all quickly agreed to accept the offer.

Earl and his friend Eddie Urbany were the first to leave. The other members of the crew were, for some reason, to follow later. The two departed from Hickam Field in an LB-30 that was well past its prime. (An early version of the B-24, the LB-30 was designated a bomber, although it was mostly used for transport purposes.) They climbed into the plane through the bomb bay doors, along with the rest of the twenty passengers, where they made space for themselves among a variety of other cargo.

Then they had to wait about an hour while mechanics worked on one of the engines which had refused to start. Eventually they took off only to have the engine quit after about another hour. They finished the flight on three engines. Since no one had told them how cold it gets at high altitudes, they were wearing their usual tropical uniforms and shivered for eleven hours until the plane made a refueling stop at Canton island. Canton is a small island of the Phoenix Islands group, about midway between Hawaii and Fiji. At its widest point it is only about four and one-half miles across.

During their Canton stopover, they were given a meal that featured greasy potatoes. Earl thought it guaranteed to induce airsickness. They were then transferred to another plane and sent on their way with assurances that the first plane would be repaired and would catch up with them later.

After enduring seven more hours in the cold, they landed late in the afternoon at Nandi Airbase in Fiji where they were to spend the night. In the transit mess hall they ran into two acquaintances from their Fort

Monmouth days, who had been on Fiji for some time doing radar work. From the two long-term residents, Earl and Eddie learned that a traditional local dance was to be performed that evening. It would be the first such performance before a military audience. Earl and Eddie joined the crowd. After the natives danced and sang for awhile, the chief's daughter approached the commanding officer and insisted that he dance with her. Even though the local woman was a good head taller than the colonel, he gamely did his best. Then other women invited other staff officers to dance as well. Eventually Earl and Eddie left the group before they embarrassed themselves by bursting out in laughter.

The following day the first plane, now repaired, appeared, and they proceeded to their assignment destination: New Caledonia.

THE PEOPLE OF THE ISLANDS

Wherever he traveled beneath the Southern Cross, Earl made a point of getting acquainted with—and indeed, making friends with—the native inhabitants. He deplored the attitude of most other servicemen who simply assumed that the natives knew no English, so the American troops, by and large, made no effort to communicate with the locals. Earl quickly learned, however, that many of the natives had been to high school and acquired a working knowledge of a very passable English. Many of the natives, Earl realized, were quietly listening in on conversations deriding them and their ways, and understanding every word. The English as spoken by many of the natives was a very sophisticated pidgin which Earl had no difficulty understanding.

On one island Earl developed a friendship with a native who was a college graduate. This man gave Earl a great deal of information about the local culture. On the islands administered by the British the best students got to go to a central high school, and the best ones from there, in turn, would get to go to college. Education arrangements were apparently quite different on islands administered by the French and other European powers. Earl singled out for particular scorn in this regard the French, who apparently tended to turn educational responsibilities over to the church.

Earl generally spoke well of the native people he came in contact with. He referred to the light-skinned Polynesians as Kon-Tiki people, a reference to the book by Thor Heyerdahl who proposed a theory that the Polynesians originally came from South America. Some of them, Earl observed, even had blue eyes. Their clothing was usually made of tapa cloth which is made from the bark of a tree. The men wore a lava-lava, and the women a muumuu. Earl describes a lava-lava as being something like a kilt; the women's garments were generally longer. The women were often beautiful when in their teens, but tended to get heavy later. Earl blamed this on the diet of poi, a local dietary staple made from the root of taro, a common local vegetable. The young girls would perform the hula dance—considerably less risqué in Earl's view than the Hollywood version. The larger, older women would play the ukulele to accompany the dancing.

NEW CALEDONIA

While exploring the southwest Pacific Ocean in 1774, the British navigator Captain James Cook came upon a large island, the mountainous profile of which was said to have reminded him of Scotland, his father's native land. In paternal tribute, he named the newfound island Caledonia, the ancient romantic name for Scotland. Although it took several decades to move into high gear, the race among European nations to colonize this find was underway. Ultimately this was a race that England lost to France, although the name assigned by Cook persisted as the island group came to be known as New Caledonia. The principal island of this collection eventually received the name Grande Terre (Big Land).

The first European settlements were established in 1841, and in 1853, on the orders of Napoleon III, New Caledonia was declared a French colony. Later a penal colony was established there, and in 1864 the first prisoners transported from France arrived. This practice continued until 1897 when the last load of prisoners came ashore. The penal colony itself was closed in 1922, and non-criminal immigration began in earnest. The new residents arrived from Europe as well as from Indonesia which provided the multitude of workers needed by the nickel mines that were by then flourishing. (It has since been determined that roughly a fourth of the world's supply of nickel ore deposits is located in New Caledonia.)

Grande Terre is a long, relatively slender island trending from northwest to southeast. It is 220 miles long, with width varying from 31 to 43 miles. A mountain range runs down the middle of the island and includes a number of impressive peaks, the highest of which is Mont Panié, rising 5,341 feet above sea level, surpassing the 5,267 feet of Maine's Katahdin. It is more than likely that during his many days of idleness while in New Caledonia, Earl would have climbed Mont Panié, perhaps not even realizing the height that he had scaled.

New Caledonia is located at the eastern edge of the Coral Sea about 750 miles east of Australia and 930 miles northwest of New Zealand.

When Hitler's advance in Europe brought the establishment of the Vichy puppet government in France, New Caledonia—after an internal struggle—elected to cast its lot with the Free French Government of Charles de Gaulle.

With the bombing of Pearl Harbor and the entry of Japan into World War II there came a worrisome concern that the advancing Japanese Empire might succeed in severing the sea lanes between the United States and its important ally Australia. This concern precipitated the hurried establishment of an American military presence in New Caledonia to forestall Japanese ambitions in this area. Earl Shaffer became a part of that military build-up.

Five Thousand Miles from Their Outfit without Orders

It was in New Caledonia that the men were dumped off at Plaine Des Gaiacs Airfield, located on the west coast of Grande Terre, halfway along the island. At that time this was still a little jungle airstrip being used as a relay station on the way to Australia. Later it was expanded by the American forces into a major base. The airfield was named for the Gaiac trees that grow in the area.

The men were still without orders. All along they had assumed that the plane crew had their orders, but when they asked for them, they were told that the crew did not have them either. All that was known for certain was that they were on the plane's manifest. So there they were, a good five thousand miles away from their outfit without orders.

The post authorities thought the men were AWOL and would not allow them off the post. For a week they were housed in a kind of shanty that was built in New Zealand. Finally an officer appeared who was from the same outfit as the confused wanderers, although they had never before encountered each other. When the situation was explained to this officer, he said, "I think I know where they're supposed to go." So he took charge of the situation and the men finally ended up at the big signal depot in Noumea, the largest city in New Caledonia, sometimes described as the Paris of the South Pacific.

After an unsettling flight they arrived at Tontouta Air Base at night. The C-47 that took them nearly crashed at take-off and again at landing. Later they learned that the pilot's previous experience had been limited to pursuit planes; this was the first time he had flown a multi-engine plane. Fortunately the head officer was still in his office, and he found them a place to stay. Otherwise, Earl feared, they might have spent the night wandering around Noumea looking for a place to sleep. The next day, at last, they found someone who knew they were coming and even had a copy of their orders. This individual obligingly made copies of the orders and gave them to the bemused men, thereby restoring to them their lost identities.

They were given quarters in a house along with a number of other GIs, and there they waited until, a week later, the rest of the crew arrived. Their assignment, they finally learned, was to install one of the massive radar units on the north shore of Grande Terre. An engineer company was already there building a road and a bomb-resistant building. Mr. Sturdy signed out a truck which turned out to be a three-quarter-ton weapons carrier with four-wheel drive. The eight-man crew along with their belongings and equipment finally got aboard and they set off.

The Black Engineers

After a few miles the two-way gravel road ended at an outpost manned by two New Zealanders who told the crew that from that point on, the road was wide enough for only one vehicle at at time, and one was approaching from the other end. This information was thanks to a phone line that had been strung between the outposts at either end. Meanwhile, the crew was invited to have a "spot of tay." The tea in question was in an old #10 can which was kept simmering and looked none too sanitary. Beside the tea was a can of sugar and a punctured can of "cow." Notwithstanding the unattractive appearance of this refreshment set-up, Earl said it was about the best tea he had ever tasted.

Later when they were once again on their way along the narrow road, rain began to fall. At one point, with Sturdy driving, they started to skid and ended up in a ditch—happily on the uphill side. Otherwise they would have plunged into a ravine. After sitting reflectively for awhile, Sturdy finally said, "Well, who's going to drive." To this Lyle, a husky farm boy from Wisconsin, responded, "I will. I used to drive a quarry truck."

Lyle managed to get them out of the ditch, and then drove them safely to the village of Thio where they found a small store. Here they bought some canned peaches and French bread. Beyond the village was a river that had to be forded at low tide. Even then it proved a daunting challenge. Lyle persevered, however, and the crew continued on their way. On the far side, between the river and another mountain they came to a meadow where they found a tent encampment.

As they drove up, they noticed a tall blond man wearing nothing but underwear and boots. They hailed him informally, "Hey, Joe, where can we stay? We're the radar crew." He pointed to an empty tent. As the crew was unloading their truck, they saw another man come up and salute the half-naked blond. To their mortification, they discovered that he was Lt. Stokes who was in command of a detachment of the 810th Engineers. This was the outfit that was building the road and erecting the steel building.

One of two Black Engineer Aviation Battalions formed during World War II, the 810th was serving in New Caledonia while Earl was there. The road they were building with little more than a worn-out bulldozer was a marvel of engineering. It passed through a swamp and up a rocky ravine before climbing to a small peak several hundred feet above the Pacific. Various other outfits had previously studied the situation and said it couldn't be done. Lt. Stokes, a product of Georgia Tech, decided to give it a try. In the process he lost all but two of his trucks, including a compressor rig, in headlong plunges. Fortunately, no one was killed. Fortunately also, he had a half-track, which was the only vehicle capable of reaching the site in bad weather.

Subsequently, the Signal Corps group named the road the Stokes Memorial Highway.

Fish Fry

Not surprisingly, the men of the 810th shared the common Southern passion for fish and chicken fries. Chicken was not to be found on New Caledonia, but fish there were in abundance. Hardly a week passed when there were not at least two fish fry excursions. These activities were abetted by one of the battalion's White officers who, being himself from the South, shared their fondness for deep-fried seafood. He it was who made available the dynamite that was used in their heavy-handed fishing technique. The engineers, fortunately, always carried an extra ton of dynamite along when they went on a job. Earl's Signal Corps group who worked closely with the engineers were generally invited to come along on these dining adventures.

The party would head for a remote section of the island and then seek out a secluded valley where they would select a spot that seemed likely to attract an abundance of fish. A bundle of dynamite sticks were tied together and tossed out into the water. The array was then detonated from a battery box, sending up a vast boil of water along with a considerable quantity of dead or dying fish. Immediately, the best swimmers in the group stripped off their clothing and dove into the water on an unorthodox fishing expedition. Subsequently, with an abundance of fresh fish on hand, the fish fry itself took place. In Earl's words, "The fish were as delicious as only an experienced southern colored boy could prepare them."

By the time the meal was well under way, plans for the next fish fry were being cooked up along with the sizzling fish in the deep, hot pans of lard.

At one of these fries Earl noticed one young man who was especially skillful at collecting fish. His dives were deeper and longer than the others, and invariably he came up with three or four fish in hand. Unlike the other swimmers, this one was wearing undershorts which puzzled Earl at first. The answer proved to be simple: the man was a native Black Frenchman, which seemed to explain both his swimming skill and his modesty.

Later when the Frenchman had changed to dry clothes, he approached the group that was clustered around the accumulated fish. In his hand he held a half dollar that Mr. Sturdy had given him for his help with collecting the fish. He showed the coin to Earl and questioningly said, *"bon"*? Earl nodded his head and responded, *"forty francs."* The Frenchman looked puzzled, and using his finger he wrote in the sand, *"forty-three."* It turned out that he was right; forty-three francs was the official exchange rate for fifty U.S. cents. The man had been questioning not the value of the coin, but its authenticity. He then used the coin to purchase *forty-three francs* worth of fish from the communal catch.

Tate

Tate was a tall, powerfully built member of the 810th, whose coal black eyes had a fearless look that along with a firmly set chin suggested strongly that he was not a man to be crossed. His home was in Baltimore, and he told Earl how he had quit school when his father died and then helped to put his brothers and sisters through high school, and some through college

At the time Earl first met him, his face was covered with recently healed scars resulting from having the jeep he was driving hit head-on by a two-and-one-half-ton truck. Although it was determined that Tate was not at fault, he was not spared a long hospital stay. Earl later commented, "He must have been too tough to die." Tate was something of a jack of all trades who tended to wind up with the most difficult jobs, all of which eventually yielded to his strength and ingenuity.

One day while shell hunting, Earl found a sea bean that was shiny and black, about the size of a quarter dollar. A sea bean is the seed from any of a number of tropical plants which are capable of finding their way into the ocean and traveling great distances before coming to another tropical shore where they can germinate and extend the range of their species. When he showed his find to Tate, the engineer got quite excited and announced that it was a "luck charm." Despite Earl's assurances that it was just a kind of bean, Tate implored Earl to bring him one the next time he found a specimen. This Earl did a few days later, after which Tate considered him a special friend.

Tate rarely had much to say to his co-workers but when he did, it was short and to the point. He never bothered anyone and expected to be treated likewise. "I ain't got no eddication," he would say, "but I got a heap of common sense."

Corporal Jackson

Corporal Jackson of the 810th was considered the best steeplejack on the island even though back home in Detroit he had been only a shoeshine boy. He had a firm faith in himself that extended even to the dice with which he had managed to win more than a thousand dollars, all of which he sent home to his wife.

When Earl first encountered him, Jackson was working on an antenna tower that extended 180 feet straight up. The tower was supported by only a network of guy lines that were anchored in the coral. Although it was dangerous work, Jackson seemed completely unafraid. One evening in the PX he was asked if he ever got scared way up there with the wind blowing so hard and the clouds scudding past just above his head. He grinned in the way he had and looked around before responding, "What do the wind say to Jackson when it whisper past up there? It say, 'Go down, Jackson; go down shoeshine boy.'"

Malaria and Mosquitoes

In New Caledonia Earl and another man who happened also to be from Pennsylvania appeared to be the only ones who did not get malaria. Actually the other Pennsylvania man merely waited until he got home to contract the disease. It seems the infection in his body remained dormant all the intervening time. In retrospect Earl was unsure if he had malaria or not. He thought he might have had either a mild case of malaria or dengue fever. Malaria was so common there that the men did not even go to the doctor with it. They knew it would last about three days and then be over.

Mosquitoes—which transmit malaria—were so bad on New Caledonia that if the truck you were riding in slowed down to about thirty miles per hour, they would swarm into the truck. Once after he first arrived Earl tried to take a shower after dark, and "it was just like a cloud hit you!" He jerked his clothes on without even washing the soap off, and headed for his mosquito bar. (A mosquito bar consists of very fine mesh netting stretched over a frame which, in turn, can be placed over a sleeping bag or other bedding to exclude mosquitoes. The mesh is so tightly woven as to keep out mosquitoes but not impede air circulation.) The authorities provided a pamphlet with information about the island; the last thing it said was: "We won't say anything about the mosquitoes; you'll find that out soon enough."

The mosquitoes would bite right through the netting, and in the morning you would find a big red welt on your arm. Looking up, you would see the ones who had been feasting on you hanging there like a sack of blood. If you shook the netting the mosquitoes would fall down and the blood would splatter all over. No matter how carefully you tried, you couldn't seem to keep them all out

Torpedo Juice

Robby, a member of Earl's crew, got word one day that one of his buddies had been injured in a truck accident and was in a field hospital far up the island. Robby wanted to take the buddy's gear up to him and was looking for someone to accompany him. Because of Robby's well known eccentric driving habits, everyone declined except big-hearted Earl. The ride was wild. Robby had heard that, when driving, you should speed up on curves rather than slow down. What he had not been told was that you should slow down before entering the curve, and then maintain the slower speed while navigating the curve. Robby's technique was made even more hair-raising by the rough gravel road which resulted in alarming skids as Robby raced around curves.

After a while they came to a hitchhiking soldier who, of course, they picked up. Next they came to a merchant seaman who likewise was picked up. It turned out that, like Robby, the seaman had in the past worked for a carnival so the two engaged in some reminiscing.

A pair of young sailors were the last hitchhikers taken aboard the truck. These two were carrying the ingredients for mixing what they called "torpedo juice." This locally popular concoction was a mixture of pineapple juice and the 180-proof grain alcohol which at that time was used to propel torpedo motors. (A variety of techniques, some problematic, were used to detoxify the denatured alcohol.) The merchant seaman, after first proclaiming that he shouldn't drink, then promptly joined the sailors in imbibing. At this point Robby, after giving Earl the keys to the truck, also became a participant in the booze party that had developed among the truck's passengers.

After a time they reached a village where the soldier asked to be dropped off. At the next village the seaman got off. Then somewhat farther along the two sailors also left the truck. It was after dark by the time Earl and Robby reached the field hospital. Robby's friend was so delighted about getting his gear that he tried to give them some of it as a reward for the delivery service. His offer was, of course, declined.

About ten o'clock Earl and Robby started back, expecting to drive all night to get to their base. By this time Robby was sober again and took charge of the driving. After about two hours on the road, a figure loomed in their headlights waving his arms. When they stopped to see what the man wanted, he identified himself as a Texan, and asked them if they had seen a native along the road who had been sent to get more wine since the arm-waver was almost out. He then asked where the two were headed, whereupon he invited them to spend the night with him at a place he was renting from a Frenchman. He still had some wine left he told them. For Robby this sealed the deal, and they gave up driving for the rest of the night. Shortly, the native turned up with still more wine and Robby and the Texan set to drinking in earnest. By morning, Robby was once again unfit to drive.

Earl took over, and soon they came to the place where the night before they had dropped off the two sailors, who were wearily walking along the road back to Noumea. Earl stopped the truck and invited them aboard. (They still had their bottles.) Next, they came to the merchant seaman and then the soldier who were both picked up. So there they were with the same group as yesterday, but going in the opposite direction, and sure enough the booze party resumed. Eventually, however, they ran out, and someone said that he knew where they could get some *vin rouge*.

At this point Earl asserted the rights of the driver, and announced, "Look fellas, I'm headed for Noumea and I can let you off if you wish, but I'm not waiting." No one left the truck, and eventually they were back in Noumea after what Earl called, "one of the strangest journeys of my entire life."

Getting Lost
With their assignment finally completed, the Signal Corps team returned to Noumea where they were told the next job would not be ready for at

least a week, and in the meantime they should "get lost." After considering their options, they finally decided to take a truck tour of New Caledonia. They managed to get a French map which showed a road along the island's shore. Five of the group set off on the tour with very little in the way of advance preparation. They had no food, no extra gas, no pick and shovel to dig the truck out if it should get stuck. Earl described them as a "happy-go-lucky gang," who would try anything.

Toward evening, after crossing numerous small streams on crude bridges that would barely support the truck, they came to a New Zealand outfit where they got some food and gas. They were well up the island when the road became narrower and rough. Bridges were washed out and Lyle gunned the truck to get across, laughing as he did so. With the advice of an American lieutenant they encountered, they found their way to a hotel on the far side of the Diahot River. (This river, with a length of sixty miles, is the longest in New Caledonia.) Before the war the hotel had been a resort with access from the sea. At this time, however, it appeared to be getting little if any business. The team parked their vehicle and crossed the river on a ferry that would not have supported the truck.

The hotel appeared to be deserted, and as they were pondering what to do next, the shutters on a window were flung open and a woman peered out inquiringly. Robby, who claimed to know a little French, attempted to engage her in conversation. Abruptly she closed the window after which she opened a door that led into a small store where they found little in stock, with the food items appearing quite stale. The men went outside again and sat down to assess their predicament.

Shortly there appeared from around the end of the building a man rather formally dressed in a dark suit and a white shirt. He beckoned for the others to follow him, which they did and found themselves before a number of rooms with outside entrances, not unlike some American motels. The man who appeared to be the proprietor had guessed—correctly—that the visitors were looking for overnight lodging. The rooms were comfortable with furnishings that included canopied beds. This feature was a welcome blessing in view of the island's vicious mosquitoes.

Robby managed to let the proprietor know that the group would like a meal, whereupon the host nodded and left. It was about nine o'clock when the man returned and gestured to the group to follow him. In a large room they were placed at a long table, and two women, one of whom was the one previously encountered, brought in their food: primarily steak, potatoes, and black coffee.

Earl's radar crew dining à la française

The proprietor sat with them while they ate; then when they were finished, the first woman returned and sat down also. Robby determined that the two simply wanted to socialize with the visitors, so the men used such talent as they possessed to entertain the two French speakers. Robby succeeded in securing a deck of cards and performed some tricks he had learned while working with a carnival. Lyle managed some tricks with a piece of string. Others did what they could, and the man and woman seemed highly pleased. They had surely seen few visitors at their hotel since the start of the war.

Before the group retired for the night Robby managed to let the host know that the five GIs would like breakfast before leaving. The next morning the man woke them to a French breakfast of rolls and black coffee. Before leaving, the men were presented with a bill which for meals and lodging for all five visitors came to only $3.50. All parties, it seemed, were quite pleased with this interlude. The following morning the group decided to return to Noumea, having concluded that the rest of the road leading to the north shore was probably little better than a mule trail, and not worth further struggles.

This "getting lost" adventure later inspired one of Earl's best poems, "Diahot Valley."

DIAHOT VALLEY

A winding trail through a lonely pass
And the river route by sea
Are the [only] means to gain access
To a valley few men see.

Where the one-way road and the river meet
By a hand-hauled ferry boat
That braves the changing tide and heat
And still contrives to float.

On the Northern shore stands a French hotel
For the hardy souls who roam;
On the southern bank in a little dell
Is a tile-roof mud-walled home.

A young girl stood by the bamboo gate
And watched us as we worked
With a wistful face resigned to fate
And eyes where shadows lurked.

Timid and yearning and wild and shy
In a faded homemade dress,
The light of intelligence in her eyes
And a look of loneliness.

Not far away in a native shack
Lives a man of doubtful birth
Who spoke of gold in the hills far back
With a smile devoid of mirth.

Past the mission house in the distant peaks
Where the springfed waters flow,
Where a man may find the things he seeks
If the urge be strong to go—

To those who were at the quickening
When the pioneer seed was sown
Diahot valley is beckoning
From realms of the world's unkown.

BELEP

Back at Noumea they learned that a new job had been lined up for them that would involve doing a radar installation on a small coral island in the Belep group, which is administered as a part of New Caledonia. Located to the northwest of Grande Terre, Earl described Belep as "isolated and remote." The 810th Engineers had already been transferred to Belep, along with all their equipment. The commanding officer had by now been advanced to the rank of captain and had two lieutenants serving under him.

Transportation for the Signal Corps team was to be by means of a yawl-rigged schooner, the *Lita Mai*, which had a New Zealand skipper, an Australian mate, and a native Hawaiian crew. The *Lita Mai* had an honorable history that included service in the evacuation of Dunkirk in 1940 when 335,000 Allied troops were ferried across the English Channel under constant German bombardment. Although supplied with an auxiliary diesel engine, the vessel unfortunately lacked either life boat or life jackets, a failing to which Mr. Sturdy (the civilian head of the team) strongly objected. He was told that since he was a civilian he could not be forced to go, but the enlisted men would go at bayonet point if necessary. So they all went.

It proved to be a wild two-day cruise up along the Coral Sea. Seven squalls were visible as they left Noumea, passing the anchored *Enterprise*, the only surviving aircraft carrier after the Battles of Makassar Strait and Midway. The flattop was being hidden from the Japanese. A brisk offshore wind filled the sails and the ancient engine labored valiantly as they began making their way up the south coast. Toward evening a dark storm approached over the island and caught the *Lita Mai* with all of her sails full. The crew reacted quickly to begin pulling down the rigging. Meanwhile giant waves began battering the vessel, and for a time Earl and his team were convinced that they were about to capsize. Eventually the ship was turned with its stern to the wind, and the mainsail was raised again. They sped along for about an hour, rising and falling with the waves until the storm passed. The sky began to clear, and by midnight all was calm and placid again. About mid-morning a line of reefs appeared and the *Lita Mai* turned in that direction. At the same time the skipper climbed as high as he could on the mainmast where he stayed for about an hour while the vessel zigzagged through the reefs, keeping to shallow water where the bottom was clearly visible.

The Signal Corps team were mystified by the skipper's performance, and it was not until he climbed down that they learned what he had been up to. The *Lita Mai*, in passing through the reefs, had followed the only known channel, which early in the war had been mined, first by the French and later by the New Zealanders. The captain from his vantage point had been spotting the mines which were clearly visible against the white bottom. The men were glad they had not known beforehand what he was doing.

The island was roughly shaped like an hourglass with a grassy area in the middle where the camp had been set up. The rest of the island was mountainous, with steep cliffs on the north side. On the south side were lushly fertile coves where rows of coconut palms had been planted. Trails had been worn through open areas where grass grew taller than a man. Oranges and papaya were found there, along with a delicious fruit they never identified. Taro, which usually is no more than knee-high, also grew so tall there that its leaves provided shelter from the sun. An old Frenchman leased the land from the government, primarily to grow coconuts, although he also had longhorn cattle, some of which had gone wild and could at times be heard crashing through the jungle with their long horns.

The 810th Engineers began building a road to the radar site but their old bulldozer finally gave out completely and they had to finish the job "the hard way." When the road was done it wound for two miles to get between two points which were only a half mile apart.

A machine gun had been brought along and it was set up on a slope near the camp. No one ever tried to fire it, however, and Earl suspected that it was inoperable. The only other available weapons were some Enfield rifles from the first World War. On two occasions submarines came so close that those on shore could see the periscopes. They never knew if the subs were American or Japanese. The few men on Belep were essentially defenseless and it was fortunate that no effort was ever made by the Japanese to take the island.

The Cliff at Belep

It was on Belep that Earl found himself in the scariest (non-military) situation of his entire Pacific tour. He had been out hunting shells along the beach, and when it came time to return he found himself faced with the choice of going back along the rocky beach for a couple of miles or climbing a cliff that would provide a shorter route back. He chose to climb the cliff; a foolish choice he himself acknowledged. When he started up he did not realize how steep it was, nor was he aware that there was an overhang at the top. He got to a point near the top, just below the overhang and found himself unable to go to either side or back down. It was go up or fall. Earl looked down into the shark infested waters, and his arms and legs took over and managed to get him up.

"I guess I have a guardian angel that brought me through that," Earl later said. "I was about six, seven hundred feet up . . . I'd have bounced about once off the boulders and dropped right in among the sharks."

The Easter Bunny's Gift

Once they got settled in, the Signal Corps crew got busy and within a week the station was on the air, and they were ready to leave. Unfortunately, they were at the mercy of an empire-building major who was intent on increasing the number of men under his command in order to justify a request for higher rank. His strategy for keeping the Belep Islands men as part of his responsibility was simply not to send transportation. Before long the military food supply on the island was exhausted, and the personnel were reduced to surviving on beans and coconuts. While he still had food to work with, the mess sergeant had been doing an excellent job, making the depletion of their food supply all the more unpleasant.

The two lieutenants who had been assigned to the Belep Islands operation had been nicknamed by the enlisted men Sleepy Joe and Skippy. It was Skippy who had radioed the colonel to request transportation after the transmission station was finished. His message was shortstopped by the nefarious major, making Skippy reluctant to initiate any more radio messages, so more food was simply not requested.

It was not long before the monotonous—not to mention unhealthy—diet made the tempers of all personnel very short. Eventually two of the cooks got into a murderous argument, resulting in one of them being kept under guard for a night before being released upon his promise not to cause any more trouble.

The following day Earl and a buddy decided to go out in the hills to see if they could shoot a goat for food, but no goats were found. When they were rounding the far end of the island on their way back to camp, they heard a shot which they assumed was merely someone shooting at bats. Shortly, however, they met the camp's three cooks hiking together, all armed with rifles in spite of the previous day's argument. They seemed to Earl to be acting strangely.

They all continued walking along together talking of various matters, when Earl's buddy observed that he was about hungry enough to kill "one of the Frenchman's cows" in order to get fresh meat. The cooks laughed and said that this would not be necessary because they already had. They had not previously told the other two about their action because they were not sure if Earl and his friend would go along with it. Earl announced that they heartily agreed and offered to help lug the dead beast back to camp.

Two teams of burden bearers were designated, and after dressing out the half grown cow and cutting off its head as well as the legs below the knees, they forced a long pole through the animal and began the long trek to camp. Using all of their shirts as shoulder padding , the teams changed places whenever the bearers became exhausted—which turned out to be about every fifty yards. On the steepest slopes they were all needed to do the carrying.

In this manner they made their way through the jungle terrain, following a narrow trail. Eventually they reached the edge of the camp where they hid the carcass in the brush while they continued into camp. Once it had gotten dark, they all returned and skinned the animal which, after lights out, was carried into camp and deposited in the small mess hall.

The next morning—which happened to be Easter Sunday—the cooks as usual all went early to the mess hall, where they promptly set off a noisy commotion. "Look what the Easter Bunny brought," they yelled. This roused the enlisted men, but fortunately, Sleepy Joe and Skippy were in the officers' tent which was separated from the rest of the encampment by a sufficient distance to keep the clamor from their sleeping ears.

During the morning nothing was said to the officers about the earlier discovery of the Easter Bunny's gift, although everyone else knew about it. The cooks used the morning to prepare a generous quantity of steaks. When the time for noon chow arrived, Sleepy Joe and Skippy arrived expecting their usual portion of beans. Instead, they had steaming steaks slapped on their mess gear. They instantly knew that something was amiss, but the temptation of the feast before them was too strong; they ate the steaks. Having themselves eaten of the forbidden meat, there was little objection they could make. They did, however, insist that such an occurrence should not happen again.

Other than the perpetrators—who never told even their best buddies—no one ever knew for certain who had been responsible for the appearance of steak on Easter Sunday. Even so, everyone had a pretty good idea, since it was common knowledge that the cooks went out for a hike the day before

In any case the camp had a brief respite from a diet of beans. Shortly afterward the ration boat arrived, and not long after that, they were able to leave the Belep Islands.

Back to Oahu

The vessel on which they left Belep to return to New Caledonia was one of the 2,751 Liberty ships turned out by American shipyards during the years 1941–1945. It carried no cargo on this trip however, since it was scheduled to take on a load of chrome ore in New Caledonia. Earl reported that the food on the ship was excellent, especially in contrast to the prolonged diet of beans endured at Belep. The ship was unarmed except for two 40 mm guns; they anchored overnight off the coast of another Belep island, where the ship drifted and tossed with the tide, making the moon appear to move about the sky at random.

Although they had been away from Noumea for about three months, their return found the *Enterprise* still lying there at anchor.

The next day they began the long flight back to Oahu with an overnight stop at Nandi Air Base on Viti Levu, the main island of the Fiji group. Viti Levu has a climate similar to that of Hawaii. From Nandi Air Base the interior mountains were visible in the distance. Of the Pacific Islands, Viti Levu is exceeded in size only by New Caledonia and Hawaii's Big Island. Earl described the native people as "dark skinned, husky, and handsome." A significant percent of the Fiji population consisted of Indians, many of whom were engaged in jewelry making, their specialty being silver pieces.

While he was there Earl decided to go shopping for the silver jewelry that he had heard was available in the area. He reports spending his last

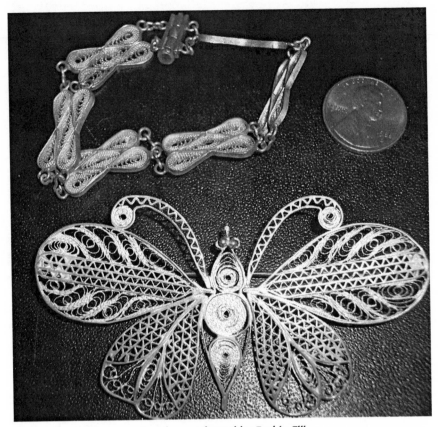

Jewelry purchased by Earl in Fiji

thirty dollars on a filigree set consisting of a clasp, necklace, and wrist band. The merchant let it be known that he would prefer payment in silver coins, not because he mistrusted paper money, but because he would melt down the coins to provide the workmen with the raw material for more jewelry.

The next morning they took off on the flight to Oahu.

Back at Fort Shafter Earl managed to collect his back pay before tending to a variety of housekeeping and other details to prepare for the next assignment, which was not long in coming. His team, he shortly learned, was to be switched to work in point-to-point radio, the long distance communications between installations. They were headed for the atoll of Tongareva where they were to install a message center at the airfield.

Earl had heard that Tongareva was a "pearl island" and that the best way to obtain anything from the natives was to trade brightly colored cloth. which was used by the local people to make lava-lavas, a traditional article of daily attire worn by both men and women. So Earl headed for Honolulu where he browsed the remnant counters of various stores and purchased a supply of brightly colored cloth.

As he was about to leave one of these counters he felt a hand grab his arm and spin him around. The hand proved to belong to Gene Bentzel, a neighbor from back home in Shiloh, who was the first hometown acquaintance he had encountered since the start of his Pacific tour. Gene told him that Lorn Hake, another mutual acquaintance from Shiloh, was also serving in Hawaii. Earl later visited Lorn. These were the only people from home he ever met while in the islands.

ATOLLS

Many of the islands on which Earl spent time while in the South Pacific were "atolls." Atolls are chains of coral reef islands that circle around a central lagoon. Generally there are channels to the sea between various islands. The creation of atolls depends on the building of coral reefs, thereby limiting them to tropical seas, most commonly the Pacific and Indian Oceans. Coral reefs are structures of calcium carbonate created by coral colonies which are made up of tiny living organisms. Atolls vary widely in size from quite small to those that are many miles wide and long.

TONGAREVA

Tongareva (or Penrhyn Island) is the largest and most remote atoll of the fifteen Cook Islands. The northern side of Tongareva is 537 nautical miles south of the equator. The anchorage at Omoka, the location of the Island Council, is almost exactly nine degrees south, so that mariners find it a good place to check their instruments.

The atoll measures 12 miles from northwest to southeast and ranges from 6 to 8 miles wide. The rim has a circumference of about 40 miles, and the enclosed lagoon has an area of about 108 square miles. The highest point on the atoll is only about 14 feet above sea level. The total land area is about 4,000 acres.

The flight to Tongareva landed near Omoka where coconut palms had been removed to make room for an airstrip, space being at a premium on this small bit of land. Indeed, the tent where Earl slept was set up on a

Reefs on Tongareva Atoll

graveyard barely above sea level, for lack of any other suitable space. The weather was hot and the men sweated all night in their mosquito bars. Notwithstanding these inconveniences, Earl found the place to have a charm and beauty such as one finds described in books set in the south seas. He acknowledged, however, that the war was damaging the idyllic setting.

The Signal Corps team's assignment on Tongareva was to install a new message center and to replace the telephone lines to the transmitter station which was already in operation. The old phone lines had been attached to trees and over time had been damaged, mostly by wind. These lines, which were taped together, had to be taken down, separated, and rolled up for salvage. The point of this elaborate process remained a mystery to Earl, but they spent some weeks complying with their orders. The new lines were to be attached to poles instead of trees. The poles that were used were simply the trees that had been removed to make room for the airstrip.

Anchoring the poles, however, proved a daunting challenge. While working in the Coral Sea Earl had learned to climb, so the climbing assignment fell to him. The poles were bone dry and difficult to climb to begin with; the job was made even more difficult because the poles had to be set in crumbly coral which was not as secure as would have been desirable. On one occasion the pole Earl was climbing started to tip forcing him to cut loose and slide down, skinning his bare chest in the process.

Johnny Ford

Earl decided that he wanted a pearl as a souvenir of his time in the islands. Before leaving Oahu for Tongareva, he bought a ukulele for seven dollars. The ukulele was made out of two coconuts fastened together, and Earl knew that where he was going it would be worth a lot more than he paid for it. He was taking it to trade for a pearl.

After Earl got settled on Tongareva, he hung the ukulele on the corner of his mosquito bar in plain sight as bait. Before long, Johnny Ford came by. Johnny was a native who spoke English better than most; he had graduated from high school and worked on ships where he had regular contact with many English speakers. Johnny, as well as his father and brother were all pearl divers. Johnny was also something of a musician; although his singing in the chanting native style was only fair, he was a skillful ukulele player. On this occasion, he stopped beside the instrument on display, which he first examined and then tested by playing "You Are My Sunshine" as he sang along. Earl said that at that time "You Are My Sunshine" was the most popular song in the world.

"How much?" Johnny asked.

Earl replied, "I want a pearl, Johnny."

On three or four separate occasions this exchange was repeated until finally Johnny said, "I get you pearl." Earl asked when, and Johnny replied, "Now."

After Earl obtained a special pass to visit the village—a requirement designed to safeguard the native girls—Johnny then escorted Earl down to this secure zone. As they walked along the narrow road that led through the palm grove up to the village, Johnny was describing for Earl the mysteries of pearl diving. "Little ones you find like this," Johnny said, pantomiming himself sitting in shallow water and groping about on the bottom for clams. "But big ones—this big," and he gravely picked up a stone the size of a small marble, "they way down." When a big spotted clam is found, the diver knows that the spots indicate sickness and the probable presence of a large pearl. "You jam knife in shell at end, then reach in for pearl. Get big pearl that way."

Unmentioned other than by implication were the dangers involved in this occupation, beginning with diving to great depths with only a basic diving mask and a long-bladed knife. Then there was the risky business of reaching an arm inside a giant clam to search for a pearl, while in the surrounding water was the constant threat of barracuda and sharks, as well as the rough water itself above the pearling beds. (The giant clams of the South Pacific can weigh more than four hundred pounds and live for as much as one hundred years.)

It was a typical, storybook tropical day with the trade wind rippling the lagoon and the tops of the palm trees. Earl had previously noticed that none of the trees on Tongareva stood upright; all leaned toward the prevailing wind. He commented to Johnny about this peculiarity and asked why all the trees leaned toward the wind instead of away from it. Johnny pointed in the opposite direction and said, "Hurricane come that way."

A violent storm had passed over Tongareva, and with it a soaking downpour that left even the highest point on the island under a foot of water. As a result, the soil was so softened that the fierce wind blew the trees nearly flat. Afterward they only partially recovered, and all were left tilted away from the hurricane's wind but toward the gentler prevailing trade wind.

As the two were discussing this matter, Johnny suddenly broke off and, pointing through the trees toward the water, exclaimed, "Schooner!" Earl turned to look and far out on the horizon, still only faintly visible, he made out the silhouette of a sailing vessel. They were already in the village by the time the ship turned into the channel that led through the reefs to the shore. Earl describes the ship as "a sleek-lined hundred footer" of the type that at that time plied regularly from New Zealand to that nation's various outlying possessions.

It was a two-masted vessel with the cabin amidship, and a sail rigged across the forward boom as a kind of awning to provide shelter from the sun. The ship visited the island about once a month. The deck was crowded with home-comers, including—Earl later learned—a number who were returning after seven years in the Fiji Leper Colony where they had gone for treatment. The passengers gazed quietly across the water toward the shore where a crowd was gradually gathering. The people on shore were unusually well groomed and festively dressed. The schooner maneuvered slowly toward the sea wall, as small boats set out to haul the mooring lines ashore.

Meanwhile, Johnny took Earl to meet his brother who lived in one of the few wooden houses in the village. He was a pearl diver, who had a white pearl—his prize possession. The pearl was kept at the bottom of a locked blanket chest. Johnny and his brother conversed for a while in the native Polynesian language. The brother then nodded his head and reached for his little ditty bag, such as was worn around the neck by all the local men. From the bag he extracted a key with which he unlocked the blanket chest. From the chest he withdrew a ball of cloth which he unfolded to reveal the pearl. "And it was the size of a small pea," Earl said, "pretty good size for a pearl, a genuine pearl. So he laid it on my hand."

The pearl divers normally sold their finds to dealers who paid a flat rate per pearl, regardless of size or quality. The going rate at that time, according to Earl, was about ten dollars per pearl. If a diver came up with a specimen he believed to be particularly valuable, he would hold it out and wait for an opportunity to sell it at a better price. Earl asked, "How much, Johnny?"

The reply was. "Ukulele and twenty dollar." So Johnny got the ukulele and his brother got the twenty dollars—roughly double what he would have gotten from a dealer.

For almost three years Earl carried the pearl all over the Pacific in his wallet because he was afraid to run the risk of mailing it home.

Back at the schooner, as these negotiations were taking place, the vessel was made fast to the seawall, and a curious ceremony took place. A group of passengers assembled amidship and began a singing ritual. The song was of the strange native variety that seemed a combination of hymn and the ancient chants of the people. It began softly at first, gradually increasing in volume as the singers swayed gently in rhythm with the song. Although he could understand nothing of the words, Earl wrote that they seemed to be of the wind and the sea. When the singing finally died away, a man arose and delivered what appeared to be a short sermon in the native language. When he finished speaking, a crude gangplank was fitted into place and the people on the shore rushed aboard to welcome the new arrivals.

The singing may have ended but the music did not. An impromptu band of drums and ukuleles assembled on the shore and beat out their oddly cadenced hula rhythms. Johnny Ford had rushed to join this group with his new ukulele. Later, by the time Earl and Johnny were leaving the village to return to camp, a group of young boys had gathered and were strumming guitars and ukuleles as another boy performed one of his people's wild dances of the olden days.

Campsite of Chaos

At one time while Earl was stationed on Tongareva the tent next to his included some men from an Airborne Air Control Squadron (AACS), one of whom was an artist who had previously taught school in Los Angeles. Occasionally this artist would offer to do someone's portrait so that he could stay in practice. Depending on his mood, he would do the work in chalk, ink, or pencil, and would invariably complete it in less than half an hour.

The teacher had read some of Earl's poems and the two of them would engage in artistic discussions that must surely have seemed anomalous in that improbable setting. Another member of the AACS crew also wrote poetry, although his was always in the sonnet form. A third crew member, the resident skeptic, was scornful of poetry and labeled it "foolishness."

One day the artist said to Earl, "Did you ever deliberately empty your mind and then write whatever presented itself?" Earl replied that he had never done so but would try it. Half an hour later he came back with the poem "Campsite of Chaos." The artist read the poem and said that it was exactly the sort of thing he had in mind.

The skeptic, who had been listening, seemed puzzled and said, "Let me see that." After reading the poem and brooding for a bit, he commented, "It does make you think." Earl noted that the skeptic never made disparaging remarks about poetry again.

CAMPSITE OF CHAOS

The glimmer upon the palm trees
The sheen of the glancing sun,
A web that splinters the sky blue
And clouds that the winds have spun.

The roar of a groaning diesel
And of surf agrind on reef
Way out where the winds once murmured
But now are shrill with grief.

A helmet of steel akimbo,
A truck where a road goes by,
The brown of a tent encampment
Where coconut husks pile high.

The blot of a rotting tree stump,
A tangle of crawling vines

And over it all the palm fronds
Like millions of sabre tines.

When their work on Tongareva was finished, all of the Signal Corps team except for Earl and another man were flown back to Hawaii. Earl and his partner were put aboard the "mail plane," a four-motor transport, for a destination unknown to them. They took off before dawn under clear skies, but shortly past daybreak, however, the weather turned bad with a low cloud cover. After flying for a few hours with no improvement, they noticed the navigator frantically manipulating his various instruments. They sensed also that their fuel was getting low. Finally the pilot took the plane down below the cloud cover which placed them only a few hundred feet above the ocean. Suddenly the plane made a sharp turn, and on the horizon they could see the white surf that indicated an island.

The stop at this island was very brief, only long enough to drop off mail and to refuel. Although the next stop at Bora Bora was equally brief, it was long enough for Earl to be captivated by its beauty and to regret not being able to stay longer. One more flight brought the two Signal Corps men to their destination.

AMERICAN SAMOA

The Samoan archipelago extends east and west for about three hundred miles in the central Pacific Ocean, midway between Honolulu, Hawaii, and Sydney, Australia. American Samoa consists of the eastern half of the chain, while the western half is the Independent State of Samoa, with the dividing line being longitude 171° west. The largest island in American Samoa and the third largest in the archipelago is Tutuila which, like all of the other Samoan islands, is of volcanic origin. The larger islands are mountainous, surrounded by coral reefs, and lushly forested. Tutuila has a beautiful natural harbor beside which is located Pago Pago, the largest city and the capitol of American Samoa. The inhabitants of the entire archipelago share a common culture. Since 1900 American Samoa has been an unorganized U.S. territory and is today the only U.S. territory located south of the Equator.

A Marine base had existed on Tutuila for some time, and about seven miles from Pago Pago a new air strip had recently been built where Earl and his partner were quartered in small barracks. They spent about two weeks there, although they were never told why they were there nor were they given anything to do.

At one point during this period of idleness Earl's partner suggested that they go into Pago Pago where he hoped to obtain some Tapa cloth, which is made from the bark of the paper mulberry tree. This cloth is manufactured at various places across the south seas, including Samoa. After the cloth is pressed from the bark it is customarily decorated in various colors and patterns using natural local dying materials. They might not get another opportunity to acquire this souvenir, the partner observed, and suggested that Earl might like to get some too. At the time Earl had only about fifteen dollars and no idea when he might get paid again, but he agreed to go along.

They hitched a ride in a truck to the village of Pago Pago which was a cluster of thatched *fales*, a typical feature of Samoan architecture, which are usually oval shaped with a domed roof and no walls (just framing) which allows the trade wind to blow through and moderate the heat. As they were walking through the village, a man came out of one of the fales and asked in excellent English if they were looking for souvenirs. Earl's partner expressed an interest in Tapa cloth, and the local merchant said that he had a couple of pieces. One proved to be extremely fine and the other only slightly less so. His price was twelve dollars for the best one and ten dollars for the other. Earl's friend took the better one and urged Earl to buy the other one. Although the purchase would leave Earl with very little money, he decided to take advantage of an opportunity that might not be repeated. After making their purchases, the two hitched back to the airstrip where Earl later mailed the tapa home. He learned much later that it took six months to find its way back to York County. Ultimately it was delivered and the family wrote to let Earl know it had arrived. "But what is it?" the letter asked.

That same evening following their return to the base, they learned that new orders for them had arrived. They were to report to an atoll far to the west where a secret base was being established as part of the "island war" which had now become the established pattern in the South Pacific. When they asked about transportation, they were told that if they hurried they could catch a DC3 that was headed their way. They gathered their things and hurried out to the airstrip where they found to their amazement that the pilot was a Marine PFC. This low-ranking pilot looked at their travel orders, which were high priority, and told them to get aboard. They asked how much baggage they could take and the PFC responded, "Anything you can get in the door." The pilot proved to be a cynical and unhappy Marine who had recently been demoted from sergeant. Nonetheless, he was still piloting a DC3.

Notwithstanding his bitterness and low rank, he clearly knew what he was doing at the controls of a two-engine aircraft, and got them safely to their destination which was an atoll dangerously close to Japanese occupied islands. On this atoll a secret airbase was being developed to help in the protection of various American islands in the South Pacific.

TUVALU

The island nation of Tuvalu (formerly known as the Ellice Islands) extends over some four hundred miles of the Pacific Ocean about midway between Hawaii and Australia. Overall, Tuvalu consists of three reef islands and six atolls. Its total land area is less than ten square miles. The highest elevation is fifteen feet above sea level. Because of this very small elevation, the expected rise in sea levels could, within the next hundred years, make Tuvalu uninhabitable. Preliminary plans have been made to evacuate the entire population to New Zealand should that become necessary. The quality of Tuvalu's soil is very poor and of little use for agriculture. Drinking water for the most part is obtained from roof runoff which periodically results in water shortages.

Funafuti and Nanumea

Funafuti and Nanumea are both atolls forming part of the nation of Tuvalu, with Funafuti being the nation's capital. Funafuti is also the largest of the reefs and atolls that make up the Tuvalu island chain. The Funafuti atoll itself consists of a chain of islands surrounding a central lagoon. The land area, however, is quite small, being only a trifle more than one square mile.

Nanumea is the northernmost of Tuvalu's nine islands and atolls and the one closest to the equator. It is a true atoll consisting of a series of small islands circling twin lagoons. In 1943 the entire population of the atoll was moved to a neighboring island to allow the construction by U.S. forces of a mile-long airfield on Nanumea. Almost half of the atoll's coconut palms were destroyed for the runway. Some 2,300 U.S. personnel were stationed on this tiny island at the time of the invasion of Tarawa in the Gilbert Islands.

Tarawa

Tarawa, an atoll which is part of the Gilbert Islands (now Kiribati) in the Central Pacific, was the scene in November 1943 of one of the bloodiest battles of World War II. Although perhaps not as famous as some of the other island battlegrounds of that war, it still offered a more than average share of mortality. At the time of the Tarawa battle Earl was stationed on Nanumea, a coral atoll now part of the Polynesian nation of Tuvalu just south of the equator. Nanumea was being used as a base for the bombers carrying out the preliminary assault on Tarawa.

From the bomber crews that landed on Nanumea following sorties to Tarawa, Earl learned more than he probably wanted to know about the horrors of that battle. The first attempt at a landing was bungled, with 1,200 marines forced to swim and wade about a mile over broken reefs when their landing crafts ran aground. Only three hundred reached shore and established a tiny beachhead of about twenty-five by seventy-five yards. They held this position for forty-eight hours without relief.

Months later, Earl saw the official movie taken following the landing. "The beach,"he wrote "as far as the eye could see was completely covered with bodies."[3]

The DC-3 delivered Earl and his partner to an atoll where they found a landing strip and an anchorage in the atoll's lagoon. This was Funafuti, dangerously close to Japanese bases on nearby islands from which bombing raids could be expected at nearly any time. Although almost every spot on the small island was being used for something, they were told they could find space in any of a number of empty tents. They were cautioned, however, that it would be better to spend the night in the revetments along the shore. The bright moon expected that night along with the white surf surrounding the island like a bull's eye would make it a prime target for Japanese bombers, in which case the revetments would be safer than tents. The two signal men had already found that most of the empty tents were riddled with shrapnel.

They succeeded in finding one tent that was reasonably intact on one side, where they proceeded to settle in. Then, happily, the weather turned rainy and the risk of bombing that night essentially vanished.

In the morning the two boarded another DC-3 and headed four hours north to the island of Nanumea, another atoll in what was then the Ellice Islands group. Before take-off, they had been given parachutes since they were headed into a region where their plane might encounter Japanese interceptors. They sat on their parachutes, however, instead of wearing

---

[3]Earl wrote two powerful poems about this battle: "Dirge of the Landing Barge" and "Who Judged the Tide?". Both of these poems are collected in *South of the Sunset*. See Appendix.

them since, as Earl cynically observed, the use of a parachute over water is generally unwise. The open chute tends to fall on the user and drown him. After landing, they learned that the place had been bombed less than half an hour before their arrival.

The plane, which was also carrying all of the heavy equipment they would need for their job, managed to land safely on an air strip that was still just a muddy runway left when the palm trees had been bulldozed aside. Take-off was another matter, and plane and pilot had to wait a few weeks until the strip could be "paved" with coral. In the meantime, they were assigned a moldy and riddled tent, and directed to dig a slit trench in case of another air raid.

The two were joined a few days later by five others who flew down from Fort Shafter. Unfortunately all but one of the new group had come down with malaria while en route, and had to be quarantined under mosquito bars. They had previously been on Guadalcanal where the mosquitoes were reported to be especially fierce. The four infected men were sent back to Fort Shafter as soon as transportation was available.

Nanumea was within only a few hundred miles of the enemy held Gilbert Islands, from which bombing raids were periodically sent to Nanumea to harass the Americans and delay the work of putting in an airstrip. The Japanese were well aware that when the airstrip was completed it would allow the Americans to return the bombing raids.

Although the Marines landed on Nanumea without opposition, the Seabees had preceded them and had to deal with a significant level of enemy opposition. A Japanese spy plane had observed the arrival of the first contingent of Seabees, and alerted his home base which triggered bombing raids that killed several Americans. It was learned later that the Japanese themselves were planning to occupy Nanumea. Our forces got there first by less than a week.

Once established, the Seabees worked at a feverish pace to complete their assignment. Within a matter of weeks they had converted a large palm grove into an airstrip where fighter planes were already parked. The bombers would come later. The continuing work involved blasting coral from the bottom of the lagoon and hauling it to the airstrip to be used as paving.

Meanwhile, the Japanese continued to launch bombing raids which generally killed a few and terrorized the rest. Near their tents the men all had favorite "personal" slit trenches where they would seek shelter when

Earl's foxhole (slit trench)

the sirens sounded to warn of approaching enemy planes. With the danger of flying debris caused by bombs bursting in the palm groves, the trenches were generally provided with roofs made of fallen palm logs left over from the airstrip building. These makeshift roofs were laid out so as to allow only a small opening just big enough for a man to squeeze into.

This strategy worked well enough at night when most of the raids occurred and the men were generally in their tents. It was quite another matter, however, when a rare daytime raid came along. Then the men more often were occupied with a job assignment that put them too far from their tents to be able to use their personal shelter. The alternative was to find a nearby trench that was unoccupied and to quickly lay claim to it.

One time while Earl was on the island, two buddies were working on a job when the sirens were sounded for an approaching raid. The two quickly scrambled to find shelter and had to make use of trenches that had been dug nearby. The two each dove into separate trenches where they huddled while the bombs burst in the area. After the planes finally left, one man crawled out of his trench and waited for his buddy. When the friend did not appear, the first man went looking for him, and found him still huddled in his trench. The first man made some teasing remarks about the buddy being afraid, but when there was no response he reached down to touch his friends shoulder and found him completely lifeless.

When others arrived on the scene, they found the first man in a state of speechless shock, and unable to communicate. The dead man was later found to have no marks of any kind on his body, and it was concluded that he had been killed by the concussion from the bomb blast. The survivor was eventually sent home because of the severity of the mental problems he had developed. For several weeks mail continued to arrive regularly for the dead soldier.

When they finished setting up the communication station and its transmitters, Earl and Frank were ordered back to Fort Shafter to pick up the equipment for a "radio range" which would provide a beam for aircraft to follow. This was a technique that had been used before the war for mail planes. Their transportation for this trip turned out to be the most luxurious either of them had ever before experienced. The plane they were put aboard was the one assigned to a general, and it was heading back to Hickam Field for maintenance. Earl and Frank were the only passengers and they got to stretch out on bunks, which is how they spent most of the trip.

Upon their return to Nanumea, the two learned that the island had been bombed while they were away, and that all of the transmitters had been knocked out.

Blue Sky

The day Earl was leaving Nanumea, as he was standing by the revetment waiting for the plane, he was talking to a young native man with whom he had previously had several conversations. The American workers had just knocked down several palm trees to make room for another revetment. The palm trees were a key part of the native subsistence diet, and natives had rushed in when the trees were knocked down to salvage the coconuts and the hearts of the trees. Near the top of the tree the hearts are tender and something like lettuce, which Earl found "very tasty."

The friend of Earl's was part of the group that came in to do the food salvage work. Earl said to him, "I'd like to drink a last toast to Nanumea in coconut juice." The native grabbed a coconut which he brought over to Earl where, with his machete, he chopped it open. The two of them then went through the "exchange of names" ritual. This involved exchanging family names and telling the names of relatives. It was in the nature of a blood-brother ritual. The exchange of names ritual was the last thing Earl did on Nanumea before taking off. When asked later what name he took, Earl replied softly, "Kalani. It means *blue sky*."

When they finally got back to Oahu after finishing the Nanumea job for the second time, they learned that the rest of their radar crew had been sent out with a convoy that was diverted by General MacArthur. Earl never saw them again. Meanwhile, Frank was assigned to a crew that was sent to Guam.

Back on Oahu Earl was assigned as a helper to a civilian engineer, and for a few weeks the two of them traveled around the island on maintenance duty. Then four more men were added to the engineer's crew, and the team of six headed for a job on Johnston Island.

JOHNSTON ISLAND

Johnston Island is a very small, desolate sand and coral atoll located in the Pacific Ocean a little more than 700 miles southwest of Hawaii. It is one of two natural islands on the same coral reef platform, along with two artificial islands that have been created by coral dredging. Johnston itself was originally only 0.07 square miles (47 acres), but has since been enlarged by coral dredging to 0.93 square miles in order to accommodate an airstrip and other mostly military facilities. The other natural island, known as Sand or Agnes Island, was even smaller than Johnston and has been only minimally enlarged. The two islands contain only three species of low-growing vegetation.

The only good thing Earl could find to say about this outpost was that, unlike most of the other islands he spent time on, it had no mosquitoes. The place was too barren to support even that staple of South Sea island wildlife.

In the late nineteenth century Johnston was briefly mined for guano until that resource was exhausted. Thereafter, until the arrival of a Marine contingent early in 1941, its human visitors were few, limited mostly to explorers and scientific researchers. The Marine force that arrived a few months before the Pearl Harbor bombing consisted mostly of teenagers who found themselves bored to distraction by this dreary assignment. When Earl arrived, after the war was well under way, the boys were pleading to be sent where they could fight the enemy—anywhere but on this forbidding pile of sand.

Earl was one of a small party of six which consisted of five Signal Corps personnel plus Mr. Sturdy, a civilian engineer, who had been sent to install an Air Corps radio station to guide the arrival of planes that were expected to use Johnston as a stopover on flights to the Marshall Islands once those islands had been recaptured from the Japanese. The arrival of Earl's group aroused great expectations among the Marines who had been hearing rumors of the imminent arrival of the Army to relieve them of their unwanted duty. It took a considerable amount of explanation by Earl and his buddies to persuade the Marines that their hopes were ill-founded.

It was actually on tiny Sand Island that Earl's crew did most of the work of installing a radar and transmission station. The island was so cramped for space that the antenna poles had to be set out in the water. The men then had to swim out to them wearing all their climbing gear in order to climb the poles to string the antenna wires. The sea around the island abounded with various species of unpleasant aquatic life including sharks, stingarees, eels, and octopuses. Occasionally, these creatures were caught in the very water in which the men had to swim to get to the poles.

The center of Sand Island provided room for only two five-inch gun emplacements and a few smaller caliber guns. Crowded into the remaining corners were the barracks, the mess hall, the equipment needed to convert sea water to drinking water and some work shops. The only vegetation to be seen was the work of the island commander—a Marine lieutenant—who was fecklessly attempting to landscape his hut. He had imported a few tree seedlings which he had planted and babied with a substantial portion of the available drinking water. Indeed, he left barely enough water for the men to shave, let alone perform any supplementary washing. Moreover, his seedlings were not thriving.

Adding to the misery of life on Sand Island were the sea birds with their endless moaning which, if anything, was even worse at night when the men were trying to sleep. There were predominantly two species on Sand. The smaller of the two, which Earl believed to be a petrel, nested in burrows and "moaned" all night long. The others, which Earl identified as a species of albatross, nested on the ground, and circled and wheeled during the day uttering their croaking calls. It was their nighttime moaning that was the worst. Earl likened it to the sound of a nursery full of crying human infants, which only served to remind the men that somewhere across the water was another world inhabited by women and babies. Often at night men could be seen armed with makeshift cudgels attempting to violently end the raucous calling of the birds. In the morning the trash cans would be filled with feathered bodies. But to no avail. Each morning to get to the day's job the men had to pick their way through the avian nesting grounds.

Exotic marine life was not the only thing to be found in the waters around Johnston. From time to time evidence was brought up of ships that in the past had come to grief on the reefs. An anchor was found and placed at the base of the flag pole where it was used to secure the halyard. Other smaller artifacts that came to light were displayed in a show case in the island library. It is distressing to contemplate the fate of shipwrecked seamen who survived the wrath of the sea only to come ashore on this barren island with no human inhabitants and, indeed, with no vegetation or fresh water. It must be assumed that they did not long survive.

Life for the servicemen stationed on Johnston was monotonous in the extreme, notwithstanding the introduction of a number of modern amenities, including ice cream, regular movies, and a variety of sport facilities. The latter included tennis courts, a swimming pool, boxing ring, and basketball court. Because of the heat there was little interest in the athletic facilities except for the swimming pool. By far the most popular of the available recreational opportunities was the island movie hall, to which every evening most of the men would migrate. There for a couple of hours they would lose themselves in a second-rate movie "presented without cost to the War Department" by the movie industry.

It was, therefore, not the least surprising one afternoon that a great commotion was aroused when a Navy man stumbled into the barracks, seemingly in a state of delirium, muttering about "women, real women on the island." Since the Navy man was too dazed to offer a coherent explanation, the men in the barracks rushed to the windows where they were rewarded with the sight of two nurses walking along the street followed by virtually all of the "brass" on the island. The men were dumbfounded and not a little awed. One bearded man even commented that perhaps he ought to shave.

The nurses, who had arrived on a plane that afternoon, were taken on a tour that included a visit to the swimming area where the men had gotten in the habit of swimming unclothed. This resulted that day in some embarrassing confrontations. Thereafter, whenever nurses were on the island, a sound truck went around warning the men to wear swimming trunks.

That first evening as the men settled in for the start of the day's movie there was a sense of anticipation in the air. Then, just as the show was about to begin, the nurses appeared in the gallery reserved for officers, accompanied by the island commander. They were greeted with a thunderous roar from the assembled enlisted men. Things settled down somewhat during the movie, but when it ended the men rushed to leave so they could watch the nurses depart. Alas, they were denied that pleasure, since the nurses had been spirited out just before the movie's end.

Only once did any of the visiting nurses cross over to Sand Island, to which they were enticed to watch a special show that was being put on for the young marines there. Most of those boys had not been off Sand Island for at least a year, and they were simply overwhelmed by this occurrence. After that occasion, visiting nurses were not encouraged to cross from Johnston to its much smaller neighbor.

Once the crew of a PBY flying boat arrived and took up quarters next to Earl. They had just been transferred from duty in the cold and forbidding Aleutians to hot and desolate Johnston. It is hard to imagine any greater extreme, but there they were. One day the man in the bunk next to Earl's asked him if he would like to go for a plane ride. Having done plenty of flying already during his time in the Pacific, Earl was not particularly interested in taking a flight that was not obligatory and he tried to refuse. This would be quite different, Earl was assured. A large convoy was en route to Kwajalein, and the PBY was heading out to help fly cover. It proved to be an offer too appealing to decline, so Earl went along. With a top speed of less than 200 miles per hour and a cruising speed of only about 125, the flying experience on the PBY was quite different from what Earl had known on the large craft that he had flown before.

After about an hour in the air, the crew of eight suddenly assumed battle stations; and it appeared that battle was imminent. Then just as suddenly everyone relaxed. The radar blip proved to be a small coast guard vessel that was "on point" out ahead of the convoy. Soon the whole spectacle was revealed. A total of about eighty ships were moving along. Those in the center were large landing craft which were surrounded by protective ships. One of the crew members commented that it looked just like a lot of toy boats in a bathtub.

About the time that the men on Sand Island were starting to believe that their dreary lives could not get any worse, a new commanding officer appeared on the atoll. This individual proved to be a strict, by-the-book disciplinarian. The relaxed rules that had applied when Johnston was considered a combat zone were quickly suspended. Full uniforms were required in spite of the heat. The barracks arrangement had to conform to approved standards. Proper salutes were expected. And so on and so on. The result was that a life of barely endurable monotony was made even more uncomfortable.

When their tours on Johnston came finally to an end, the men left without the least regret and with no wish to ever see it again. Empty moonlight, coral, water, and the wail of the moaning birds were their chief memories, along with the sheer desolation and loneliness—and meagerness beyond description.

Back on Oahu they learned that Signal Corps responsibilities were being reorganized with the Air Corps assuming responsibility for their own communications work. At the same time a "Joint Communications" concept was being implemented. Under the new program Earl became part of a team of eight enlisted men and two lieutenants—for whom Earl had no high regard. This crew was assigned to go with a large convoy headed for a landing on an island somewhere near the Philippines. The convoy's mission was to establish an air base to support General MacArthur's return to those islands. Earl's crew would go ashore on the second wave following the combat troops for the purpose of establishing communications systems. The crew traveled with their own trucks loaded with all the equipment they were expected to need.

Along with some 2,000 other support troops of various descriptions Earl's crew embarked on the *Sea Sturgeon* for what was to be a voyage of forty-two days, with only one break on land that lasted a grand total of four hours. The men witnessed two full moons during this extended cruise.

THE *SEA STURGEON*

The SS *Sea Sturgeon* was a troopship that had been converted from one of the many standard freighters that were being launched before and during the war. Built at San Francisco in 1944, the *Sea Sturgeon* saw service in the South Pacific during the war and later in the Atlantic. In 1947 she rejoined the commercial shipping fleet under the name *Hawaiian Farmer*. Twenty-four years later the vessel was scrapped in Taiwan.

In view of the long time Earl and his team spent on the vessel, it was fortunate that the *Sea Sturgeon* proved to be the best ship Earl ever traveled on. It was both well designed and well run for carrying the large numbers of men crowded on board. The food proved to be above average both as to quality and quantity. Even sleeping below deck was less unpleasant than his other shipboard experiences. Nonetheless, except in the worst weather, Earl generally chose to find a place to sleep on deck.

The *Sea Sturgeon*

The life rafts on the ship were tipped up in such a way that they would be easy to launch if needed. This made the space beneath a raft one of the choicest for spending the night on deck, since the raft provided shelter from any rain squalls that might come along Space under the rafts quickly filled up at night, rewarding the early comers. One night Earl was early enough and got a good spot under a raft along with many others. After it got dark, a voice said, "Hey, Red, how about some music tonight."

The redheaded man to whom the request was directed replied, "OK, go get my fiddle." He proved to be a conservatory graduate who was an accomplished singer and a skillful violinist. Earl and his under-raft companions were treated that night to a classical music concert in the middle of the Pacific Ocean. In the morning the redhead walked away and vanished among the vast numbers of men on board. Earl never saw him again—and never learned his name.

After some days, the *Sea Sturgeon* came to the enormous coral atoll of Kwajalein—one of the world's largest in terms of the area of enclosed water. The lagoon covers 839 square miles and is surrounded by ninety-seven islands and islets. By contrast, the total land area is only 6.33 square miles. Kwajalein Island is the largest of the ninety-seven. The convoy passed through the middle of the enormous atoll which is about eighty miles across. When they were in the middle of the lagoon, they were unable to see any land in any direction.

At that time some of the islands on the Kwajalein atoll were still held by the Japanese, because of which a routine of "abandon ship" drills was implemented. These required every man aboard the *Sea Sturgeon* to have a specific spot to which he would immediately go when the alarm sounded. This procedure was intended to minimize confusion in case of an emergency evacuation of the ship. These drills were repeated every morning at dawn for about a week while the ship passed through this dangerous region. The men would remain at their designated places until after sunrise. The reason for this was a concern that the twilight time of the morning was when attacks were most likely to occur. Earl observed that during the drills, with the deck packed full of standing men, the ship developed an odd motion, as though it were top-heavy.

Eventually they came to the north side of New Guinea where, at a long offshore reef, they anchored for several days. Here was a vast assemblage of ships, an armada beyond counting, destined to become a part of General MacArthur's return to the Philippines. During this lay-over Earl's team along with many others were allowed ashore on a small island for four hours—their only time on land in forty-two days. When the *Sea Sturgeon* finally moved on, they sailed for half a day through the vast fleet, and Earl counted forty aircraft carriers alone—mostly of the smaller variety.

At last they came to their destination: the Palau group of islands where on Angaur and Peleliu the landing was already underway

ANGAUR AND PELELIU

The only landing under fire in which Earl participated was at Angaur and the nearby island of Peleliu. Angaur is a tiny volcanic island only three miles long and separated from neighboring Peleliu by a six-mile strait. Both Angaur and Peleliu are part of the island nation of Palau. Earl's unit participated in the building of airstrips on both islands. The airstrip on Peleliu was used by fighter planes while the Angaur strip was used by bombers intended to cover General MacArthur's return to the Philippines. Earl and his team were originally scheduled to go ashore on D-Day plus one, just twenty-four hours after the landing troops, but because of extremely rough water caused by a passing hurricane, as well as the unexpectedly stiff Japanese resistance, they did not land until ten days later. As they waited off the coast of Babelthuap Island—the largest of the Palau group—which was still held by the Japanese forces, they could watch the enemy guards patrolling the shore, obviously anticipating a landing. The islands had been shelled so heavily that they were "nothing but a mass of debris." All of the buildings and trees were shattered, including a massive stone lighthouse built by the Germans when they held the islands.

Palau

In 1899 Spain sold Palau along with other islands to Germany. In 1914 Japan took control, and in 1944 during World War II Palau was taken by the United States. When Earl was there German gravestones were still scattered about. The Germans during their control profited from phosphate deposits found all over the island.

Earl recalled seeing a gravestone for a young woman who was about twenty-five at the time of her death. On the back of the stone was the word *warum*, the German word for why. Earl thought the answer to that question was easy: "Well *why*, because the place was about the most disease ridden place on earth, that's why."

Nonetheless, one of the finest singing voices he ever heard was on this island: a woman who was part of a local singing group. The locals who had survived the bombardments of the invasion would have a meeting of the Red Cross on Sundays. One week this singing group came out and sang in the traditional local way—a mixture of hymn melody and native chant. "It was three-part harmony," Earl remembered. "The bass would take it some of the time, the alto another time, and then the soprano would take it. And they never stopped; they would phase each other out. And some of it went way, way up. And when they went way up they'd all fade out but her and she'd just increase the volume and take it up. It was like an opera singer. Yet she lived on that little island out there."

When the landing barges were finally lowered off the coast of Angaur, the sea was still extremely rough. Earl described the motion of the barges in the turbulent water as being like that of a surfboard. The fighting on shore was so close that the men in the approaching barges could see the flash of rifle fire. Once ashore Earl's team was directed to a part of town that was little more than a heap of rubble following the massive naval bombardment. Each man had been provided with a shelter-half, but there was hardly any topsoil, although lots of hard coral, making the driving of stakes a futile endeavor. Finally, Earl and his tent partner collected some scrap wood from which they fashioned a crude frame over which they placed their shelter-halves.

On the way up to the ruins of the town a man popped his head out of a hut and asked Earl, "How are the states, buddy?"

Earl replied, "I wouldn't know; haven't been there for three years." Nothing more was said.

Several weeks after they landed, the village area was bulldozed, and regular tents were erected. The men had no bunks, however, but did manage to improvise enough to keep themselves off the ground which tended to be damp as well as infested with snails and other undesirable sleeping companions. Mosquito bars were absolutely essential. It was, all in all, the least attractive island Earl had ever been on—as well as the only one where they lived under battle conditions.

The six men collected in Earl's tent were somewhat unusual in that each one had separate, clearly identifiable characteristics. Along the wall across from Earl was a half Cherokee from Oklahoma. Next to him was a two-year medical student. At the back was a Dutchman from eastern Pennsylvania. On Earl's side of the tent, at the back, were a tall, nervous ex-basketball player and a nineteen-year-old who was the only son of a Hollywood playboy. This young man had always attended private schools. When his father finally drank himself to death, the boy was left with an estate on the New Jersey shore, a ranch in Wyoming, and various holdings in Hollywood. The young man always laughed when he was handed his monthly pay of fifty dollars.

And then there was Earl to fill up this distinctive tent.

Each of the tent's inhabitants had strong opinions on a multitude of topics, and they often stayed up late at night arguing about their various views. At times the men in neighboring tents who were more interested in sleeping than in arguing resorted to violent threats to silence the disturbers of their peace.

All of the men had carbines except for the nervous one at the back who had a tommy gun, which he kept loaded and hanging on the corner of his mosquito bar. Sniper action had been sporadic at times, and he wanted to be prepared. One night Earl awoke with a sudden feeling of dread. He looked toward the back of the tent and immediately froze. The nervous man was crouched beside his bunk with the tommy gun pointed in Earl's general direction and a wild look in his eyes. After several seconds his eyes changed and he stuttered, "Where is he? A Jap was in that tent door, I swear he was." Evidently Earl's tent mate had been having a nightmare. There was no sniper in or near the tent.

Actually, a Japanese officer had been killed a few weeks before not far from their tent. He had apparently been hiding in one of the many bunkers before being spotted and killed by a three-man patrol. The three had promptly gotten into an argument about who got his pistol and sword. Claims were asserted by the sergeant, the driver, and the gunner. The record does not show how the dispute was finally resolved.

In any case, the closest Earl ever came to being shot was by a tent mate who briefly mistook him for a Japanese soldier.

Another time, the occupants of Earl's tent were awakened by bullets ricocheting overhead. They learned later that a sniper had sneaked into an adjacent area carrying a pistol and hand grenades. He had an infected wound and, apparently realizing that he was dying, decided in typical fanatic fashion to take some of the enemy with him. Fortunately no one was hit by the grenades, and his bullets ended harmlessly in the ocean.

Those few Japanese who decided they wanted to surrender found that this was not an easy thing to do. The Americans had become very suspicious as the result of an assortment of subterfuges that had been employed by enemy soldiers pretending to surrender and then attacking their supposed captors. GIs now had become more inclined to shoot than to accept offers of surrender at face value. Attempts at surrender thus required ever more imaginative techniques for getting past American suspicion. One variation of a popular surrender strategy was employed by a group of three soldiers who emerged, hands upraised, from the jungle near where the Americans were waiting in a chow line—without their weapons. To further allay suspicion, the three Japanese were stark naked. The leader of the group of three later told interrogators that he had watched for several days before hitting on this idea.

A similar surrender was engineered a few days later when during the night three Japanese quietly entered a tent where there was only one man present, and he was asleep. The three lined themselves up—all completely naked with their hands in the air—before making a noise to rouse the sleeping GI. The flabbergasted soldier leaped from his bunk, grabbed his carbine—unloaded as it happened—and marched the prisoners to the nearby stockade.

Trigger fingers had become very nervous, and the story was widely circulated of a guard who one night well past midnight, while walking his post, heard a sudden clamor in the nearby jungle. Unhesitatingly he raised his rifle and blasted away in the direction of the noise, whereupon there appeared the fleeing form of a small white, thoroughly terrified cat.

————————

The job of Earl's crew was to install a high frequency relay station on the far side of the island, about a mile from their camp. They rode back and forth to the job site in a truck along a road that had been bulldozed through the jungle. By this time they had grown so inured to the war's hazards that they stood up in the truck even though they knew that Japanese snipers were in the area to the left of the road. They knew also that the snipers would not fire at the workers in the truck because that would betray their position and subject themselves to machine gun fire from the Americans to the right. The same was true at the work site itself, where the workers had to climb 70-foot poles to string antennas. Japanese snipers were known to be in the area, but if they fired they would reveal their positions and invite return machine gun fire. The workers on the poles never did get shot at.

As the few remaining Japanese soldiers were gradually eliminated, things quieted down considerably. After a few months, when the battle was virtually done, Earl decided to venture alone onto the hill where the enemy had held out the longest against constant mortar shelling. Although by the time Earl went souvenir hunting, there were not believed to be any remaining Japanese holdouts, warnings were still being issued that anyone wandering around the island wearing a canteen was at special risk, because any remaining enemy personnel would be desperate for water. Earl did not encounter any live Japanese, but he saw the remains of many dead ones. The stench, he reported, was often over-powering. In places, the ground was literally covered with bones. He came upon one place where a mortar shell had apparently scored a direct hit on a man. What remained was a heap of clothing and body parts, in the middle of which were his shoes, the feet still in them.

Eventually the time came for Earl and his team to leave Angaur and head back to Hawaii, marking the end of his adventures in the southern islands. Their plane stopped briefly at neighboring Peleliu and then for a few hours at Guam before taking off at dusk with a full moon rising. They flew all night through a partly clouded sky, stopping at Kwajalein to refuel, and then again at Johnston where they found the island so much enlarged by coral dredging since Earl's last visit there that it could accommodate B-29s. At last they arrived at Oahu and returned to Fort Shafter.

Waiting To Go Home
Earl came back to Hawaii hoping that he would finally get a furlough. Instead, the war ended not long after his arrival. With the fighting fin-

ished, the military presence in Hawaii quickly increased as personnel from all over the Pacific were sent there to await processing for transportation back to the mainland. The wait proved unexpectedly long because of the U.S. West Coast dock strike which seemed to drag on endlessly. In this tense atmosphere, with frustrated servicemen on one hand and crowded locals on the other, fighting between the military and civilians began to break out.

Earl nearly got involved in one of these brawls on the main street of Honolulu near Waikiki. That incident involved a merchant seaman who was being attacked by several native Hawaiians who were attempting to jab the seaman's face with broken bottles. Earl was on the brink of intervening to try to save the seaman when a policeman arrived and put an end to the fracas. Later he saw brawls on Waikiki beach itself. These never seemed to involve locals of Japanese ancestry (of which there were many living in Hawaii) but rather other races. Earl returned to camp in a hurry to avoid getting involved and did not venture into town thereafter.

The wait in Hawaii lasted ten days which were spent on Sand Island, which Earl described as "a barren coral strip." The island lies at the entrance to Honolulu harbor, and was at one time known as "Quarantine Island" because of its use in the nineteenth century to quarantine ships believed to carry passengers infected with contagious diseases. Quarantined indeed—also tedious and frustrating—Earl and his companions were further afflicted with young, self-important officers who had never been beyond Hawaii. Since the officers could not safely be defied, fights tended to develop among the enlisted men.

Having, on average, spent between four and six years on dangerous duty in the Pacific, usually with no leave or passes, these men found their morale at a low point and made worse by the attitude of the officers. "Being told we were lucky to be going back so soon was the ultimate insult," Earl wrote.

CHAPTER 15

ANECDOTES

SOUVENIRS

When Earl eventually got home after the war, the pearl joined a number of other souvenirs he had acquired. These included a tapa, which is a traditional cloth made throughout many of the South Sea islands, usually from the bark of the paper mulberry tree. Other souvenirs included silver filigree jewelry from the Fijis, mats from the Coral Sea, and seashells that he gathered himself in various places. He also had a few cat's eye shells that he found himself along with one that was given to him. Cat's eyes were actually the covering of a certain type of shell that resembled the eye of a cat. When the mollusk died, the eye would separate from the rest of the shell, and sometimes wash ashore. Earl used to sit along the beach and watch for a flash of green and white. When he saw the flash he would rush down to the water to grab the eye before the water came back. He considered himself lucky never to have been caught by a returning wave.

WOMEN ON THE ISLANDS

Women's Army Corps

Once while Earl was on Angaur a plane made an emergency landing there. As it happened, the plane's cargo consisted of Women's Army Corps personnel (WACs). The women were en route to the Philippines where they were to assume duties at MacArthur's headquarters. There happened to be an outdoor movie scheduled for that night to which they took "these nice, young girls." According to Earl's account, "They had to put guards on them. They practically had to put guards on the guards! Those guys would come out and try to proposition them in front of everybody."

Eleanor Roosevelt

Once when Eleanor Roosevelt was touring the South Pacific Theater she landed unannounced on one of the islands. Just as she was leaving the plane, one of the men walked out of the barracks stark naked, carrying only a towel. This particular enlisted man, like most of the others, was what Earl called "island happy" and shrugged it off, making no effort to cover himself. Earl claims that Eleanor was so offended that after she got back to Washington she announced that any man who had served in the South Pacific should go through a six-month reorientation before being allowed back into the country.

On another occasion she visited Nanumea while Earl was there. To provide her with the best possible overnight accommodation, the officers had to give up their usual thatched huts (which were much cooler than tents). The officers then requisitioned the quarters of the non-commissioned officers, who, in turn, had to move into tents. After spending the evening at a big luau in the local village, Eleanor then returned to her plane which had been outfitted with sleeping facilities for her. All the shuffling of officers and men had been in vain.

"We hated her because of the remarks she made," Earl said. But "she was a wonderful woman. You could hardly blame her because these guys acted like savages."

KILROY

When asked about the Kilroy phenomenon, Earl replied: "If you draw a line like this (a straight line) and what looked like a nose in the middle and two eyes. And it's like he was peeking over a wall and his nose was hanging over and his eyes were popping up with a dot in each of the eyes. You could make it in a second. It really was a spectacular thing when you think about it."

SNOW PLOWS IN THE TROPICS

Although not personally involved, Earl tells of a bizarre incident described to him by a source that he considered reliable. A cargo ship left Seattle carrying a two-part cargo, one part of which consisted of anti-aircraft ammunition destined for a battle zone in the South Pacific. This portion of the cargo was stored below deck where it was protected from the weather. The second part of the ship's cargo consisted of a quantity of rotary snowplows destined for Alaska. The second part of the cargo was carried on the deck.

Shortly after leaving port headed for Alaska, the ship received a radio communication informing them that the need for the ammunition had become urgent. Accordingly, the ship changed course and headed for a destination in the South Pacific. Upon arrival the snowplows had to be unloaded first in order to get to the ammunition. However, immediately after unloading the ammunition, the area became so dangerous that the cargo ship had to get away from the region forthwith.

The upshot was that until the end of the war a consignment of snow plows sat undisturbed in the tropical jungle.

CHAPTER 16

RECREATION

WRITING

It didn't take Earl long to realize that in the Army he would be spending a lot of his time sitting around with nothing to do. He quickly decided to fill up his spare time with writing poetry. He wrote all the way through the war: in the dark and by moonlight, by candlelight, and flashlight. He wrote on anything that came to hand, and he wrote wherever he was—sometimes in a slit trench or a foxhole with light provided by flares. For one three-month period it never got dark because the flares never stopped. As soon as one started to fade, another would be sent up; it was the only way they could control the Japanese snipers who would take advantage of any dark moment to crawl up and sneak in.

It was near the start of his Army career, while he was at Fort Monmouth that he first decided to become a writer. He was near the seacoast, and he could get a six-hour pass on the weekend with no difficulty. Earl took advantage of this option to walk the roads of the seacoast. In his walks he often crossed drawbridges where people would wave to him, and he would wave back. He was always alone, and it was on these walks he decided to become a writer.

SPORTS

Earl always enjoyed sports both as a spectator and a participant. While in Hawaii he would sometimes go to wrestling matches of a type that he described as "dirty wrestling." He remembered that there was often more fighting in the stands than in the ring, and he and his buddies would turn their backs on the match in the ring to observe the more exciting action in the stands.

While waiting to come home after the war ended he would, on occasion, go to a baseball game that featured professional ball players who were in the service but never did anything but play baseball. He remembered seeing PeeWee Reese along with other stars. On one memorable occasion on Palau he actually played in a game with Vic Wertz, who was one of the American League's top sluggers throughout the 1950s. Wertz is perhaps best known as the batter who in the 1954 World Series hit a 450-foot fly ball to dead center field in the Polo Grounds only to see it caught by Willie Mays. In almost any other ball park it would have been a home run. Coincidentally, Vic Wertz was born in York, Pennsylvania, as was Earl.

Partly for recreation and partly as a survival strategy he turned to boxing. He had done some at home before entering the service, but now he decided to get better at it in order to keep from being taken advantage of.

Another very personal style of recreation took him on foot to see the countryside and towns wherever he was. While at Fort Monmouth he often spent his weekends wandering the country roads all over central New Jersey. Throughout his tour in the Pacific he made a point of seeing, usually by walking, what each particular island had to offer.

CHAPTER 17

COMING HOME

GETTING OUT

When Earl was finally separated, he had only what he was wearing plus a hundred-dollar discharge bonus. Although he belatedly received a Good Conduct Medal after his discharge, he never received any of the other medals to which he believed himself entitled. This resulted in part because of paperwork's apparently getting lost, and in part because civilian supervisory personnel were less than diligent in submitting needed forms.

They had been flying across the country supposedly headed for the Newark airport. When they got there, however, the weather at Newark was too bad to allow them to land. Since the plane was scheduled to go on to Fort Dix from Newark, the crew simply took it directly to Fort Dix, but without telling the men where they were. They stood around in the early morning waiting for something to happen. Nothing did. They hadn't eaten for about thirty-six hours. Finally around noon one of the men said, "Well, we better find out what this is all about." They walked to the headquarters building where they discovered that no one even knew they were there. The plane crew had never let anyone know that a load of men had been dumped off. At least they were finally given something to eat.

That evening they were put aboard a DC-3 headed to Newark where they landed in the dark near a Red Cross facility. They went inside to get a cup of coffee but before it was cool enough to drink they were informed that they were about a mile from where they should be. So they climbed back aboard the plane which taxied a mile to the proper destination.

Earl's last journey on a plane, until after his 1998 Appalachian Trail hike more than fifty years later, was only a mile long and never left the ground.

The following day Earl and the others were put on a train to Indiantown Gap, Pennsylvania. The train was a slow-traveling local, and it took them nearly twenty-four hours to go from Newark to Indiantown Gap. When they got there in a cold and wet September, they were assigned to a barracks and given just one blanket. For four days the men loitered around their barracks doing nothing at all. At last they were called for the physical examination that was required before discharge. The ritual examination was strictly pro forma. He was told, "You need eyeglasses, but you don't want to wait around for that." And that item was checked off. "You need dental work, but you don't want to wait around for that." Again the item was checked off. Earl felt that he was being "railroaded right out."

The men being separated were supposed to turn in their old uniforms and get new ones. The one they gave Earl was "about ten sizes too big, so I just turned it back in and kept the one I was wearing." About eleven o'clock at night the men were marched through the rain to the post chapel where the final ritual was performed. They saluted the officer in charge and got their discharge papers. Then they were marched back and put on a train to Harrisburg. "I came the whole way down to Harrisburg in a wet uniform," Earl said. "And by that time I told myself I'll never, never wear that uniform again."

Earl got back home in the middle of the night on a train that used to run from Harrisburg to York. His father and sister were the only ones there waiting for him.

Looking Back
Earl's already unfavorable impression of the Army caused by its bureaucratic ineptitude was certainly not improved by the multiple bunglings that accompanied his discharge. "I was just one of them that fell through the cracks," he said. " I never got a fair break. If you were willing to work in the Army you worked. If you didn't want to work they'd put you in charge of the guy that would work. That was their philosophy." The difficulty Earl had in readjusting after the war was one of the main reasons for his decision to set out on his first Appalachian Trail hike. Initially his main feeling was one of restlessness and hopelessness. He viewed the hike he was planning as "a kill or cure, it would either make me worse or make me better."

He decided not to go to college on the GI Bill because he feared it would force him into the same mold as everyone else. It was his insistence on affirming his own individuality that led to the trail trip and to his writing.

Military Inefficiency
Earl and many of his companions concluded that the other armies must have been really terrible if with ours, even as unorganized as it was, we could still win the war

War's Purpose
In Earl's view the only purpose war serves is to reduce the population. The First World War was horrible, and brought on the Second World War which was even more horrible. Future wars can be expected to get steadily worse. Nuclear power has not really solved anything.

Resentment Toward Japan
After the war Earl felt no resentment to the ordinary Japanese people. The Japanese people that he encountered in Hawaii impressed him as good Americans. Of the Japanese from Hawaii who served in the U.S. Military he said, "They were the most decorated outfit in the whole Army. So I respected the Japanese." As for the Japanese soldiers, they were, like American soldiers, just following orders and doing what their country wanted them to do. "They grew up that way and didn't know any better."

HOME FINALLY
One of the first things Earl did after getting home was to take a walk along Honey Run where he and Walter had so often wandered. In particular, Earl wanted to see again an ancient pine that towered above all the other trees thereabouts. Although it was clearly past its prime and steadily deteriorating when he last saw it, the tree's upper branches had been still green and full, providing homes for squirrels and the occasional raccoon. On even the calmest days there was always a gentle soughing that drifted down from the top of this forest monarch. As Earl's homecoming walk neared the site, however, the pine's looming presence was not visible, and shortly his worst fears were confirmed. The tree had collapsed into a heap of rubble, with only about ten feet of trunk left standing. Three years later, during a night in Vermont's Green Mountains, he was to hear the sound of such a forest giant's fall.

An ancient pine tree nearing its end

His first labors after getting home were directed toward fixing up The Old Place which he found suffering from lack of maintenance. Among other things he rebuilt the winding stairway that his sister liked so much. He also tore down and rebuilt the old barn. In addition to his labors around The Old Place, he took some outside jobs working as a carpenter, doing stone masonry, and other construction work.

THE HARLEY DAVIDSON

Now that he was home Earl needed some means of transportation. The U.S. Army was no longer available to move him around, and although he was by instinct a walker, there was a limit to walking's utility in a rural day-to-day routine. When he entered the Army, he had sold his Model A Ford panel truck for a nominal amount to his youngest brother, John, who used it in his radio repair business until about 1951. Once back home Earl discovered that the car market was dramatically changed. Price controls were still in effect, with prices set so low that owners were unwilling to sell. Eventually Earl decided to get a classic 1934 VLD Harley-Davidson motorcycle, which he bought for $250. This vehicle had previously been owned by the Harrisburg police department and was in very good condition. Earl used it for relatively short trips; he never took it more than one hundred miles away from home. In the winter when the temperature approached the zero mark, he would attach a windshield to diminish the impact of the icy wind.

Earl found riding a motorcycle a wonderful experience, adding, "As long as the weather is good and the drivers of cars give you equal treatment." As for the weather, in the summer there were thunderstorms with drenching rain, and in winter snow and ice with accompanying slipping, sliding, and struggling to stay upright. The air flowing past your face in the summer was cooling and refreshing; in the winter it was chilling or even freezing.

On a Sunday afternoon when the weather was nice, Earl would invest two dollars to fill the gas tank before setting off to tour some back country roads and, on occasion, detour into the woods themselves. Sometimes when he was being especially troubled by war memories, he would ride to one or another of the nearby trail shelters and spend the night. Gradually, "the old hiking habit" began to revive along with renewed thoughts of hiking the whole Trail.

One balmy day Earl was cruising along on a narrow blacktop road when he came to a curve where a dense hedge along the side blocked his view. As he rounded the curve, he was confronted by two boys pushing bicycles on his side and a Model A Ford coming up on the other side. Somehow he was able to swerve the 700-pound Harley to avoid hitting the boys but in the process managed to bounce off the rear wheel of the Ford. Earl and the motorcycle slid down the road for about fifty feet, "just like sliding into third base" he later wrote. Fortunately the heavy motorcycle did not land on top of him which, he thought, would probably have killed him. As it was, he quickly righted the Harley and pushed it off the road. The boys fled. The driver of the Ford pulled over and came back to check on Earl and asked to see his leg which he thought must surely be broken. Meanwhile, the woman who lived in the house behind the hedge came out with a basin of water which she used to wash off the blood and tar that he picked up as his arm scraped along the road.

Eventually, when everyone was assured that Earl was not seriously injured, he mounted his Harley and headed for home. The next time he rode past that spot he found the hedge gone.

The following weekend, to Earl's astonishment, the driver of the Ford appeared at Earl's door to check on him and to see if he was still in the hospital.

He kept the Harley for two years until he got involved in auction work and needed a larger vehicle for hauling furniture and other bulky items. The motorcycle was sold for

Earl on his 1934 Harley-Davidson

$150, an action that he often regretted later, as the market value of classic old Harleys steadily escalated.

REJECTION SLIPS
During this immediate post-war period Earl put together a manuscript of his war poems which he submitted to various publishers. From all of them he got rejection slips. The usual comments were: "Nobody wants to hear about the war." or "Poetry is not profitable." This too contributed to his feelings of depression. Later, following the hike, he had a similar experience with the book that came out of that adventure: "Nobody wants to hear about hiking."

A DOORWAY TO HISTORY
Before the war he and Walter had talked about someday hiking the whole Appalachian Trail. But with Walter gone, Earl initially found the thought of doing it alone too disturbing. One day, however, he happened to pick up an outdoor magazine, the name of which near the end of his life he no longer remembered. In it was an article called "The Long Trail's Challenge," written, he thought, by either Jean Stephenson of the Appalachian Trail Conference or a retired major who was very interested in the trail. The article stated that although various people had tried to hike the entire Trail, no one had even gotten halfway. The author wondered doubtfully if anyone would ever succeed. This implicit challenge was one that Earl could not let pass, and provided him with his doorway to history.

PART FOUR

THE WILD LONESOME

Meanwhile people began to drift in, probably to get a look at the stranger. One was a little old mountain lady wearing an ancient shawl. "You ain't agonna sleep on Old Bloody Mountain tonight, be ye?" she queried. I said I didn't know. "Well I wouldn't no how," she declared. "It's too wild lonesome up thar."

—Earl Shaffer
Walking With Spring

CHAPTER 18

GETTING OVER
THE WAR

arl came home in 1945 after four and a half years of military service. In all that time he had neither a furlough nor rest leave; his only time off consisted of a few three-day passes. Most of his time in the Army was spent on dangerous duty in the South Pacific islands. He returned unsettled, depressed, and embittered with no clear plan for his future. The one firm plan he had carried with him into the war had perished in the maelstrom of Iwo Jima along with his best friend, Walter Winemiller. The two of them had talked often of hiking together the entire 2,000-mile length of the Appalachian Trail. In his present state of mind, however, he could not even consider the possibility of pursuing such a dream alone.

He rattled around at loose ends for two years, gradually exhausting the modest savings he had put together from his Army pay over those years. By the time two years had passed his resistance to an Appalachian Trail hike had softened. This work of time coincided with his receipt finally of three hundred dollars in bonus money that Congress had authorized. Earl decided that if he was ever to hike the Trail, now was the time. His decision was further prompted by information he had been reading suggesting that after the neglect necessitated by the war years, the Appalachian Trail was in real danger of fading out of existence. As he put it later:

> And I thought, well I'll do it to get over the Army, and I'll take pictures and keep a notebook so I could write a book about it. It was all planned the way it turned out. Everything went according to plan.

Of course the plan had not included finding a publisher for the book, but we will return to that problem later.

The Appalachian Trail had been initially completed in 1937 under the direction of Myron Avery whose dynamic leadership was the key factor in achieving this goal. The following year, however, the "Long Island Express," the great hurricane of 1938 inflicted massive damage to great stretches of the newly completed Trail. Then a few years later came the war. Between the limitations imposed by gas rationing and the drastically reduced manpower available for volunteer trail maintenance, the Appalachian Trail was slowly fading away. Trail managers up and down its entire length expressed a concern that it might already be beyond recovery.

Earl envisioned his proposed walk as something that would generate publicity for the fading trail and help renew interest in its restoration. This publicity would be further enhanced by the book that he planned on writing. He would not wait any longer, Earl decided; he would do the hike the following year.

Having made his decision, Earl was confronted with the problem of preparing for a journey of more than two thousansd miles on foot over a time period of at least four months. Even with the government windfall of three hundred dollars he had precious little money available to finance such a trip. Extreme prudence was called for. The biggest expenditure, he knew, would be for the camera that he felt was essential for illustrating the planned book and also for documenting the very fact of the hike itself.

Earl went to Philadelphia to do most of his supply shopping. In a hock shop he bought for sixty-five dollars an old pre-war German Kodak Retina that he suspects some service man brought back from Germany after the war. Near the end of his life he still proclaimed it "the best camera I ever owned. I still have it and it still works." After taking one roll of film to be sure it did work, it became more or less a permanent part of his backpacking equipment. He said that the main reason for "splurging" on this item was a desire to make his planned hike truly worthwhile.

At the other extreme, he paid only five dollars for a surplus mountain troop rucksack and no more than a dollar or two for various other items. Earl bought a new rucksack at the start of each trip and never paid more than five dollars for one. By the end of each trip the rucksack was pretty well worn out.

All told, he spent about $150 for all of his equipment and supplies, including the camera. During the trip he spent an additional $100 for film. So his total cost for equipment and supplies came to approximately

$250. He later estimated that at current prices he would have spent at least ten times that total.

On his first trip Earl used wood for both cooking and warmth on cold nights. With his poncho he would set up a kind of "half teepee" with the fire in front of it. Before retiring for the night he gathered enough wood to see him through to morning and trained himself to wake up before the fire went out, so that more wood could be added.

For additional warmth at night he carried a "paper mill blanket." This is a piece of the large felted wool blanket used in paper mills to press the water out of the paper. When such blankets became too worn to be usable for paper-making purposes, they were cut apart and made available to employees and others for little or no cost. Most likely the blanket Earl carried was acquired from the Glatfelter Company, whose headquarters at that time were in Spring Grove, Pennsylvania, not far from where he lived.

His cooking specialty was what he called "pan bread" or sometimes— jokingly—"wonder bread" because he wondered what would be included in the next evening meal. The recipe was simple, and vague enough to assure a somewhat different taste every time. He would take cornmeal, oatmeal, and flour and mix up a batter that he would bake in a pan. "If you have a small hand," he said, "use two hands full; if it's a big hand, only use one." If the mixture was mostly cornmeal, the result would be cornbread; if mostly flour, biscuits; and if mostly oatmeal, it would be bannock. Depending on the season and on what he might be able to forage en route, special treats such as berries or apples might be added.

The 1948 hike was still in the era before plastic—which Earl acknowledged to be a boon to long-distance hikers. He carried a Marine Corps poncho which weighed a couple of pounds; whereas today an equivalent tarp would weigh a few ounces. Heavy cloth bags had to be used rather than the near weightless plastic ones available today. Cloth bags had the further disadvantage of tending to get wet which added even more weight.

Other items carried included an Air Corps survival tent which, after about a week, he sent home because it was too heavy. Among the things that stayed with him for the whole trip were a rain hat, a match safe, a compass, a sheath knife, small hand axe, sewing kit, snakebite kit, Mountain Troop cook kit, and a week's worth of food.

Clothing items included T-shirts, a Navy turtleneck, mountain cloth pants, and wool/cotton socks. Earl never wore shorts when hiking. In his

*Earl's Birdshooter boots at
the end of the hike*

view they made no sense considering the insects, poison, briars and snakes that had to be guarded against. On his feet he wore Russell Birdshooters boots made of elk hide, from which he removed the heels. He believed that this provided more natural foot movement and also eliminated the possibility of the heels catching on something and causing a fall. He has a similar objection to modern lug sole boots. The Russell Birdshooters lasted the whole trip. In what has become one of his trademark idiosyncrasies, he never wore socks when he was hiking. He carried them to use as gloves when his hands were cold.

Early in 1948 he ordered maps and other information from the Appalachian Trail Conference, but for unclear reasons that Earl blamed on the Post Office, these items did not reach him, with some being returned to the sender marked "Moved. Left no forwarding address." Earl went to the York post office where a recent personnel change had replaced the former postmaster with a new acting postmaster. He was unable to actually talk to the acting postmaster and attempted to explain the situation to a clerk, but apparently with little success. He ultimately delayed the start of his trip for a week in hopes the ordered material might appear, but he finally had to set off without it.

Near the beginning of April he took a bus to Georgia where he succeeded in obtaining at a gas station an oil company map on which a dotted line showed the approximate route of the Appalachian Trail. With that in hand, along with a compass, he set off. Earl learned later that the maps and other information he had requested from the Appalachian Trail Conference were finally delivered a month or two later when he was already well on the Trail.

CHAPTER 19

THE LONG CRUISE

With nothing but an oil company map and his compass to guide him for more than two hundred miles at the start of his journey, Earl frequently got lost. Blazes were mostly non-existent and where they were found they were badly faded, and the compass was of limited value. While the general overall direction of the trail was north, it twisted and turned along the way. At times he would find the trail again after having lost it, only to head off in the wrong direction because one of the twists had trail-north heading south for a while. Many hours were lost one way or another. Frequently he found that the only reasonable strategy was to head north until it got dark and then stop. Sooner or later—usually later—he would find the trail again. This method of finding his way somewhat resembled the point-to-point navigation system used by old-time seafarers, which led the wandering hiker to refer to his trek as the "long cruise."

When he reached the Great Smoky Mountains National Park Earl was able to obtain a park map that showed the Trail route and the location of shelters with reasonable accuracy. Beyond the Smokeys, however, he was once again traveling without navigation tools. The Skyline Drive was being built at that time, and in that area the Trail was thoroughly disrupted. One way and another he finally reached Maryland where Trail conditions improved, as was also the case in most of Pennsylvania. From there on northward there was less problem with losing the Trail. In New England, for the most part, the Trail was better maintained and better blazed than had been the case in the south. Even Maine was pretty well marked.

His goal was to cover twenty miles a day, but as a practical matter he acknowledged that he would settle for fifteen.

GEORGIA

On Saturday, April 3, 1948, Earl Shaffer arrived near sundown at the summit of Georgia's Mount Oglethorpe, at that time the southern terminus of the Appalachian Trail. He had come by bus as far as Jasper, Georgia and then set off on foot toward Mount Oglethorpe, a few miles to the east. Earl was spared the need to walk the entire distance when a logging truck came along and gave him a ride. The truck let him off at a gravel road along which he walked the rest of the way to the mountain's crest. After observing the board sign marking the southern starting point of the trail, as well as the native marble obelisk honoring James Oglethorpe, the

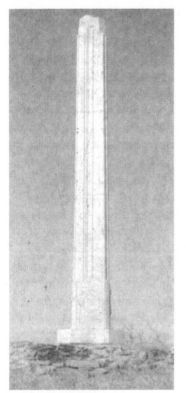

Marble obelisk at Mount Oglethorpe

founder of the colony of Georgia, Earl backtracked a short way to "a rickety lean-to near a rickety fire-tower," where he spent the night.

The following morning his first stop was at the road crossing where the loggers had let him off the evening before. At this point, with delayed action shutter release and a contrived tripod Earl took a photo of himself from the back, showing his large and heavy pack and the lake at Connahaynee Lodge in the background. This photo was used on the cover of the first Appalachian Trail Conference edition of *Walking With Spring*, Earl's description of his 1948 hike. A modified version of the photo was used on a later edition.

That evening Earl made the first of the daily entries in a journal he kept in a small notebook that he referred to as his *Little Black Book*. This practice was one that he believed should be a requirement for any hiker claiming recognition as an Appalachian Trail through hiker:

April 4. Started early from Mount Oglethorpe, weather cold and raw. Made good time over fair trail till about noon. Met family of three having picnic near a water reservoir. Man said "Luck to ye." Lady said, "I'se glad I got sense." Passed Amicalola Falls, arrived at Frosty Mountain fire tower. Had difficulty finding trail beyond, but finally reached the slope of Springer Mountain where I bedded down under a large fallen tree. Began to rain lightly.[4]

Before starting off again the contents of the pack were rearranged to shift the weight forward, and the large exterior pocket on the pack was discarded.

After only a couple of days into the hike, Earl's feet developed a generous crop of blisters. In trying to adjust his walk to favor the blisters he managed to put undue strain on his ankles and other joints, thereby adding to the pain. "Hiking had become an exquisite kind of torture," he writes. The usual way to deal with such a problem would be to go barefoot, but the weather was too cold and the footway too rocky to allow for this approach. Instead, Earl elected to put sand in his boots and remove his socks. He also used generous quantities of foot powder. Although painful at first, calluses did form eventually and thereafter he had no more foot problems. He later determined that the sand was not necessary, and he simply hiked with bare feet inside his boots.

When making camp one wet evening, Earl used all but one of his matches before getting a fire started. The following morning as he walked, he pondered the match problem and wondered how to resolve it. Shortly, he came upon a small farm in a cove and a young man outside digging a trench for a water line. He explained his match problem to the man who immediately handed over the few matches in his pocket and even went inside the house to get more. After declining payment for the matches, the farmer directed Earl to a narrow woods road which would take him back to the "government trail"—which is how local people tended to describe the Appalachian Trail. Earl headed up the road and soon spotted a faded blaze where he turned to resume his trek. After some time, he suddenly stopped in stunned amazement; before him was the site of his camp of the night before. The explanation, he later determined, was that the road intersected the Trail at a switchback, and Earl turned the wrong way.

---

[4]The *Little Black Book* now resides in the Smithsonian Institution along with Earl's Bird-shooter boots and most of his other papers and artifacts.

Earl's Little Black Book

It was on Georgia's Tray Mountain at the end of a 25-mile day that Earl came closer to total collapse than at any other time on the entire hike.

The first of a number of brushes Earl had with moonshiners occurred in Georgia. He reached Snake Mountain Cabin in mid afternoon and found it to be one of the best shelters yet. He was low on supplies, and his map showed a nearby road leading to a town. This seemed like a good opportunity to replenish his supplies. Leaving his pack at the cabin he struck off across country to find the road. He very quickly regretted his decision when he entered an area of dense, damp laurel thickets, heavy with the pervasive odor of moonshine. At this point he had little choice but to hurry on without looking to either side. When he finally found the road and reached the town he saw many people outdoors, but none seemed to even notice him. This made him quite nervous.

Over time he developed a useful strategy for dealing with moonshiners, all of whom tended to be very suspicious of strangers. Those who would buy and drink their illegal product were—at least at that time—considered just as guilty as those who manufactured it. Such customers were therefore accepted. It was the ones who would not buy or drink who aroused the suspicions of the moonshiners. Earl would tell them that his mother was very much against drinking, and she made him swear that he would never take a drink. The moonshiners accepted that explanation and Earl was not molested.

Finally, beyond the town, he reached the store, which posed new problems. The shopkeeper was nearly blind, so Earl had to find everything himself and even read the price tag aloud to the proprietor. He prudently decided to stick to the public road when he returned to the Trail at the top of the ridge. When he had gone perhaps halfway to the Trail a mountain man offered him a lift. In conversation they learned that they had both been serving in the South Pacific at the same time. Finally the mountain man asked with what seemed to be sincere concern whether Earl was not concerned about hiking alone in the hills in an unknown region—even if it was on the government trail. He acknowledged that he himself had practiced the art of moonshining for a couple of years until he and his partner had nearly been caught one night. He even pointed out to Earl the spot where they had dumped their contraband that risky night.

When they passed the area where Earl had caught the scent of "Mountain Dew," the man commented that four stills had been raided there the week before, thereby accounting for the strong odor Earl had noticed. After declining the mountain man's invitation to Earl to join him in town for a "high old time," Earl hastened to the shelter where, we may assume, he probably spent a less than wholly restful night.

On April 11, exactly a week after his start, Earl crossed the state border into North Carolina. He had averaged fifteen miles per day—the minimum distance his goal had established as acceptable.

NANTAHALA

Although his feet had toughened and his pack load had been streamlined, Earl nonetheless felt his strength ebbing as he entered a region of dense growth, rough terrain, and extensive blowdowns. Something was clearly wrong, although he was mystified as to what might be the cause. One time when he stopped to prepare his midday meal he decided to cook a double portion and save half for the evening when it could be eaten cold if a fire proved impossible. When he sat down to consume his lunch, he was at first startled to see the entire double portion disappear along with half a pound of brown sugar, a can of milk, and some raisins. Almost immediately he began to feel his strength returning, and he realized that he had simply not been eating enough—a failing that he resolved to correct. Thereafter his strength increased along with his food bill.

When Earl reached Wallace Gap he encountered a Nantahala Forest game protector who gave him a ride to a store in Rainbow Springs. Later, at the game protector's invitation, he spent what promised to be a stormy night in an empty ranger shack nearby. Hanging on the wall in a corner of the shack was a small mirror. Upon glancing in the mirror he got the first look at himself in two weeks; he drew back in amazement. His face had become drawn and thin; his eyes were wide and staring; and his hair had gone wild. Hiking the Appalachian Trail alone leaves its mark on a person.

At Wesser Bald around midday, Earl yielded to the shouted entreaties of the fire lookout up in the tower to come up and visit. The man was in the midst of preparing his lunch to which he added considerably more food which was then offered to Earl who hungrily accepted. The fire watcher carried on a steady stream of conversation throughout the meal and on into the afternoon. Finally, with evening beginning to fall, the lookout triumphally announced that it was too late for Earl to leave now, so he would have to spend the night and make use of an extra bunk that was part of the tower's facilities. The two continued their conversation well into the night before finally getting to sleep around 12:30.

At breakfast the next morning the fire warden was still urging Earl to stay for a day or two. His entreaties were eloquent: "Well, we fought about three wars and four election campaigns and hunted nigh every critter in the woods last evening, and I enjoyed every minute of it. Why don't you stay over a day or two? We got lots more to talk about." Having lost more time the day before than he should have, Earl was adamant this time and departed promptly after breakfast.

Where the Trail met the main road in Wesser, he found a ramshackle grocery store packed with all manner of food and other goods. One thing the store did not have was color film, which Earl needed, so he caught a ride on a lumber truck to Bryson City where he found the needed film. He also bought a small spoon and spatula which he thought would be more convenient for turning pan bread than the axe he had been using. "After all, you can go only so far for simplification," he later wrote.

After some unpleasant bushwhacking as the result of again losing the Trail, Earl came to the village of Tapoco where he was directed to a grocery about a mile up a side road, to which, after hiding his pack, he duly headed. The storekeeper's regular customers always provided their own containers in which they carried home their purchases. When Earl completed his buying, however, he had nothing in which to put the items. The only thing the proprietor could find to serve the purpose was an old potato sack, which was loaded up and flung over Earl's shoulder for the trek back to the Trail. This gunny sack subsequently went with him all the way to Maine and proved useful in a variety of ways.

At the post office in Tapoco he obtained a map of the Great Smoky Mountains National Park which he was about to enter. For the next few days he would have, for the first time, a reasonably precise idea of where the Trail went and where the shelters were located. Although battered and bruised as he left Nantahala, his spirits soared. The weather had improved and he had finally hit his stride. He knew now that nothing other than some incapacitating mishap could prevent him from reaching Katahdin.

THE SMOKEYS

The Great Smoky Mountain range is the highest in the United States east of the Mississippi River. More than two dozen peaks in the range rise above 6,000 feet. A number of these are on or near the Appalachian Trail, including Clingman's Dome which, at 6,643 feet, is the highest. The abundance and diversity of flora and fauna here is extraordinary. The national park covers some 521,000 acres and straddles the crest of the range, along which the Appalachian Trail itself runs. Notwithstanding the high elevation, the ridge crest is unexpectedly level and the footway rarely rough, making for quite pleasant walking along most of its length.

Earl's first night in the Smokeys was spent in the open somewhat beyond Deal's Gap. To compensate for the weather which had turned cold and windy, he was looking for all available means to keep warm, thus providing him with the first opportunity to make use of the Tapoco storekeeper's gunny sack, which he put over his feet. "I fell asleep," he wrote in *Walking With Spring*, "to the lullaby of the wind in the trees and the somewhere calling of a whip-poor-will."

Although many complaints are heard about the rainy weather encountered in the Smokies, Earl's four days there consisted of sunny days and moonlit though cold nights. Actually his main complaint about the weather in the Smokies had to do with the sunburned face that the clear weather caused him.

For Earl's second night in the Smokeys he planned on reaching Spence Field Shelter, which he did after sunset, although with the help of a full moon. As he descended to the shelter he neither saw nor heard any evidence of its being occupied, but under the bright moon he could see tables laden with food: canned goods, jars of jam and other food, enormous pancakes still on the skillets, and plates of partially consumed food. His first thought was that the (very quiet) people must be inside the shelter in the dark. When he approached, however, and struck a match, he found the shelter empty. There was a dark mystery here, he realized, but he was exhausted and already half asleep. He decided that solving the mystery could wait until morning, and opted for a good night's rest.

The following morning the mystery was still there but the light was better. The scene had something of the eerie look of a ghost town. It appeared that a group had hastily departed in the middle of a meal, leaving all kinds of litter "strewn from here to yonder." Earl cleaned up the mess somewhat including a number of empty whiskey bottles which likely had some bearing on whatever had occurred. After restoring a semblance of order to the area, he rewarded himself with a bountiful breakfast from the abandoned food.

At Newfound Gap Earl took a bus to Gatlinburg to replenish his supplies. There were two drivers on the bus who seemed to delight in regaling the reckless hiker—and everyone else on the bus—with numerous tales about people being attacked by bears. When Earl informed them that he carried no gun, they took a philosophical attitude and concluded that with bears it was probably best to just run anyway. In Gatlinburg, with only a few minutes available before a bus going in the opposite direction was due, Earl raced to a store across the street from the bus station, and quickly stocked up on his needs.

The driver on the returning bus was more concerned about snakes than bears, and trotted out an assortment of stories about the many unfortunate encounters he knew of people dealing with venomous serpents. He too seemed to think Earl should have a gun. When Earl left the bus in Newfound Gap the driver wished him well, and the passengers seemed to believe that he was going to his doom.

At Davenport Gap Earl left the national park. Of the Smokies he later wrote, "Nowhere else on the Appalachian Trail do I feel so strong an urge to return."

NORTH CAROLINA/TENNESSEE

From Davenport Gap the trail headed north mostly along the North Carolina–Tennessee border. After crossing the Big Pigeon River at Waterville on a cable bridge that swayed and rocked alarmingly as he crossed, Earl came to a small farm where a man sitting on the porch firmly urged him to "come and set for a while." The farmer insisted that Earl must know Dick Lamb from Philadelphia who appeared at the farmhouse door one rainy night and asked to be allowed to sleep on the porch. The farmer would have none of it and took Mr. Lamb inside to sleep in the guest room. At this point he insisted that Earl do the same. Earl countered with the observation that it was still only mid-afternoon and he had miles to go. Here the farmer's wife appeared and expressed outrage at the thought that she would let someone sleep on the mountain when they had a perfectly good bed available. Earl finally yielded and was rewarded the next morning with "one of the most elaborate breakfasts imaginable." Apparently it even surpassed the mystery breakfast he had enjoyed one morning in the Smokies.

Earl was to hear more of Dick Lamb when he reached Vermont and to actually meet the man some years later.

When he stopped at the District Forest Service Headquarters near Hot Springs, the man on duty there studied him closely before commenting, "You must be that lone trail hiker we've been hearing about." Apparently the first Forest Service lookout he had encountered had passed the word northward. From then on, for more than five hundred miles until he left the northern end of the Shenandoah National Park, Forest Service and Park Service employees were always watching for Earl and offered him any help they could provide.

Once when Earl was hiking along a rural road a teenage boy on a bicycle caught up with him from behind and slowed down to ride beside him. A conversation was struck up and the two were soon talking like old friends. This continued for several miles until they came to a house where the boy said he lived as he turned into the yard. "Well, be seeing

Big Pigeon River

you," the boy said; then paused for a moment to add in a low voice, "though I know I never will." Later Earl would write, "The memory of that parting, after so brief an acquaintance, has haunted me ever since."

Earl went into the town of Hampton in hopes of finding a cobbler who could resole his boots which had worn quite thin. He found one who obligingly half-soled the boots, but Earl asked him not to do anything with the heels because he wanted to try walking without heels Indian-fashion. "He finally agreed," Earl writes, "but joined the growing list of people who doubted my sanity."

The next to last night in Tennessee was spent in a "small ramshackle lean-to," with a leaky roof. The night was windy and rain began to fall, but these proved to be the least of Earl's problems. Although he had been forewarned about the shelter's resident mouse, he naively believed that by keeping the pack next to his head he would keep it safe from depredation. This seriously underestimated the boldness of Appalachian Trail wildlife. The next morning he found that the mouse had gnawed a hole in the pack and left droppings everywhere, including in his salt. Most of his supplies had to be thrown away, making the need to find a store unexpectedly urgent.

He hurried on that day, covering some twenty miles on Holston Mountain before stopping for the night in a Forest Service shed at Maple Springs. After a cold and windy night he rose at dawn to hurry the few remaining miles to Damascus across the border in Virginia.

SOUTHERN VIRGINIA AND THE BLUE RIDGE

After passing through Damascus, Virginia on May Day in the midst of a carnival and general festivities, Earl came to Feathercamp Fire Tower where the watchman on duty was not surprised to see him. The back country communications network was working most efficiently. The next day he camped at a spring near Skulls Gap and the following morning as he headed out he passed a long black stick which suddenly moved and revealed itself as an eight-foot black snake. In this area herds of cattle were grazing, each herd with a giant bull supervising. He carefully circled around these beasts, and wrote later, "Even a bear or a mountain lion will not attack such a monster."

When he reached Fries Junction, Earl stopped at the local railroad station and struck up a conversation with a man waiting for a train. The man told him that years before he had been bitten by a "spreadhead"— the local term for a cottonmouth moccasin—but because he had gotten to a doctor within fifteen minutes he had survived. However, the sickness

One of the two Pinnacles of the Dan

he experienced returned every year during hot weather, and he believed that this was the result of some of the venom remaining in his body. Earl reports having heard similar stories from other snakebite survivors.

Earl had reached Fries late in the day, after the ferry that crossed the river to Galax had ceased its daily operation. A storekeeper invited him to get out of the rain at his house across the street from the store. This eventually led to an invitation to supper, after which the storekeeper drove Earl by way of a road bridge around to Galax where Earl took a two-dollar room in a tourist home, his first night indoors since Waterville. This marked the completion of just about five hundred miles. He was still firmly on track to complete his trek within the timetable he had set.

The next day Earl encountered the recently constructed Blue Ridge Parkway which had thoroughly disrupted the Appalachian Trail. The Trail crossed back and forth across the Parkway and was often lost. This all contributed to Earl's walking the longest day of the entire trek—an estimated thirty miles.

Just as Earl was growing thoroughly weary of road walking, the Trail abruptly veered eastward into a gorge from which rose a spectacular pyramidal peak: the Pinnacles of the Dan. Crossing this peak was mostly rock climbing, and not only difficult but often downright dangerous, particularly the descent on the far side. His forty-pound pack became more than just a burden; it was a serious hindrance. Earl wrote later, "This couple of miles was probably the most rugged and most spectacular segment of the Trail, which now has been relocated far to the west." The Pinnacles of the Dan is still visible from the Blue Ridge Parkway.

As the advancing season moved toward the middle of May, Earl experienced the first mosquito attacks. As if to compensate himself for the resultant loss of blood, it was at about the same time that he encountered the first ripe wild strawberries, encounters that decidedly slowed him down. "Not even a thicket of green-briers," he wrote "can stop me as effectively as strawberries."

In a sporting goods store in the town of Salem he acquired mosquito repellent, but they had no mosquito netting. A visit to the local department store found no mosquito netting as such, but he did turn up some fashionable black netting which he reluctantly decided would serve his purpose.

As Earl approached Rockfish Gap at the southern end of the Shenandoah National Park, he was accosted by an engineer on the Blue Ridge Parkway project who struck up a conversation. When he learned about Earl's long trek he announced that he was a personal friend of the editor of the *News-Virginian* newspaper in nearby Waynesboro. The editor, it appeared, was greatly interested in adventures like Earl's and the engineer asked Earl if he would agree to be interviewed. Since Earl had made Waynesboro a designated mail stop, he agreed to think about the interview proposal.

At the post office Earl picked up some letters that were waiting—the first thus far on the hike—whereupon the clerk informed him that the newspaper editor had called and requested that he come right on over to the office. Earl did so. The editor, Earl noted later, had something of the enthusiasm of "a kid on a picnic." At the conclusion of the interview a photographer was instructed to drive Earl back to Rockfish Gap and get some photos there. The article along with a photograph appeared on the front page of the next day's paper.

MR. HANDY

Throughout his hike Earl's chance encounters with local people provided as much mental and emotional nourishment as did the wonders of the natural world through which he stepped. An example is a family he came upon somewhere in the vicinity of the Blue Ridge Parkway in southwestern Virginia.

One day while trying to make progress against a fierce headwind that had come up, Earl noticed a farmer who was plowing his field with a team of two mules and a horse. The man saw Earl and waved; then, stopping his team midway along in the furrow, he walked over to the fence to talk. This in itself was an unusual act by any farmer in the midst of his spring plowing. The man identified himself as Handy—no first name given. (It later was learned that Handy's first name was Euwel.) "I ain't got no eddication," Mr. Handy stated, "that's why I'm followin' the plow, but I like to talk to everyone as sensible as I can." He owned two hundred acres of farmland and one hundred acres of pasture; he also rented additional land that he worked. After starting from scratch, he had eventually built a large new house to replace the tiny cabin in which he and his wife had started out. He invited Earl to join him for his noon meal. Even though his wife was in the hospital for an operation, his "girl" was coming over from her place "to fix a little somethin'." Although Earl would ordinarily have declined such an invitation in the interest of time, this case, he felt, was somehow different so he accepted.

As the farmer finished plowing the interrupted furrow and headed toward the far end of the field, Earl walked along and talked about his own work on farms as a boy, including some "walk-plowing." When they neared the fencerow Earl noticed a young man moving around aimlessly as though unable to keep still. "That's my boy," Mr Handy said, "got throwed in the war," by which he meant the boy was shellshocked. The farmer had recently brought him home from the Veterans Hospital in hopes that the familiar surroundings might help improve his condition. "Maybe it'll do him good if you talk to him," he said to Earl. When the farmer introduced the two, however, the boy scarcely seemed to notice, clutching the back of his neck as though from pain or numbness.

When the team was unhitched, Mr. Handy instructed his son to take the horse to the barn and feed it while the farmer himself tended to the mules. Walking along with the boy and the horse toward the barn, Earl asked how old the horse was. In a voice that was barely above a whisper the boy said, "Two year." Those were the only words Earl ever heard the boy speak. In the barn after the horse was fed and they were waiting for Mr. Handy to come up with a hay cart, Earl was startled when the boy took off his corduroy cap and put it on Earl's uncovered head. Earl retrieved his rain hat from his pack and, in turn, put it on the boy's head. "That made him laugh a little," Earl later wrote.

They quickly unloaded the hay and hurried to the house to beat an approaching rain squall. Inside they found that Mr. Handy's daughter had indeed fixed "a little somethin'." The meal included fried ham, spoon gravy (made from the fryings), stewed apples, goat's milk, and real southern cornbread, "the kind that is broken, not sliced."

Earl and Mr. Handy talked for at least an hour and Earl was invited to stay for the night "or a week for that matter." Earl firmly declined, observing that spring was steadily moving north and he was committed to going along. Mr. Handy agreed, but it still took another hour for Earl to get away.

As he resumed his hike, Earl mused to himself that for a man whose wife was in the hospital for an operation, and whose son was almost hopelessly shellshocked, Mr Handy was remarkably cheerful.

SHENANDOAH

Before Earl could get away from Rockfish Gap a Park Service patrol truck stopped and the ranger, Pete Johnson, greeted him by name. (The network was still working.) The two talked for nearly an hour and before leaving, the ranger gave Earl a fire permit. The following day when Earl reached Swift Run Gap another ranger was waiting for him and gave him a copy of the *News-Virginian* containing the article and photo. While eating breakfast in the town tavern, Earl noted with some bemusement that the article included questions that had not been asked along with answers that had not been given. (This was likely Earl's first introduction to real-world journalism.)

One of the invented questions asked how Earl found springs along the trail. The answer given in the newspaper was that he just stumbled on them. Earl's reaction was to mail a postcard to the editor informing him that actually he (Earl) used a peach stick—presumably a reference to the divining rods said to be effective in finding underground water when used in the hands of a "water witch."

Another week's walking brought Earl to Harpers Ferry, West Virginia, where he was within another week of reaching the trail's mid-point. In spite of delays caused by strawberries and time spent talking, the long cruise remained on schedule.

SOUTH MOUNTAIN

From Harpers Ferry it required only two days of hiking along South Mountain to bring Earl into his home state of Pennsylvania. South Mountain is actually an extension of the Blue Ridge although with considerably more modest dimensions. Another day brought him to the Stony Mountain Fire Tower just as a violent storm broke. Earl took shelter on the porch of the ranger cabin and waited. This was to be the meeting point with his father and this was the specified date, but no one was there. Earl was not surprised, given the violence of the storm. After about an hour the rain stopped and Earl moved on to find his father waiting at the first road crossing. "He stared as though he couldn't believe his eyes," Earl wrote. "His middle son, roaming the mountains on foot, had actually turned up, alive and well."

At that time Earl's sister Anna was working at the nearby Mont Alto Sanatorium, and she too had planned on meeting him at the same time and place as their father. The violent storm turned her back, however, so Earl and his father drove to Mont Alto to talk with her. After the brief visit with his sister, Earl and his father decided to drive home so that Earl could see some material that had arrived from the Appalachian Trail Conference, and also so that he could see the color slides that had been processed and returned. The distance from the meeting place along the Trail to Earl's York County home was about one hundred miles, so it was finally agreed that Earl would spend the night at home and be driven back to the Trail the following morning. He was at first uneasy about this arrangement, fearing that once off the Trail and at home for the night he might be reluctant to return to the Trail. That fear was misplaced, however, and the long cruise was duly resumed.

As it turned out, this was the only night on the entire trip that Earl spent away from the trailway. The following morning his brother John drove him back to the trail crossing where Earl had stopped the previous day. Their sister Anna was waiting there with a picnic lunch. The food that was left over when they finished eating Earl gladly took with him.

The next day Earl met an old friend, Woodie Baughman, at the Quarry Gap Lean-tos. The two had planned on hiking together for a few days. They shortly began encountering a peculiar feature of South Mountain: giant ant hills five or six feet across and up to two feet high. Many a hiker has been deceived by their attractive appearance and sat down on one to rest. The ants would quickly make their presence known and send the hiker uncomfortably on his way.

A few more days brought Earl to Center Point Knob, so named because originally it was calculated to be the center point of the Appalachian Trail. Since then the many relocations have shifted the actual center point one way and then another. It was here that Earl took one of the three self-portraits taken during his long walk, using a contrived tripod and delayed shutter release. The photo shows him standing in front of the rock to which the bronze plaque had been affixed. The plaque itself disappeared sometime in the 1940s. It was not until the mid 1960s that a farmer digging post holes unearthed the missing plaque

Earl at Center Point Knob, 1948

which is now displayed at the Appalachian Trail Museum in Pine Grove Furnace State Park.

Near Dillsburg, South Mountain abruptly ends at the northernmost limit of the Blue Ridge. Here the trail turns north to cross the Great Valley and head for the Alleghenies. Earl turned with it as he began the second half of the long cruise. It was exactly two months since he started in Georgia, and he remained safely on schedule.

BLUE MOUNTAIN

In 1948 the dozen or so miles of trail required to cross the Cumberland Valley mostly followed secondary roads that remained at that time picturesquely rural. At the center of the valley Earl's otherwise pleasant walk was punctuated by the life-threatening crossing of the heavily traveled U.S. Route 11. Today the trail has been largely relocated onto land acquired by the U.S. Park Service, and the dangerous Route 11 crossing has been eliminated by the construction of a footbridge that carries the trail above the racing traffic.

As a result of the Pennsylvania Railroad's refusal to allow hikers to cross the Susquehanna River on the railroad's Rockville Bridge, a sign directed hikers to go downstream to Harrisburg and cross the river on the Market Street Bridge. Earl wanted to visit the city anyway and took advantage of this opportunity to find a cobbler shop where he could get his boots repaired and another store where he could replace some worn-out clothing. The cobbler added an extra layer of sole before attaching half soles to the bottom. With these repairs his Birdshooter boots took him the rest of the way to Katahdin.

Standing in Swatara Gap with a storm approaching, Earl faced a dilemma. He was running short of supplies and had planned on going in to Lickdale to replenish his stock. If he did so, however, he was likely to get soaked. But if he chose to hurry on in search of shelter he would be left with very little to eat. In the midst of his pondering, he noticed an old man on the porch of a nearby house waving for him to come over. Earl hastened to the shelter of the porch just as the storm broke. The old man, it turned out was Pennsylvania Dutch and had very limited English, although he could understand the latter language well enough. Earl, on the other hand, could understand the old man's Dutch but could not himself speak it. The two of them waited out the storm while engaging in a most unusual conversation. The old man spoke Dutch and Earl spoke English. But they did manage to communicate.

When the rain stopped, Earl left his pack on the porch and started for Lickdale to acquire fresh provisions. He quickly got a ride with a man in a Model A Ford. As it happened, when Earl had finished his shopping and was starting back, the same Model A Ford was also heading back, so Earl got a ride in both directions. After reclaiming his pack, Earl set off again, leaving his elderly new friend with the customary Dutch farewell, "*Leb wohl.*"

At the Matz Valley Lean-to Earl encountered the first of a series of trail registers erected by "Sam and Flo" who turned out to be individual members of the Appalachian Trail Conference. Months later he received a letter from them informing him that they had been hiking in the Nanta-halas at the time that he was passing through their trail register area in Pennsylvania. One of the fire wardens down south had told them about Earl, but they were never able to meet him.

At another of the Sam-and-Flo registers Earl read an earlier entry bemoaning Pennsylvania's legendary rocks: "What are these, the Appalachians or the Rockies? My feet feel like hamburger." A more upbeat entry by a hiker from Easton quoted some lines of verse by the American poet Henry Herbert Knibbs:

> Sun and wind and the sound of rain!
> Hunger and thirst and strife!
> God! To be out on the trails again
> with a grip on the mane of life!

At the Delaware Water Gap Earl encountered an old man strolling up the Trail. The man was dressed in a dark suit and white shirt, "straight as a ramrod, and swinging a beautiful blackthorn cane." He said that he had been coming to the Delaware Water Gap for more than fifty years, and still considered it his favorite resort. He and Earl conversed for a while, the old man talking about his travels in Europe and the Americas, and Earl about his wartime adventures in the south Pacific.

As they headed down the Trail together, the man quoted the biblical adage: "Young men shall see visions; old men shall dream dreams." After a pause he added, "I come here to dream." When they came to the side path leading to the old man's hotel, he left with the traditional Spanish farewell, "*Vaya con dios.*" A few days earlier Earl's parting from one old man had taken the form of a Dutch farewell, and now from another old man had come a Spanish farewell.

KITTATINNY RIDGE

From Wind Gap in Pennsylvania the northbound hiker climbs to the crest of the Kittatinny Ridge which will take him to the Delaware Water Gap before he crosses the Delaware River and climbs again to the top of the New Jersey continuation of the same ridge.

Earl's camp his first night in New Jersey was made in haste as both darkness and rain began to fall together. He called it "one of those impromptu arrangements that turn out right." In hurrying to make a shelter before the ground got wet, he found a nearby pole and slanted it into the fork of a tree. Over it he threw his poncho, then found two more poles which were leaned in the fork against the first one. After tying the three poles together he had a true half teepee, and realized that the tree would not have been necessary since the three poles in effect formed a tripod. His rain hat was placed over the center opening and he was snug for the night. Such an arrangement became his standard shelter for the rest of the hike whenever no other shelter was available.

The following morning he came to Sunfish Pond, the first natural lake he had encountered thus far in his trek. They would become more and more common as he moved north.

In New Jersey the law forbade open fires and Earl obeyed the law, meaning that no matter how cold it got at night or how hungry he was he could not make a fire. When he stopped for supplies in the Garden State he tried to find items that required no cooking. Nonetheless, he was often hungry. "Sure am glad to be out of New Jersey," he wrote. "That no-fire law has me on the verge of starvation and pneumonia."

NEW YORK

Earl's problems in New York were of a different nature from those in New Jersey. Fingerboard Mountain Lean-to is made of stone with a tin roof and a fireplace in each end wall. The water supply being far downhill, he brought back an extra container of water which he placed on a ledge in the shelter so that it would be readily available in the morning. After his evening meal, he hung his pack overhead to discourage mice, and with a bright moon shining, settled down for a good night's sleep. Sometime later the sound of the kettle being rattled woke him and he raised his head to see a ringed tail scurrying around the corner. This scenario was repeated again later except the second time the raccoon didn't bother running away and just sat blinking when Earl shined a light. Even further emboldened, the raccoon in its explorations discovered a package of spaghetti that someone had left in the shelter. Taking the box in his forepaws he hopped outside where, sitting in the moonlight, the beast noisily ripped the package open and began devouring the contents. After a spell of eating, the raccoon apparently got thirsty, so he went back inside the shelter to get a drink from the extra pail Earl had put there. The creature then returned to the business of consuming the remaining pasta. Earl writes, "My only regret was lack of flash equipment for the camera."

The trail crossed the Hudson River on the Bear Mountain Bridge. Although this bridge marked the lowest elevation on the Appalachian Trail, being only a little above sea level at this point, it also featured the highest pedestrian toll—actually the only toll: five cents. This onerous levy has since been abolished and trail hikers can now cross the Hudson without charge.

At one point the Trail turned between some rundown old buildings beyond which the footway became well worn, and where Earl noticed a wire that had been placed on poles beside the trail. Here he perceived a little old man with a long pole coming toward him. The man's head was inclined in the direction of a robin that was singing off in the mist; his face bore a rapt expression. Earl spoke to the man who, at first, did not seem to have heard, but then after a pause spoke "with a gentle smile and downcast eyes." It was only then that Earl realized the man was blind and someone had set up the wire so that the man with the aid of his pole could enjoy a walk in the woods.

A MOMENTOUS DUTY

At the village of Holmes, New York, one afternoon Earl interrupted his hike to "perform a momentous duty." So far on the long cruise he had sent no communication to the Appalachian Trail Conference, but the time had now come. Within a few days, he knew, the Conference was scheduled to hold a meeting at Fontana Dam in North Carolina. This would be an appropriate time, Earl believed, to send a greeting and make the Conference aware of his hike and his progress thus far. He folded a sheet of paper and on the outside sketched a likeness of Pinnacles of the Dan. Beneath the sketch he wrote the following lines:

> The flowers bloom, the songbirds sing
> And though it sun or rain
> I walk the mountain tops with Spring
> From Georgia north to Maine.

Inside the folded paper Earl put the date he left Mt. Oglethorpe and the date he expected to arrive at Katahdin. The message was duly deposited in the mail at the Holmes post office. Months later he learned that the message was indeed received by Conference officials, although what later became of it is not known.

SOUTHERN NEW ENGLAND

The natural features along the approximately 140 miles of Appalachian Trail that pass through Connecticut and Massachusetts are not without beauty. Unfortunately, however, the persistent rainy weather that marred the eight days Earl spent in these two states reduced—and sometimes totally eliminated—his ability to appreciate them. "Sage's Ravine is said to be beautiful," he writes "but I didn't notice."

Despite the more modest dimensions of its mountains and the more populated nature of its countryside, it was in Connecticut that Earl saw the only bald eagle that he could positively identify as such during his entire trek. As he was hiking along the Housatonic River, he entered a clearing from which he saw a large specimen of this magnificent raptor species perched on a rock in the river. As soon as the bird spotted Earl it took wing and soared away above the trees.

At his first stop for supplies in Connecticut Earl began encountering typical New England food, and on this first exposure he even bought some Boston brown bread.

It was near Salisbury, Connecticut, that as a result of the seemingly endless rain, Earl's morale reached its lowest ebb on the entire hike. He continued on, however, and came to a barbed wire fence with no visible indication of where to go. In desperation he started crawling under the fence in the hope of getting information at a nearby house on the other side. He was already halfway under the fence when a voice from the house announced that there was a gate to his right. At this point Earl decided it was the easier course to continue his tunneling. The man invited Earl inside in spite of his soggy condition, and coffee and cookies were quickly provided. It turned out that the man had served in the South Pacific with the Marines during the war and had spent time on some of the same islands as Earl. They had a pleasant conversation while Earl dried off.

At another house—this time in Massachusetts—where he stopped for directions, the door was opened by "a husky young man wearing Marine fatigues." When Earl asked about the Appalachian Trail he first had to do some explaining about what it was, whereupon the man said that now he knew the reason for the white marks he had noticed on posts and trees. He then advised Earl that the trail followed Bow Wow Road and indicated a sign at a nearby intersection. The unusual road name, the man explained, was originally Pow Wow Road because it was along this road that Indians used to hold councils. Later residents considered "Pow Wow" a silly name so they changed it to "Bow Wow" which apparently they believed to be less silly.

VERMONT

At Bromley Mountain near the Snow Valley Ski Center Earl came upon two young men who were loading their gear and provisions into the trunk of a car. The two had been working on a new road then under construction, but upon finding themselves incapable of digging a straight post hole they had decided to quit before they were fired. While working on the road construction crew the young men had been staying at Bromley Lodge from which they were in the process of removing all of their belongings. They had one more trip to make to get everything transferred to the car so Earl walked along with them. Once arrived at the lodge, however, they decided to "celebrate" by fixing one more meal for themselves and Earl before they left.

Watching those two college boys start a fire, Earl writes, "was a sight to behold," provided, he added, the observer was at a safe distance. First they poured some gasoline from a bottle into a dish which they emptied into the chunk stove. Then, standing back, they struck a match and threw it in the stove. The result, Earl says, "was a ball of fire, a roar, and a dancing stove." Following a brief interval during which he was struck speechless, Earl tactfully suggested to them that they would not start many fires that way.

After preparing a meal that "would have fed a small Army," they followed up by producing an impressive array of clean-up materials. Earl concludes his description of this celebratory occasion by commenting, "No wonder they needed two trips to carry out their gear."

One evening as Earl was walking a section of Trail beside a brook where high water had washed out a portion of the footway, he startled a large mink and her kits, all of whom scurried away—except for one kit. This reckless infant remained in the center of the Trail twitching its nose and watching Earl suspiciously with tiny beadlike eyes. The mother who had taken refuge behind some driftwood made anxious clucking noises apparently in an effort to get the kit to join her. He remained on the Trail, however. Although the light was poor Earl tried to get a picture of the recalcitrant tiny mink. When the shutter clicked the sound apparently set off some alarm in the creature's head. He immediately ducked his head as though avoiding a shot, opened his mouth and began making vociferous squealing sounds. At this point the mother raced over to check on her little one before returning to her shelter where she resumed the clucking sounds. After a few moments the mother emerged again but this time she headed straight for Earl who caught her with the toe of his boot and flipped her over. As far as she was concerned, that was the last straw. She turned her back, lifted her tail and sprayed, not unlike how a skunk would do. She then gathered together her family, including the squealer, and left. The odor of a mink's spray is not as powerful as that of a skunk, but it is bad enough. Earl wrote, "My clothes smelled minky for several days."

THE MISSING LINK

In September of 1938 a hurricane more powerful than any previously recorded in New England raced through the region at unprecedented speeds of up to 60 miles per hour. The damage was extensive over a vast area. Ten years later as Earl struggled to find his way, the signs of the mammoth storm were still plainly visible, especially in Vermont. Exceptionally hard-hit was the stretch of Trail between the Long Trail and New Hampshire, which for much of its length had all but vanished, and was being referred to within the hiking community as "the missing link."

Knowing that the Trail turned east at Sherburne Pass, Earl searched but could find no blazes or any other indication of where to go. He finally decided to follow a road that led to Gifford Woods State Park through which he knew the Trail passed, whether marked or not. Beyond the park an occasional faded blaze would be seen which took him to the village of Sherburne with a steady heavy rain falling. After passing through the village, and turning down a farmer's invitation to spend the night, he came to a faint blaze that indicated the Trail turning up a ravine. Here Earl found himself struggling through a tangle of blowdowns and dense scrub growth. The rain continued and darkness was falling, so he was forced to set up a makeshift camp at a flat spot beside an ancient stump. Of that dreary night Earl wrote, "I heard for the second time in my life the awesome sound of a giant tree falling somewhere in the stillness." He decided that his declining the farmer's invitation had been well rewarded.

NEW HAMPSHIRE

After crossing the Connecticut River and passing through the town of Hanover, home of Dartmouth College and its Dartmouth Outing Club who maintain much of the Appalachian Trail in this area, Earl headed toward New Hampshire's storied and forbidding White Mountains. It was near the summit of Mount Moosilauke that he found himself for the first time above true timberline. This experience came at the end of a five-mile climb that required three hours. As the Trail climbed higher and higher the trees grew smaller and smaller until the few that still remained were no more than shrub size.

Near the edge of the timberline he came upon a shelter that was bolted with a cable to the rocks because of the violent winds the structure had to withstand. Earl found it an eerie world of silence since even strong winds make little noise when there are no trees to impede their progress. His first time above timberline, he writes, "gave me a strange feeling, as though it were possible to fall off the earth."

For the hiker heading north, Greenleaf Hut is the second in the chain of eight such huts to be encountered. The huts are maintained and staffed by the Appalachian Mountain Club during the hiking season to provide meals and overnight accommodation for hikers on the Appalachian Trail in the White Mountains. All supplies for the huts were brought in either by donkey pack train or backpacked in by the hut crew members themselves.

As Earl approached the Greenleaf Hut he was waving a spruce bough over his head to ward off the black flies which were unusually bad. This peculiar maneuver caught the attention of two college-age brothers who were pitching horseshoes near the hut. Earl hastily assured the boys that he was not demented, just allergic to flies. He then stopped to talk briefly with the brothers and a couple from Ohio staying at the hut, as well as the three on-duty crew members. When asked if he would be staying the night, Earl replied that he planned on continuing for a couple of miles before stopping. The others looked at the ominously threatening sky closing in about the top of Mt. Lafayette and assured Earl that his plans for the night were not a good idea.

At this point Earl confessed that the real problem was that he had only one dollar in his pocket, which was not enough to cover the $5.00 fee being charged at that time for a night's lodging and meals. (Today the fee approaches $100 per night.) Although the man from Ohio offered to cover Earl's cost, the three crewmen conferred and came up with a better idea. Eventually they produced a document which was worded as follows:

> Attention, All Huts:
> This man has already walked 1,700 miles of the Appalachian Trail and is about to do the last 300 of it. We at Greenleaf, in view of his tremendous accomplishment, feel that Joe would be only too willing to deadhead him through any of the Huts in the system. We know that you will all follow suit in aiding him to reach the end of his trail.

The document was then signed by all three crew members and presented to Earl, who offered to forward payment later. His offer was firmly rejected. In a final gesture of generosity, even though the regular meal time was well past, the crew set about preparing a special supper for Earl.

Rain arrived during the night and continued into early morning. When the weather finally improved the other guests left first and then Earl continued on his way, with the three crew members lined up watching him leave until he was no longer within sight.

MAINE

The Maine–New Hampshire state line was crossed on July 20 at about 2:15 in the afternoon. The Long Cruise was approaching its end and still on schedule, averaging better than seventeen miles per day.

Earl's first experience with Maine's daunting challenges came in Mahoosuc Notch where as he struggled through, he encountered in the crannies, even in July, ice that had turned yellow with age. He had passed up Full Goose Shelter because Speck Pond Shelter was "only" five miles farther on. Five miles in Maine, he learned, tends to be a good bit farther than five miles in most other places. Before he reached Speck Pond, darkness was descending and a storm was unmistakably approaching. He had just about decided that he would have to make the

Ice at Mahoosuc Notch

best of a rainy night in the open when he heard an unexpected (and cheering) sound: the piping of tree frogs. These water-loving creatures could only be at Speck Pond, so Earl followed the sound as he made his way, cautious step by step, in the darkness. In due course, he reached the shore of the pond and followed it around to the shelter.

Of this experience Earl wrote: "Ever since, when the homeland meadows are turning green and the silvery lilt of those tiny peepers livens the night, I think of the time when they helped me 'come to port' on the Long Cruise."

After replenishing his supplies in Rangeley, Earl found increasingly bad Trail conditions, the result of the fierce hurricane ten years before. At Orbeton Stream he was confronted by a sign informing him that the Trail was closed from Orbeton to Bigelow because of bad conditions. "Travel at your own risk," he was cautioned. For the next twenty-five miles the only Trail markings he found were the original axe blazes. He fell several times but managed to come through with no serious physical harm.

———————

Earl's crossing of the treacherous Kennebec River was considerably less dramatic than that experienced by many other Appalachian Trail hikers. As he was hiking along the tote-road that the Trail followed from

Pierce Pond Camps to the Kennebec, a man in a buckboard came along and offered advice about getting across the notorious river. Earl was unable to get the ancient phone at the crossing to work, so he put himself across using the boat and pole he found resting along the shore. The process went reasonably well except that when he got to the other side he found himself several hundred feet downstream from where he started. After dragging the boat and pole back to the designated landing place, he was still faced with the problem of getting them back to the other side.

While pondering this problem Earl heard what turned out to be target shooting nearby. A little exploring discovered a Maine guide and the District Fire Warden engaged in this activity. Earl's problem was explained and the two men promptly offered to put the boat back where it belonged. The warden took the boat across while the guide followed in a canoe to bring them both back again.

The guide then walked along with Earl as far as Caratunk where, upon following him into the local restaurant and general store, he announced in a loud voice, "This guy has walked all the way from Georgia." The few diners there scarcely interrupted their eating. The proprietor was a stereotypical New Englander who spoke little. In this case, however, there seemed a sharper twinkle in the owner's eyes. When Earl had purchased the supplies he needed and was about to leave, the proprietor suddenly became talkative, delaying Earl's efforts to be on his way. Suddenly a younger man hurried in the door, bringing a smile to the face of the owner, who cautioned Earl, "Be careful what you say now, he's from the paper." Needless to say, Earl's departure was still further delayed. The resulting article appeared in the *Bangor News* and was picked up by regional radio stations.

SUDDENLY I SAW KATAHDIN . . .

At Monson, the last town along the Trail before Katahdin, still more than one hundred miles away, Earl loaded up with supplies that raised his pack weight to sixty pounds. Then he trudged on.

At White Cap Mountain he climbed the fire tower, where he found on duty a warden who was startled at receiving a visitor atop this rugged, isolated peak. Earl turned to survey the expansive view and, as he later wrote, "Suddenly I saw Katahdin, the goal of my walk with spring." Although the mountain was still about seventy trail miles away, it already dominated the surrounding scene.

A little farther on, with evening approaching, the lone hiker came to a lumber camp that had set up shop astraddle the very trail. Here he accosted a man sitting on a bench and asked which way the trail went. The man, apparently believing that Earl was in the grip of a great hunger, declined to answer his question until he went to the nearby cook shack where the cook, Old Johnny Boyle, Earl was assured, would see that he didn't go hungry. Johnny turned out to be a non-stop talker who kept up a steady stream of chatter while he assembled for the famished hiker a meal consisting of a platter of roast turkey, a big bowl of pea soup, blueberry pie, and a gallon pot of tea—all the while apologizing for not having "better grub" on hand. When Earl could eat no more, even declining another piece of pie, Johnny insisted that he spend the night in the bunkhouse and join the crew for breakfast before setting out the next morning.

Breakfast was every bit as abundant as the previous evening's dinner and included baked beans. Earl declined the latter dish, explaining that at one time during the war in the South Pacific he had eaten almost nothing but beans during one three-week stretch, an experience that had left him allergic to that vegetable. Big Johnny took offense at this comment and insisted, in his booming voice, "Ain't no one gets sick from eatin' my beans. You take a plateful." Obediently Earl did as he was ordered and suffered no ill effects. Later Earl wrote in *Walking With Spring* that Old Johnny afterward told him the secret for "taking the poison out" of beans. Unfortunately this valuable secret is not passed along to the reader.

When Earl set off following all this elaborate feasting, he noticed a sign that pointed the way to the trail. It had been obscured the evening before by the body of the man sitting on the bench. The Long Cruise continued.

As the mileage countdown approached the sixty-mile mark, Earl had a confrontation with a cow moose and calf. The first sign he saw was fresh moose tracks, muddy water still in them. Earl took his camera in hand and eased around the next bend where he was greeted with a sudden thrashing in the brush and a series of explosive snorts which he took to be a warning signal. Then a large cow moose—"surely one of the homeliest critters on earth"—stepped into the trail and turned to look at Earl. He quickly snapped a picture and began looking for a tree to climb. The moose, however, decided to trot away with a second, smaller moose that appeared to be a yearling calf. The gait of the departing moose was described by Earl as being like that of a bowlegged horse, "if there is such a thing."

At Nahmakanta Lake, with forty miles to go, he could not resist the temptation to stop at a sandy beach for a cleansing swim. He had barely gotten wet when he was routed out of the lake by a low-flying seaplane. With still a couple of hours of daylight left, Earl came to Nahmakanta Camps where he spent so much time in conversation that he wound up spending the night there instead of pushing on, as he had originally planned, to Rainbow Lake Lean-to which would have left him an easy day's walk to Katahdin.

The next morning he could have pushed himself and finished up in one more day, but he found himself almost dreading the time when it would all come to an end. He lingered.

As he approached Katahdin Stream Campsite, he wondered a bit apprehensively what the recent newspaper and radio publicity might produce there. Although the campground was crowded with campers, Earl was too inconspicuous to attract anyone's attention. Earl Shaffer stood a modest five feet, seven inches tall, less than the American male average for that era; his usual hiking outfit was a dull gray; and he carried his belongings in a surplus Mountain Troop rucksack. This was far from the popular conception of the long-distance backpacker as a Paul Bunyonesque giant standing at least six and a half feet tall and wearing a bright red checked shirt. To the many campers all around he was all but invisible as he made his way toward the Hunt Spur Leanto where he planned on stopping for the night.

He was just about to cross the campground boundary when he heard a booming voice call out, "Earl!" It was Bill Biddle of Philadelphia, a man he had previously met on the trail, and probably the only person in the campground who had ever seen him before. One of the campers had asked Bill if the inconspicuous man easing along over there could be the hiker. As it turned out, Bill explained, the Hunt Spur Leanto had burned just a few days previously, and Earl might as well spend the night at a leanto in the campground where Bill himself had settled in.

Then Fred Pitman, the head ranger, appeared and asked if Earl was "the man walkin' the Trail." Ranger Pittman informed Earl that he had promised to call "the lady reporter in Millinocket" as soon as Earl arrived, regardless of the time of day or night. The phone call was made and about 11:00 that night Mrs. Dean Chase accompanied by a photographer appeared and Earl was interviewed and photographed for the Associated Press. Earl insisted that she not release the story until he returned the next day and could confirm that the trek had, in fact, been completed. Mrs Chase agreed and, in her turn, required that Earl not speak to another representative of the media before she got her story in.

Biddle brothers

THE SADNESS OF A GREAT ADVENTURE'S ENDING

The next day, the fifth of August, dawned with a clear sky and near ideal weather. Someone suggested that Earl could leave his pack behind since he would be returning before the end of the day. This proposal was firmly rejected; the battered old pack had accompanied him every step of the way so far and would not miss out on the last five miles.

The lone hiker climbed the Hunt Spur approach to Katahdin, reaching the summit about 1:30 in the afternoon, 124 days after leaving Oglethorpe. He stood alone before one last weatherbeaten sign "on a post held up by a heap of gathered stones." Using his camera's shutter delay feature, he took the now iconic picture of himself standing beside the sign atop Katahdin. His mixed feelings included the sadness that inevitably accompanies the ending of a great adventure. And the more successful the adventure, the greater the sadness.

CHAPTER 20

AFTERMATH

A BEAUTIFUL PILE OF ROCKS

The climb from Katahdin Stream Campsite to the top of the mountain, and the return descent take the best part of a day, so it was approaching evening when Earl finally got back to the camp ground. He promptly checked in with Fred Pittman, the head ranger, to let him know that the Long Cruise had ended as planned. Although Earl estimated him to be in his seventies, Pittman was a very tall man who, at six-foot-six, must have towered over Earl.

While the two were talking there came a knock on the door of the ranger cabin. When Pittman answered, he was faced by a man who asked, "Can you tell me where I can find this guy that just finished hiking the trail?"

"He's right here," Pittman replied, "come on in." The visitor introduced himself as Emlen Cresson from the Philadelphia area, who happened to be vacationing in the shadow of Katahdin.

Turning to Earl, Cresson said, "I'm this man you met at Madison Hut." Earl had forgotten the meeting until hearing Cresson's reminder.

Emlen Cresson was a prominent lawyer from the Philadelphia suburb of West Chester where, Earl later learned, he lived in a mansion. This level of affluence was never apparent from meeting and talking to the man. Earl was favorably impressed.

Cresson announced that he and Ward Hinkson were planning on climbing Katahdin the next day and wondered if Earl would like to join them for another visit. The lure of the mighty mountain was powerful, and Earl would have loved to go back to its top. Unfortunately, he had already promised Mrs. Chase, the local reporter who had fed the story of Earl's hike to the Associated Press, that he would go to Millinocket the next day to meet with the town's Chamber of Commerce.

After spending another night with Bill Biddle in a camp shelter, Earl hitchhiked the next morning to Millinocket where he met with the Chamber of Commerce. Following the meeting he set off to hitchhike back to the camp ground. This time, however, he had little luck in his efforts to get a ride on what was at that time a dirt tote road. He had just about resigned himself to spending the rest of the day just getting back to the camp when he was picked up by a couple of men described by Earl as "kooky." Not long after picking Earl up, they came to an area where road improvement work was under way and highway equipment was standing idle. No one was in the area when they got there so the two "silly, stupid son-of-a-guns stop the car and they're trying to start the bulldozer." At that point a state official appeared on the scene and the three of them nearly ended up in jail. After concluding that his benefactors were half drunk, Earl got away from them as quickly as he could and set off once again on foot.

As he was trudging along toward the camp, Earl heard the roar of a motor behind him. When he turned to look, a pickup truck came speeding around the bend. Upon catching sight of Earl, the truck's driver slammed on the brakes, sending dirt and stones flying. The driver who jumped out was of a height pretty much the opposite of Fred Pittman's. (Earl estimated him to be no more than five-five.) He introduced himself as Junior York from Daicey Pond.

York's Camps on Daicey Pond were about two and a half miles south of Katahdin Stream Campsite. Beyond the pond the view was dominated by the massive hulk of Katahdin—described by Junior York as a beautiful pile of rocks. Earl had passed the camps on his approach to the mountain but declined to stop, wanting to get a little closer to his destination before stopping for the night. Junior told Earl that Cresson and Hinkson were stopping at York's Camps, not having climbed Katahdin after all because the mountain was completely covered by clouds, and was not even visible from below. They were planning instead to do the climb the following day, and once again invited Earl to accompany them. As a further inducement (if one were really needed) Junior offered Earl free lodging for the night. Earl unsurprisingly accepted.

The following day dawned clear and beautiful. Junior York took the other two to Chimney Pond from where they took the Knife Edge approach to the crest, along the way picking up Bob Stockbridge and Bill Tarbert of the Mountain Club of Maryland. This group of five made their way to the top of the mountain, but only one of them had been there only two days before.

Bill Biddle headed for his home in Philadelphia the next morning, taking Earl along with him. After visiting his brother Dan, who was living at that time in Philadelphia, Earl caught a bus for York, and the end of his life's second great adventure.

DUE DILIGENCE

On August 6, 1948 an item appeared in the *New York Times* under the headline:

> Hikes Appalachian Trail.
> Man Who Left Georgia April 4
> Tops Mount Katahdin in Maine

This news broke just as the September 1948 issue of *Appalachian Trailway News*, the thrice yearly newsletter of the Appalachian Trail Conference (ATC), was about to go to press. Jean Stephenson, the newsletter editor, managed to insert a brief notice about this development. The insertion did little beyond quote from the *New York Times* article, essentially reserving any further judgment, and concluding with this brief statement: "Earl Shaffer is a Class D member of the Conference. He bought all the Guidebooks and other literature. Conference Headquarters has no other information at present as to his trip. Further developments will be reported in the next issue."

Four months later, in the January 1949 issue of the newsletter, a more extensive discussion of Earl's journey appeared in which it becomes clear that the report of his epic hike had been accepted by Conference officials as fact. In the same issue also appeared a piece by Earl himself, in which he tells of his preparations and on-the-trail improvisations that made the venture work.

So what happened during the four months between September 1948 and January 1949 to confirm Earl's veracity and convert most of the many skeptics into believers?

Shortly after Earl's return home in August 1948, he met with Jean Stephenson to discuss his recently completed hike and to convince her of the accuracy of his report. As Earl later described this interrogation, "Jean Stephenson put me on the witness stand a couple hours."

In addition to being editor of *Appalachian Trailway News* and supervisor of the Conference's publications program, Stephenson was a key figure in the ATC hierarchy. If she could be persuaded, it was very likely that Myron Avery, the ATC Chairman, would accept her judgment, with other Conference officials mostly falling into line. As it happened, Earl never did meet Myron Avery. Earl commented later, "we were both on the go and never in the same place at the same time."

Earl atop Katahdin, 1948

With a systematic prudence, Earl had made himself known to park and forestry officials all along the way and signed every Trail register he encountered. There were occasional meetings with representatives of various news media and others. Not least was the abundance of photographs that he had taken to document his passing.

Not long after meeting with Earl, Stephenson, accompanied by Madeline Fleming of the York Hiking Club, called on Earl's sister Anna who was asked a lot of questions by the two gentle but stern inquisitors. Fleming was active in the York Hiking Club and later in Keystone Trails Association. Anna herself had only recently become a member of the York Hiking Club.

The women were persuaded; Avery agreed; the others—mostly—concurred. Earl's feat became accepted dogma and he himself became an Appalachian Trail icon. Until the end of his life he believed that his historic hike, in combination with other factors, succeeded in saving the Trail from fading into oblivion after the years of wartime neglect and a number of natural disasters. Among the other factors that helped revive the Trail, he believed, were articles that appeared in the *National Geographic* magazine and the *Reader's Digest*, as well as the Fontana Dam ATC gathering that took place while Earl was hiking. That was the first such meeting since before the war.

CHAPTER 21

WALKING
WITH SPRING

Almost immediately after completing his 1948 hike, Earl began writing a narrative describing the trip. This first version of the text was a basic day-by-day description of events as they occurred. When the initial draft was completed, he sent it to Jean Stephenson who read it herself before circulating it among others at Conference headquarters. All seemed to be generally pleased and assumed that the book would be published. At this stage in the process only a few editorial changes were made, mostly to correct errors relating to statements about individuals. The people at Conference headquarters went over it page by page and identified a number of typing errors; these too were duly corrected.

When Earl's efforts to find a publisher continued to be unsuccessful, he proposed to the Conference that if they would help find a publisher, he would assign to the Conference one half of all the royalties earned by the publication. To this offer he never received a reply.

Finally, in a kind of desperation, he "tore it apart and did it all over again." In his efforts to reconstruct the manuscript, Earl made it shorter and clarified passages that he decided were not as clear as they should be. When this was finished he returned to his efforts to round up a publisher; efforts that continued to be fruitless.

One prospective New York City publisher not only wanted Earl to subsidize the publication costs, they also wanted him to cover the expense of hiring a ghost writer who would write "romance" into the story. This served to anger Earl who noted that he could write romance into the book himself if he wanted it there. In total, this publisher wanted about $3,000 dollars, which, Earl dryly observed, "I didn't have."

Most of the publishers from whom he received replies seemed skeptical that the book would sell enough to be profitable. Among the publishers to whom he submitted *Walking With Spring* was Stackpole Press of Harrisburg. They declined to publish the book because they said it did not fit in any of their usual categories. Following the Fiftieth Anniversary Hike in 1998, however, Stackpole approached Earl with a request that he write a book for them to publish. By that time, however, he had entered into an

Cover of first (1981) edition of Walking With Spring

arrangement with Westcliffe Publishers to write the book that later appeared under the title *The Appalachian Trail: Calling Me Back to the Hills.*

It appears also that some indeterminate number of publisher responses were lost in the mail, either because Earl did not provide an adequate address or because there were at that time a number of other individuals in the general area who also bore the name "Earl Shaffer" or something similar. Earl learned later, after the fact, that National Geographic Magazine had tried to reach him for six months to discuss a possible article with pictures. By that time the public interest was waning and nothing came of it. This all left Earl with a sense of bitterness toward the Post Office, which may or may not have been wholly justified.

In 1981 the seemingly endless process of tinkering with the text came to an end. Having resigned himself to the hopelessness of continuing the search for a commercial publisher, Earl had five hundred unbound copies printed at his own expense. Of these, he himself bound one hundred copies and gave them out to trail people wherever he encountered them. One recipient of such a copy was Thurston Griggs, a member of the Mountain Club of Maryland and a longtime activist in trail activities with the Appalachian Trail Conference as well as with Pennsylvania's Keystone Trails Association. At the time Griggs was given a copy of the privately printed copy of *Walking With Spring,* he was a member of the Conference's Board of Managers. Earl credits Griggs with being the driving force that eventually caused the Conference itself to publish Earl's book. Griggs argued that *Walking With Spring* was an essential document recording the history of the Appalachian Trail in its earlier days.

Near the end of his life, when speaking of Thurston Griggs, Earl observed, "He's retired now; he's very old, older than I—which is pretty old." Griggs subsequently died in October 2011 at the age of ninety-five.

The earliest version of *Walking With Spring* included a brief poetic epigraph at the beginning of each chapter. Later, when he completely revised the work, he eliminated these flourishes, having been persuaded that poetry was no longer popular with the general reading public. Still later, when ATC was preparing the work for publication, the editor at that time, Florence Nichol, decided that the poetry should be restored. Subsequently, people often told Earl that the poetry was one of their favorite parts of the book.

Throughout his life, Earl said he re-read *Walking With Spring* about once a year, usually in the winter "just for the heck of it."

He firmly believed that if he had orchestrated the process better, his first book would have been a commercial success that made enough money to change his later life significantly. As it was, when the Appalachian Trail Conference finally published the book, Earl stipulated that all income from sales would go to ATC. As a consequence, Earl's only personal income from *Walking With Spring* was secured when he purchased books at the author's discount and resold them himself. This happened mostly following the Fiftieth Anniversary Hike, when he attended various gatherings and took a supply of books to sell. Several hundred were sold in this manner. The Conference itself saw its sales of *Walking With Spring* increase manyfold in the years following that landmark hike.

CHAPTER 22

CASCADE CREST TRAIL

aris Walters was a man Earl first met at an auction house where
Earl was working as a tally clerk. Paris brought consignments of
antique furniture, usually about a truckload a week. The two
struck up an acquaintanceship, and as time passed their conversations
lasted longer and longer. Paris seems to have been a glib storyteller whose
accounts of his early years tended to vary from one telling to the next.

He was born somewhere around the turn of the twentieth century,
give or take a few years either way. In one version, he was born a hillbilly
in the mountains of North Carolina and at the age of fourteen ran away
from home with a traveling show that had come to town. He stayed with
the show for some time, eventually becoming the pianist who provided
background music, his specialty being jazz. Later he said he traveled
with big bands as his piano playing steadily improved. When he joined
the Army at the start of World War II, he abandoned music almost
entirely; it was only rarely and reluctantly that he could later be persuaded to play the piano. Earl said that he only heard Paris play on two
occasions; both times the playing was superb. Paris's musical skills seem
to have been confirmed by Earl's having actually heard him play.

In another variation of his life story, Paris was born in the Arizona
cattle country to a mother from Pennsylvania and a father from the
southwest, providing him with relatives scattered across the country. At
the age of twelve he got his first job with a photographic shop in a town
six miles from his home. For the handsome sum of three dollars a week
he picked up photographic film for processing and later delivered the

finished prints. He made the daily twelve-mile round-trip commute from home on a bicycle. Before long he had learned how to do the developing and printing.

Paris had worked with horses at home, so when a neighbor jokingly offered him a horse if he could break it, he readily accepted the challenge, and soon was able to make his daily commute on horseback rather than on a bicycle.

He was not yet twenty when he had achieved the status of a fully qualified photographer. Then World War I came along and further progress in this occupation was delayed by military service. After the war—the story continues—he was hired by the *Saturday Evening Post* as a roving photographer, with the freedom to choose for himself where he would work. He decided on the western U.S. and its backcountry. This led to Paris's reports of a fanciful series of adventures.

Benefitting from his earlier experience with animals, he traveled by pack train around Canada, the U.S., and Central America. He photographed the Prince of Wales rather clumsily shooting a buffalo during a royal visit to Canada. The beast was butchered on the spot by some Indian women. In the Cascades he reported seeing the tracks of Bigfoot, but not clear enough to justify a story. He photographed pueblos, cliff dwellings, pyramids, and other Aztec ruins. After about three years of roaming on this job, he turned to other things.

For a time he worked on a wildcat oil rig in the desert, where once they struck hot salt water instead of oil. In the heat the salt rapidly crystallized, covering the landscape to a depth of six inches with what looked like a weird snow scene beneath the blazing sun. While working with the oil outfit, Paris traveled once to the canyon near which Boulder Dam was in the early stages of construction. After boring deep below the surface without success, the crew shifted their operation to Black Rock Canyon where the results proved better. He decided to quit this job when the truck caravan that took the men back to their lodgings at the end of the day was halted by a great split in the earth that had appeared. This crack was so deep that they were unable to see the bottom. Paris feared the crevice might trigger an avalanche, causing the canyon wall to collapse on top of their work site.

Eventually he came to Pennsylvania where there were relatives on his mother's side, and he took up carpentering, along with dealing in cattle and horses. One day when he was negotiating with a hog farmer, he happened to notice a bureau in one of the pens. The drawers, except for one that was missing, were being used as feeding troughs for the hogs. He

Paris Walters on the Cascade Crest Trail

went over to examine the piece of furniture more closely, and quickly identified it as a Chippendale. Although it had been badly abused over the years, Paris judged that it was still reparable. When he offered to buy it, the farmer—who referred to it as "that old thing"—told him that if he wanted it he could have it. Paris finally persuaded the reluctant farmer to take five dollars for the piece. Back home, he scrubbed it clean, had a replacement drawer made, and sold it for $90. The antique dealer who bought the bureau, refinished and eventually resold it for $350.

The foregoing account is based on Earl's notes, which at times suggest skepticism on Earl's part. In general, however, Earl's reporting comes across as a neutral narrative. This writer offers no judgment.

When Earl first knew him, Paris was about sixty and not in the best physical condition, although he claimed to have hiked much of the Appalachian Trail over a period of years. He also said that he served for three years in Alaska during his World War II military service. Nevertheless, in 1963, with these slim credentials he convinced Earl that the two of them should go out west and hike the five hundred miles of the Cascade Crest Trail, which constitutes the Washington State portion of the Pacific Crest Trail.

In the advice that Earl had been giving to aspiring A.T. hikers, he regularly told them not to undertake a long hike with a partner before testing the partner on a relatively short hike to insure compatibility. To his later regret, he chose to ignore his own advice in this case. Although something of a character, Paris seemed qualified for the proposed undertaking, in spite of being somewhat out of shape.

They knew that the Washington State trail officials did not normally sanction hiking in the Cascades before July because of snow danger. Paris wrote, however, citing their extensive experience and requesting approval to start their hike two weeks earlier than would ordinarily be allowed. The Washington authorities were not only convinced to grant the request, but even went so far as to suggest that two such experienced hikers could provide the patrols that would later be on the scene with information about any trail damage the two easterners might come across.

At this stage of their planning even Earl did not know that Paris had no first-hand experience at all with wilderness camping. By the time of their departure Paris claimed to have acquired all the suitable clothing that would be needed; a tent that had been custom made by a company in New York City; and a telescoping fishing rod. None of this was actually shown to Earl, however.

The two traveled west by Greyhound Bus and the trip took five days going by way of Salt Lake City. Paris had stuck the fishing rod in the side of his pack where it was found to have a tendency to catch on everything, especially bus doors. The travelers got very little sleep and arrived in Portland at mid-afternoon.

They found a room for the night; whereupon Paris suddenly realized that he would need a Washington State fishing license, so he caught a cab and headed to the other side of the Columbia River. In addition to the fishing license, he also bought a reel, some other fishing paraphernalia, and a supply of salmon eggs. Upon his return to Portland, he informed Earl that they would live on fish and berries during their hike. Long afterward, Earl commented, "I should have known."

The following day they took another taxi across the river to the starting point of the Cascade Crest Trail. At the time there was a brilliant rainbow hanging over the river. They took it for a sign of a good hike—a false harbinger as things turned out.

When asked later if the Columbia Crest was similar to the Appalachian Trail, Earl responded:

> It's completely different. There are no steep grades and it's completely graded for horse travel. So you have no rock climbing, no boulders in the way or anything. It's longer but it's far easier than the Appalachian, except for the possibility of snow and bad weather. They used dynamite where necessary to remove any of the dangerous places; they had to for horseback travel. And on the Cascade Crest the horses have the right of way for obvious reasons; a horse might jump off a cliff.

The trail led up through rainforest, with lizards and salamanders visible in the dense undergrowth. As they climbed, the size of the trees gradually increased until they were much larger than those usually found in the forests of the eastern U.S. By dusk they had come to an area that was entirely on a slope with no level ground on which to pitch the expensive tent Paris had acquired. Finally Earl decided they had no choice but to make the best of what was available. Although the tent was presumably designed for many types of uses, Paris had not the vaguest idea of how to deal with it, so he asked Earl to set it up. After experimenting with it in various ways, Earl gave up and proclaimed it a monstrosity not good for any thing but use as a tarp. He finally devised a rudimentary wickiup for their shelter.

Meanwhile, Paris had been trying without success to get a fire started in the steady rain that was falling. Earl then assumed the fire-starting task and told Paris to get the food ready for cooking. Shortly Paris asked Earl how much salt should be used. In exasperation, Earl said that he should be collecting guide wages since he seemed to wind up doing everything.

The next day they came to a shallow pond which was rapidly drying up in preparation for disappearing during the summer. Nonetheless, Paris gathered up his fishing supplies and announced that he would get some trout for breakfast. Within half an hour he was back in camp without any fish, and announced that he would probably not get any fish on the whole trip. This proved to be a self-fulfilling prophecy since he never went fishing again. As it turned out, the only trout they had was given to them by a Boy Scout troop they encountered. Once Earl himself decided to try his luck in a marsh-bordered pond they came to. The reel collapsed at one point and some of the parts were lost in the mud. That was the end of anyone's fishing for the remainder of the trip.

Paris insisted on leading when they were walking, but he walked very slowly which irritated Earl, who suggested that a faster pace would be less tiring. The response to this observation was an unbelieving stare from Paris.

Once they came around a bend and saw a large bear ahead of them. Earl whispered to Paris that he should ease to one side so Earl could get a picture of the beast. Paris replied that he would talk to the bear which would bring him closer. When Paris started talking the bear instantly fled. "Don't worry," Paris said. "We'll see lots more bears." As it turned out they never saw another one. Paris seemed to think that bears everywhere were like those in the Smokies.

At Snowgrass Flat they came to a narrow snow-covered ridge that started at Packwood Glacier and extended for about three miles. The weather was threatening, and they had no really suitable footgear nor any implements that might be used to keep them from sliding on the snowy slope. The situation seemed impossible, so they decided to take a side trail down to the town of Packwood to replenish their supplies and to bypass the dangerous section of the trail.

In Packwood, Paris insisted on getting a room at a plush motel. Earl resisted this proposal and said that it would just make returning to the trail more difficult. Once again he was confronted with the by now familiar, unbelieving stare.

The next day the proprietor of the motel drove them up to a ski resort where they rode the ski lift to the top. Although they tried to backtrack to cover the portion they had missed walking, this proved impossible because of dense fog that had rolled in.

Another time during a wet snowstorm they came to a ski resort "half frozen and miserable." Since this location was not far from the city of Everett where Paris had an old friend, Paris decided to call his friend for help. Unfortunately there was no phone service at the resort because the phone line had been routed through a railroad tunnel that went under the mountain far below. Eventually a delivery man appeared who agreed to call Paris's friend from the foot of the mountain and explain their predicament. To their great relief the delivery man must have done as he promised since the friend, after a time, appeared. While driving them down to his home in the valley, the friend decided to stop and purchase a large salmon so that they could "have a feast."

It turned out that the friend, like Paris himself, had in the past been a professional musician and traveled with big bands. His house contained a grand piano which Paris, with some reluctance, finally agreed to play.

His performance was excellent and was one of the two times Earl heard him play. (The other time was at Paris's home in Delaware.)

Before heading back to the trail, Paris decided to lighten the heavy load he had been carrying by leaving some unnecessary items in Everett to be reclaimed on the way home after the end of the hike. Earl offered to help in the selection of the items to be left behind, but Paris declined the offer, telling Earl to go for a walk around town and do some sightseeing. When Earl returned an hour later, Paris had accumulated a pile of items to be left behind. The only undecided item was a hairbrush. After weighing the brush reflectively in his hand, he concluded that since it weighed only an ounce or so he would take it along. The next day the friend drove them back to the trail.

A few days later they came to a group of cars with horse vans. The driver of one of the cars opened the window to inform the two hikers that they had been snowed out at Pear Lake and were heading home. Paris and Earl walked on for a ways when they came to a haphazard accumulation of gear. They were puzzled at first until they noticed a sign nailed to a tree: "Pear Lake." After putting the puzzle together, they figured out that the horse people had panicked at a few inches of snow in July, to which they responded by abandoning all of their gear and supplies.

After finally becoming weary of constantly following Paris at the latter's slow pace, Earl insisted on going ahead at his normal much faster pace. When he had walked for a time and gotten far ahead of his partner, Earl would stop and wait for Paris to catch up. Once he stopped at the junction with a side trail, which he decided to explore while waiting for Paris. A short distance along the side trail he came upon a beautiful, but dead, bay horse sprawled along the trail. The hugely bloated animal was still wearing a silver studded saddle. Earl passed by and went on to see what more he might find. Shortly he came to a mining camp where he told the workers what he had found. They knew the horse's owner who had been searching for it. Their assumption was that the horse had eaten some poisonous plant.

After he had been assured that the owner would be radioed about the animal's whereabouts, Earl returned to the main trail, where his lagging partner shortly appeared. Paris was on the point of exhaustion. He had removed his shirt in the heat and was sweating profusely. Blood was dripping from his bald head as a result of the abundant mosquitoes. Earl had bought Paris a mosquito net, and asked him why he wasn't wearing it, since along with protection from mosquitos, the net would also provide some shade to block the sun. Paris replied that the mosquito net had been among the items left behind in Everett. He had kept the hairbrush even though he had little hair left on his head, but had abandoned the net.

At this point Earl lost his temper and spent several minutes calling Paris every kind of fool that came to mind. The latter's only response to this tirade was, "You knew I was a fool before we ever started this trip."

The hike was not all suffering and folly; it had its moments of pleasure and beauty as well. One evening when they had settled in for the night, a small buck deer walked into the light of the campfire and unconcernedly pranced around for a time before moving on. Another time, as they approached a pile of rocks, three eagles spiraled up and glided off into the distance.

Near the end of the trip they caught up with two high school boys who had "lost their nerve" in the northern Cascades. Earl and Paris calmed the boys down and accompanied them to the end of the trail in Canada where the boys were put on a bus to take them home.

Earl did a lot of hiking in his lifetime, but the trip on the Cascade Crest Trail was one of the very few that he was glad to see the end of. At the finish he told Paris he would never take a long hike with him again.

The return bus trip was just as long and tiresome as the starting one, but on the way home he did not even have the company of Paris, who decided to spend a few days with his friend in Everett, since he feared this might be the last opportunity he would ever have to visit with him.

Paris started the hike in pretty poor physical condition. He spent a lot of time—especially early in the trip—complaining about how awful he felt. Several times he insisted that he was sure he would die on the trail. Things gradually improved, however, and by the end he was much stronger. Actually, when he got back to his home in Delaware, he joined the YMCA, started swimming and otherwise working out every day, and got himself in good shape. He maintained this regimen for as long as Earl knew of him afterward. Earl believes Paris must have been near ninety when he died, even though he thought he was finished at age sixty.

CHAPTER 23

ENCORE

At loose ends and restless in 1965, and still a relatively young and vigorous forty-six, Earl decided to do a repeat hike. This time, however, he would go in the opposite direction, starting at Katahdin and ending in Georgia, where in the interval since his last visit the terminus had been changed from Mt. Oglethorpe to Springer Mountain.

Why exactly did he make this decision? In his own words, much later:

> Because I thought the Trail was finished. And I was in the prime of life and I wanted to see how it had changed and so forth. And I really liked it. I liked the trail the second time better than the first or the third time; really, really liked it . . .

Earl believed that by 1965 the serious problems he had found in 1948 had been corrected, and the new problems that he found in 1998 had not yet been imposed on the Trail. In Virginia, for example, the trail had been taken off roads and turned into a "beautiful trail." Later it was changed again but this time for the worse, making it unnecessarily difficult. Similarly in Maine where the trail had passed through a number of pleasant, useful towns, it would be re-routed to avoid them, to what Earl considered the detriment of the trail. In Earl's view the blame for these undesirable changes rests solely with the Park Service, whose reasons for such actions he could not understand. They were, he concluded, basically make-work projects designed to justify the Service's involvement.

It is, in its way, ironic that of his three through-hikes, the one that Earl most enjoyed has received the least public attention.

To reach the summit of Katahdin for the start of his southbound hike in 1965 Earl chose the steepest of all the approach trails. He set off in July on the Cathedral Trail, which starts at the Chimney Pond Ranger Station. From there the trail passes through forest and then climbs steeply on boulders to the ridge where there is a junction with the Saddle Trail which goes on to the summit. Earl immediately turned south on the Appalachian Trail.

When he came down, Earl encountered some people who had been camping by the Penobscot River. One of the party had been out fishing and had caught some trout. He invited Earl to join them for breakfast, which featured fried trout that could hardly have been fresher. Later the same day, Earl saw a bear with a cub—the only time he ever met a mother bear with a cub in the woods.

By the time Earl crossed the border from New Jersey into Pennsylvania his boots needed resoling. He got word to his brother John who, with his two sons and a nephew, drove up to meet Earl at a shelter and pick up the ailing boots. John took the footwear back to a shoe repair shop in Dover, Pa., where they were equipped with a new sole and returned to Earl a few days later in Duncannon. In the interim, Earl wore sneakers.

A BEAR AND A BUG

It was October when Earl finished his 1965 hike, and the nights in the Georgia mountains were turning cold. Earl's brother John and sister Anna had decided to drive down to Georgia to meet Earl at the finish and bring him back home to Pennsylvania. They knew approximately when Earl expected to get to the end, so allowing themselves some leeway, John took time off from his job and they set off on a Tuesday in John's VW Bug, driving directly to Amicalola Falls State Park, the main Trail portal to Springer Mountain.

They saw nothing of Earl, so they wandered around asking everyone they encountered if they had seen an Appalachian Trail through-hiker in the area. No one had. Next John and Anna drove to another road crossing farther north to enquire for their errant brother. With no luck so far, and with darkness falling, they finally made use of the sleeping bags they had brought with them and slept directly on the Trail. In the morning there was ice on a nearby pond.

Early that day they finally met someone who believed that he had seen a hiker fitting Earl's description who had passed through a day or two before. With this encouraging news, John and Anna headed back to Amicalola Falls State Park to wait. They calculated that Earl might be still a day's trek away. While at the park they met and talked with the Park Superintendent who after making some phone calls determined about where Earl was last seen—a good day's hike away. That night John and Anna accepted the Superintendent's offer to let them stay in one of the camp's lodges.

The following day they drove to a road crossing that was only about a mile from the Park where they settled down to wait. The hours went by and eventually dusk began to fall with still no sign of Earl. John was under very rigid time constraints regarding when he had to get back to his job. He finally set a specific time and told Anna that if Earl did not turn up by then they would have to go home without him.

As the darkness continued to thicken, Anna found herself worrying about bears as was often the case when she was in the woods. Suddenly she saw a lumbering creature coming out from among the trees. Turning to her brother she said, "Johnny, I think there's a bear down there."

John looked in the direction she was pointing and replied, "No, that's Earl."

After the initial greetings, John quickly informed his brother that they had to head home right away so that John could get to an important sales meeting the next day. Earl, however, refused to leave until he walked the remaining mile and signed the register. John finally agreed to wait until Earl could complete this formality, but insisted on walking along with his brother because he thought Earl seemed a little unsteady on his feet. Taking flashlights along, the two walked to the end of the Trail and then back again. Earl had originally planned to continue hiking the old trail from Springer to Oglethorpe, but in view of John's urgency and the fact that Springer was now the official southern terminus, he agreed to forgo the additional hiking.

In the meantime, Anna remained alone with John's VW Bug and her concern about bears. At one point—perhaps to stretch her legs—she decided to get out of the car for a while. Anna was very uneasy alone at the edge of a bear-infested forest so she kept the key in the ignition for a fast getaway if she were attacked. According to John, his sister was obsessed with keeping doors locked. Consequently, when she got out of the car, she automatically locked the door, forgetting that her only key was still in the ignition.

Fortunately John and Earl shortly returned to alleviate their sister's fear, but they were then confronted with the problem of gaining access to their only means of getting home, since John did not have a spare key. Happily, the Bug had a cloth roof. (John later commented jokingly that "the roof was worth almost more than the car." Using Earl's pocket knife they cut a slit in the roof. Then, using as a tool a small twig that they whittled down to the necessary size and shape, they finally managed to get the door open.

The three of them were all dead tired; Earl after a long day's hiking; John and Anna after many hours of anxious, sleepless waiting. Finally, for whatever reason, it was decided that the driving would be done by Earl who, incidentally, had never driven a VW Bug before. After an uneasy and briefly dangerous start, things settled down and they all got home. John was a little late for his meeting, but at least he was in one piece.

On the first day of his north-to-south hike Earl saw a mother bear with her cub, and on the last day he was himself mistaken for a bear by his own sister.

PART FIVE

PRESERVING THE TRAIL

CHAPTER 24

THE APPALACHIAN TRAIL CONFERENCE

S hortly before starting his 1948 hike, Earl joined the Appalachian Trail Conference as what was known at that time as a Class D member—the Conference's designation for what was, in effect, an individual membership. Many years later he was voted an honorary member of the organization.

In 1952 at the Conference's general meeting Earl was elected Corresponding Secretary, a post in which he served until 1958 when he was succeeded by Florence Nichol who more than twenty years later was to be responsible for preparing the manuscript of *Walking With Spring* for publication by the Appalachian Trail Conference.

Earl's chief responsibility as Corresponding Secretary was to respond to inquiries sent to ATC requesting information as to what was required to undertake a backpacking trek on the Appalachian Trail. In those days such inquiries were few, and at first Earl provided personalized responses to each one. Later, as the number increased, he prepared a mimeographed sheet of suggestions for hikers which he used to answer such questions. Generally, he would also add some personalized comments.

He recalled one such inquiry from a school teacher in Iowa. Not far from retirement, she had taken a bus tour through the Smokies, and thought it might be nice to follow that up with a hike covering the entire Appalachian Trail. She had never hiked a day in her life at this point. Earl responded by tactfully pointing out all that would be involved in such an undertaking. He concluded by saying, "Don't underestimate this Trail. It is rugged; it is long and hard. Take a trip of a couple weeks or so before you ever decide to do the thru-hike."

In due course the school teacher wrote again, apologizing to Earl for putting him to so much trouble, and concluding her letter with, "I had no idea what it was all about."

Following is the text of the mimeographed sheet that Earl prepared and distributed with his responses:

ADVICE FOR LONG DISTANCE HIKERS
ON THE APPALACHIAN TRAIL

Good planning, a sturdy physique, exceptional determination, and ingenious adaptability are essential on a long and strenuous foot journey. Most attempts to travel end to end on the Appalachian Trail fail within two hundred miles. Above all do not underestimate the difficulties involved or overestimate your own capabilities. Both good luck and good management are necessary. Preliminary experience on shorter trips is very helpful.

The weight and bulk of the pack load should be kept to a minimum, yet the necessary equipment must be carried. The pack should be rigged low so the weight rests mostly on the hips and is kept as near the body as possible to reduce the backward pull. Food supplies should be as free of cans as possible to reduce weight, yet maximum nourishment is absolutely essential.

There should be no exact day-by-day schedule set in advance. Conditions of weather and terrain prevent this. But a steady pace, if persistently followed, will result in a good daily average. Don't expect a picnic stroll. Mountain hiking is hard work.

EQUIPMENT: total weight approximately twenty pounds.
Frame pack—Mountain troop or similar, with large pocket removed.
Poncho—serves as raincoat, parka, ground cloth, shelter cloth, etc.
Rain hat—indispensable because of variable weather.
Sheath knife—small size. Pocketknife as auxiliary.
Small axe—necessary for maintaining campfire in rainy weather.
    Compass, waterproof match safe, snakebite kit—just in case.
Cook kit—Mountain troop or similar (two nested kettles and fry pan).
Sleeping bag—blanket type (April–October), down or kapok in winter.
Extra set of clothing—for added warmth, rather than heavy underwear, and as a dry change after a rainy day.

Socks—(heavy) reinforced wool or spun nylon.

Canteen—flat, one quart, slung to side of pack.

First aid kit—include foot powder such as Quinsana, insect repellent. Head net, flashlight, and plastic food bags.

FOOD:

Recommended staples: cornmeal, oatmeal, flour, brown sugar, salt, raisins, potatoes, powdered milk, rice, dried meats, dried fruits, dehydrated vegetables (if available). Diet can be varied by immediate consumption when visiting stores.

FOOTGEAR:

Moccasin-type leather boots with nine-inch tops (protect ankles from sprain, bruise, snakebite). Avoid low shoes, sneakers, knee high tops, rubber footgear. Use lots of foot powder.

AVOID:

Tent, bulky sleeping bag, cans and jars, air mattress, large sheath knife, large axe, bulky jacket or overcoat, conventional raincoat, firearms.

Guidebooks are available from the Appalachian Trail Conference for those desiring detailed information. These are rather bulky and heavy for long distance hikers however. National Forest and National Park maps are helpful. Most road maps at least show the general route of the Trail. The Guidebooks contain sectional maps, which could be detached and used.

WILDWOOD FLOWER

The fourteenth general meeting of the Appalachian Trail Conference took place in 1958 in southwestern Virginia at Mountain Lake, which is one of only two natural lakes in the state. Mountain Lake covers an area of about fifty acres and, at an altitude of 3,875 feet above sea level, is reportedly at the highest elevation of any lake east of the Mississippi River. It is also the only natural lake in the southern Appalachians.

It was late spring, and Earl had loaded up his old station wagon, piling hiking gear and sleeping bag in the back. On top of this collection he placed his guitar. As he was navigating the mountain roads that wound toward his destination, he came to a fork without markings, leaving him uncertain as to how he should go. Beside the road to his right he saw an older man relaxing on the porch of his rustic home. Earl leaned across the empty passenger seat to roll down the window and call to the man, "Which road goes to Mountain Lake?"

Instead of shouting a reply, the man got up and sauntered over to Earl's car, which he looked at carefully, taking particular note of the contents of the back seat. He seemed pleased with what he saw and called to a neighbor on the other side of the road, "Get your banjo and come on over here. He's got a guitar."

That was the start of about a two-hour session of mountain music on the porch where Earl had first spied the man resting. Much of what they played and sang came from the Carter Family's collection, with "Wildwood Flower" being everyone's favorite. It is sometimes incorrectly claimed that A. P. Carter wrote this song after seeing a beautiful mountain girl gathering wild flowers high up on the mountain. Actually the song dates back to 1860 when it was composed by Maud Irving and Joseph Philbrick Webster, and carried the name "I'll Twine 'Mid the Ringlets." Nonetheless, the song's current fame rests on the performance recorded by the Carter Family, a trio consisting of A. P. Carter, his wife Sara, and his sister-in-law Maybelle, who was both married to A. P.'s brother and a first cousin to Sara.

The men played and sang on the porch paying no attention to the occasional passing cars that carried trail enthusiasts headed to the forthcoming conference. These hikers stared at the performing musicians, probably completely unaware that one of the guitar pickers was well on his way to becoming an Appalachian Trail icon.

At Mountain Lake one evening that weekend, another, larger hootenanny assembled for more singing. This one, Earl later reported, was even attended by Murray Stevens, who was then the chairman of the Appalachian Trail Conference. It was also, in Earl's view, the last conference that was small enough to encourage such a gathering. Thereafter, as the membership of the organization continued its steady growth, ATC's meetings inevitably got too big and unwieldy to be conducive to such informality.

CHAPTER 25

ORGANIZING PENNSYLVANIA

The 1950s were a decade of feverish activity in Pennsylvania's hiking community. In 1952 Earl Shaffer was elected to the office of Corresponding Secretary of ATC, which put him in a position to attend staff meetings in Washington (where the Conference's headquarters was then located) and to have a direct influence on Conference policy and planning. As a native Pennsylvanian, he pushed vigorously for a number of actions relating to the Appalachian Trail in the Keystone State. First and foremost was the need for a major sixty-mile relocation to get the trail away from the Indiantown Gap Military Reservation. In order to provide the manpower needed to accomplish this task, he argued that a trail club should be established in Harrisburg, since the existing Appalachian Trail maintaining organizations were based too distant from the area where the relocation work would be taking place.

Earl contended that when the relocation was finished a new guidebook for the area would be needed, making this an ideal time to create a guidebook specifically for Pennsylvania. To accomplish this goal Earl advocated the creation of a statewide hiking organization somewhat on the order of the New York–New Jersey Trail Conference (NY–NJTC).

Thanks in no small measure to Earl's persistence, three of these four goals were accomplished with astonishing speed. In 1954 the Susquehanna Appalachian Trail Club was launched at Hawk Rock high above the borough of Duncannon on the west shore of the Susquehanna River. In 1955 the new relocation was dedicated; and in 1956 the first organizational meeting of Keystone Trails Association took place in the city of Harrisburg. Earl was present at all three events.

Unfortunately, the preparation of a single guidebook covering all of Pennsylvania encountered a number of unanticipated stumbling blocks, and the actual publication was delayed for a dozen years. Prior to this time, the Appalachian Trail in Pennsylvania was divided between two different guide books. The Trail north of the Susquehanna River was included in a guidebook published by the New York–New Jersey Trail Conference, while the trail south of the river was included in another book published by the Potomac Appalachian Trail Club. The proposal for a single Pennsylvania guide met with strong initial resistance from Jean Stephenson who was ATC's editor-in-chief. During KTA's organizational phase Stephenson had been a strong supporter of the new group, but later when she thought that KTA was trying to grow too fast and to overextend its resources, she dug in her heels and attempted (with some success) to slow the process.

For twenty-five years Stephenson edited *Appalachian Trailway News*, at that time the newsletter of ATC, which appeared three times a year. Even after relinquishing the editorship of *Trailway News*, she continued to edit the ATC-published guidebooks. It is reported that she worked at her editing task until her death in 1979 at the age of eighty-six, even continuing her work from a hospital bed. Her knowledge of the Appalachian Trail was reportedly "encyclopedic." It is clear that her opinions would carry considerable weight within the organization.

When Stan Murray became ATC Chairman, however, he proved more receptive to a larger role for KTA in the guidance of A.T. affairs in Pennsylvania and encouraged the guidebook project. There was also some level of opposition to the guidebook project within KTA itself. This eventually was overcome, and bolstered by Stan Murray's support, planning moved ahead. By 1963, coordination was begun to mesh the publication date of a new Pennsylvania A.T. Guide with the publication schedules and inventory levels of both New York–New Jersey and PATC. At last, in 1968 the first edition of *Guide to the Appalachian Trail in Pennsylvania* was published by Keystone Trails Association.

DELAWARE WATER GAP

Following its fourteenth general meeting in 1958 at Mountain Lake, Virginia, ATC began planning for the fifteenth meeting to be held in 1961. The regular rotation of meeting locations being followed at that time called for a site somewhere in the central area, and the still young KTA was urged to host the gathering in Pennsylvania. Delaware Water Gap was chosen as the location, with the Glenwood Hotel as the setting for meetings and lodging.

As planning progressed for the event, some members of the KTA Council began to feel overwhelmed by the amount of work they saw would be involved. The Council was approached and urged to reject the hosting responsibilities they had tentatively agreed to. At this point Earl stood up and announced that if KTA backed out of this commitment after preliminary announcements had already been made, they might as well disband and admit publicly that they were incapable of playing the state-level role they had marked out for themselves.

Earl believed that by shaming the others into continuing with the sponsorship work, he fell into general disfavor at KTA and was thereafter eased out of a leadership role. This estrangement persisted for many years until eventually there came a reconciliation of sorts, and Earl was made an honorary member. Nonetheless, the six-day general meeting at Delaware Water Gap was the largest general meeting up to that time with more than 275 in attendance. KTA had established itself as a major player in ATC affairs.

SUSQUEHANNA APPALACHIAN TRAIL CLUB (SATC)

In the meantime, SATC was getting started. Sometime in 1953, both Earl Shaffer and Ralph Kinter had independently approached George Gruber about starting a local trail club. Gruber, whom Earl had previously met in Maine while hiking the Appalachian Trail, was president of the Natural History Society of Harrisburg. Having heard that Earl was planning on doing some trail work on Blue Mountain, Gruber went looking for him one Sunday afternoon. And, as Earl later reported, "sitting on that mountain is when we planned to start the Susquehanna Appalachian Trail Club. I suggested starting it the first Sunday in April on Hawk Rock. And George was the one who suggested the name of Susquehanna Appalachian Trail Club, instead of Harrisburg or something else. I don't remember if he ever mentioned Ralph Kinter or not, if he did I don't remember." In any case, George Gruber, Ralph Kinter, and Earl Shaffer were all key figures in the establishment of SATC.

On Sunday, April 4, 1954, eighteen people met behind the State Education Building. Earl had arranged a hike to Hawk Rock, high above Duncannon. Elmer and Ruth Bolla met the group in Harrisburg but were unable to join the hike because of another commitment. After two more hikes in April, the group established the Susquehanna Appalachian Trail

Club on April 25, 1954, with Ralph Kinter as President, Earl as Vice-President, and Thelma Marks as Secretary/Treasurer. A Constitution and By-Laws Committee was established and plans were made to join the Appalachian Trail Conference.

Earl and Ralph Kinter agreed that the new club should have a newsletter, with Earl as editor. After some searching, Earl came up with an ancient mimeograph machine and a name for the publication: *Bushwhack Bulletin*. In October 1954 the first edition was produced. Unfortunately Earl had neglected to tell Ralph how to spell "bushwhack," which resulted in the first issue's appearing as *Bushwack Bulletin*. Jean Stephenson spotted the error and pointed it out to the editorial team. She decided, however, that the aberrant spelling made the newsletter more distinctive, and she urged that the flawed spelling be retained. It was.

Earl wound up writing much of the material for the early issues himself—sometimes unsigned and sometimes with the *nom de plume* "Sylvanis." A feature of those first issues was occasional four-line snippets of verse appropriate to the season or some other aspect of the publication. Once Ralph commented on the verse to Jean Stephenson and wondered where Earl came up with them. Jean smiled knowingly and said, "Well, maybe he just writes them himself."

Several early copies of the *Bushwack Bulletin* are among Earl's papers that are now in the collection of the Smithsonian Institution.

CHAPTER 26

THE GREAT
RELOCATION

When Earl Shaffer was doing his first Appalachian Trail hike in 1948, he encountered two major problems related to the route of the Trail in central Pennsylvania. One had to do with the Indiantown Gap Military Reservation through which the Trail had once wandered. The other involved the difficulty of getting across the Susquehanna River.

At that time there were two distinct segments of the Appalachian Trail, with the Susquehanna dividing the two. Coming from the south the Trail ended at Overview, above the river, at the west end of the Rockville Railroad Bridge. The Trail, coming from the north, reached the river on the opposite side at Rockville. The Pennsylvania Railroad had made it clear that it would never allow its bridge to provide passage for the Appalachian Trail. The thru-hiker was thus left with no alternative but to walk downriver (or hitchhike if lucky) to Harrisburg where the river could be crossed on one of that city's bridges. Of course, the weary pedestrian was then faced with the need to retrace the same five miles upstream, this detour being itself no part of the Appalachian Trail. (At least the scenery would be different.)

The Indiantown Gap problem was of a quite different nature. In 1931 the Gap had been established as a training facility for the Pennsylvania National Guard. With the coming of World War II, the federal government assumed control of the camp and turned it into one of the nation's most important Army training camps, and the Appalachian Trail was evicted. Even where the Trail was not on Indiantown Gap real estate, it was often close enough to put the passing hiker at risk from artillery practice. In any event, the outcome was many miles of road walking as the hiker circled around the new Army post.

After his return home from his big hike, Earl mulled over this problem off and on, especially as he became increasingly involved with Trail matters both in Washington and in Pennsylvania. He spent many weekends over a period of a couple of years scouting adjacent areas on both sides of the river. He regularly discussed his explorations with Murray Stevens, who was at that time Chairman of the Appalachian Trail Conference. As the number of viable options were steadily narrowed, Stevens began coming over to Pennsylvania from time to time to assist in the job of assessing the pros and cons of each possibility.

Eventually, they decided on a relocation of nearly seventy miles that would alter the Trail's route from Center Point Knob on the west (Trail south) side of the river to Swatara Gap on the east side. Roughly half of the relocation would be on each side of the river. Coming from the south, the Trail from Center Point Knob would steer a more northerly course than previously, reaching the river at the Clark's Ferry Bridge, well north of Overview.

After crossing on the Clark's Ferry Bridge, the Trail then would slant up Peters Mountain, the crest of which it would follow for a dozen miles or so before descending into Clarks Valley to start a climb up Stony Mountain. From Stony, the Trail would pass quickly to the adjacent Sharp Mountain, passing through St. Anthony's Wilderness on the north side of Indiantown Gap Military Reservation. At Swatara Gap the Trail would reach Blue Mountain and resume its former route.

U.S. Rep. Daniel Hoch, Earl Shaffer, and Murray Stevens at the dedication of the Pennsylvania trail relocation, March 1955

With the route decided, the work of clearing and marking could begin. This, too, became primarily Earl's task. Murray Stevens came over to help on weekends as he was able. Help from the various trail clubs other than SATC was sporadic and not as enthusiastic as Earl had hoped. Thanks to Ralph Kinter, SATC did organize some work trips to help with the relocation.

When work was done and the new trail ready for use, Jean Stephenson took the lead in organizing an elaborate dedication ceremony on the weekend of March 19–20, 1955. She arranged for use of the Harrisburg Civic Club on the riverfront for the indoor ceremonies. (When Earl asked her where the money was coming from to pay for all this, she replied, "Oh, it's taken care of." Earl remained convinced that once again she had dipped into her own financial reserves for the benefit of ATC.)

Stephenson also orchestrated a major publicity campaign in connection with the dedication. "The response," according to an article in *Appalachian Trailway News*, "was overwhelming," with widespread newspaper coverage throughout Pennsylvania. Former Congressman Danny Hoch of Pennsylvania, the first Congressional advocate of federal trail protection for the Appalachian Trail, was on hand along with ATC Chairman Murray Stevens, and a host of other Trail dignitaries. A total of 125 persons attended the formal dedication ceremonies on each end of the Clark's Ferry Bridge on Sunday morning, after which many of the participants climbed Peters Mountain to hike a portion of the new trail on the east side of the river. In the afternoon a group climbed Cove Mountain on the opposite side to enjoy the spectacular view from Hawk Rock.

CHAPTER 27

SHELTERS

The compulsive trail builder was also a compulsive shelter builder. Over a span of half a dozen years Earl was the prime mover in the construction of four shelters, only one of which remains, although no longer in use as a trail shelter.

SUSQUEHANNA LEAN-TO
At a site a little less than a mile east (trail north) of the Susquehanna River, Earl constructed a basic Adirondack shelter which he named the Susquehanna Lean-to. It no longer exists, having been replaced by the Clarks Ferry Shelter.

DARLINGTON SHELTER
Using native stone, Earl built the first Darlington Shelter in 1956, mostly working alone, with only occasional assistance from other trail club members. The site on Blue Mountain, about a dozen miles trail-south of the Susquehanna River crossing at Clark's Ferry, was chosen primarily because of its proximity to a spring. The shelter's name was selected because it stood less than a tenth of a mile from the Appalachian Trail's intersection with the Darlington Trail. Given the construction material Earl used, the building of this shelter cannot have been an easy task. On erecting a stone structure, Earl later commented, "That takes a lot of work."

By 1977, however, the annual "Status of the Trail Report" published in that year's May issue of *Appalachian Trailway News* included the terse statement: "Darlington Shelter is barely usable." Later the same year the shelter was replaced.

Decades later, in a taped interview, speaking of the existing Darlington Shelter, Earl ruefully observed, "That's not the one I built. Now it has been destroyed, the stone shelter that I worked hard building. That one is gone."

THELMA MARKS SHELTER

In 1960 at a site about five miles west of the Susquehanna River, Earl built a shelter which he named Thelma Marks in honor of a longtime activist with SATC. Near this site Earl found a number of small chestnut trees which, although they had been killed by the chestnut blight, had remained standing, thereby avoiding decay. The walls of the Thelma Marks Shelter were made entirely of these chestnut logs. The Mountain Club of Maryland provided some help in dragging the logs to the construction site. Otherwise, Earl did all of the work himself. This shelter no longer exists.

EARL SHAFFER SHELTER

In the course of his crowded career Earl Shaffer built four Appalachian Trail shelters, of which the last survivor was the one on Peters Mountain in Pennsylvania between Clarks Valley and the Clarks Ferry Bridge. The exact date of construction of this modest but functional edifice is a matter of disagreement among various authorities, with dates ranging from 1955 to 1961. It was named the "Earl Shaffer Shelter" by SATC, the maintaining club for the Trail in that area.

In an undated memo provided by Earl's brother John, Earl writes:

> The shelter on Peters Mtn. was built in the manner of the traditional Adirondack Lean-to, small, low, and without a floor, to accommodate four to six persons. This type is easy to build and maintain and adequately fulfills the basic needs of backpackers in bad weather.

Some years after construction, however, it was suggested that the shelter be provided with a floor, a proposal which Earl firmly resisted. In the same memo cited above, Earl states, "My reasons for opposing a board floor in a lean-to are, mainly: snakes, spiders, mice, rats, trash, discomfort, picnickers, and squatters." The floor was nonetheless installed. Earl's reaction was predictable: He demanded that his name be removed from the structure. In July 1983, SATC's Board honored Earl's request and renamed his shelter the Peters Mountain Shelter.

Eventually, a new shelter was erected nearby to which hiker use shifted with little complaint since the new edifice was larger than the original one and considerably more elaborate. Earl's handiwork then began the slow process of deterioration. Many in the A.T. community, however, recognized the historical significance of the "Earl Shaffer Shelter," and determined to take action to save it.

The Appalachian Trail Museum Society took the lead in formulating a proposal to dismantle the shelter and transport it to a secure storage location where eventually it could be restored and reassembled for display in an Appalachian Trail Museum, plans for which were then being developed. The approval of the National Park Service was sought for this disassembly and removal.

After complying with various Park Service requirements, the necessary agency approval was received and disassembly was completed in August 2008. Eventually, the shelter was put back together in the new Appalachian Trail Museum on the grounds of Pine Grove Furnace State Park, where it is currently on display.

WORKING ALONE
Earl seems to have had mixed feelings about all of his shelter work. Obviously, he took great satisfaction in it or he would not have persisted through the construction of four shelters, one of which was a stone structure with all the work that entailed. He did complain, however, about the little help he received in the actual work and also in financing his endeavors.

Years later—near the end of his life when he was often seriously depressed—he commented:

> I was never paid a red-cent for all that work that I did. Never. Paid my own gas and everything. One shelter, the Mountain Club of Maryland helped pay, I had bought some corrugated tin at a farm sale. And I carried that up the trail about a mile by myself. In fact all my shelters had tin roof and I carried it all up the mountainside."

MURDER AT THELMA MARKS SHELTER
In September 1990 a young hiking couple in their mid-twenties were murdered at the Thelma Marks Shelter in a particularly vicious fashion. The subsequent autopsy revealed that the woman had been raped before

being killed. After the murders were discovered by another hiking couple, the police solicited the help of local people and hikers familiar with the area to assist in a search for the murderer. Earl participated in the search. The assumption at the start of the search was that the perpetrator had probably left the Trail to get off the mountain.

Earl helped on "the roughest part of the mountain." The police, who were in charge of these activities, were the only ones permitted to carry guns, although as Earl later reported, "Of course one of the guys had a gun concealed." Earl believed that if the murderer had been found, the man with the hidden gun would have shot him on the spot. As it turned out, the murderer had stayed on the Trail and headed south, wearing the murdered man's boots and carrying his pack. The killer was finally apprehended in Harpers Ferry a week after the killings.

During the search, Earl was accompanied by a much younger policeman. At one point Earl overheard the man comment to a fellow officer, "Dog-gone guy is twice as old as I am and I can hardly keep up with him." Recalling this incident near the end of his life when his strength was failing, Earl ruefully observed, "He could now, oh could he ever."

In May 1991, Paul David Crews of South Carolina was found guilty of the two murders and sentenced to death. In December 2006, after fifteen years of appeals, Crews was sentenced to two consecutive life terms with no possibility of parole.

CHAPTER 28

TRAIL THOUGHTS

THRU-HIKING

Although the term "thru-hiking" has gradually spread, over time, to encompass many kinds of long-distance walking on many different trails, for many hikers and backpackers it is inextricably associated with the Appalachian Trail. Even when limited to the Appalachian Trail, however, there are many definitions of what exactly thru-hiking means. For the most part, Earl Shaffer was a purist. "A thru-hike," he once said, "is when you start at one end and go through to the other end without skipping and without any unnecessary delays. In other words, do it in one season from one end to the other in a continuous journey. That is a thru-hike."

Earl found most of the frequent variations on this theme to be illegitimate. One popular variation, the so-called 'flip-flop thru-hike' fails Earl's legitimacy test. A flip-flop hike is one in which the hiker starts at one end of the Trail, goes part way, and then travels to the other end to walk back to the point at which the first portion was interrupted. Earl likened this to trying to walk part way through a tunnel and then going to the other end to walk back. "It just doesn't work that way," he said. "You don't go through." In his view, it is two trips, not one.

He grudgingly accepted "slack-packing" as permissible—for other people, not for himself. Slack-packing involves a hiker's making arrangements to have his gear transported by car or otherwise from one end of a trail section to the other, thereby greatly minimizing the weight that the hiker must carry. "I don't exactly approve of it," he said, "but I don't disapprove of it." At least the hiker is walking the entire way, even if carrying less weight. "I always said wherever I go, the pack goes with me."

MOTIVATION

Earl had more than enough trouble sorting out his own motivations for thru-hiking; the motivations of other people remained, for the most part, a complete mystery to him. His years in the Army taught him patience, which helped. He found that he spent most of his time in or on his bunk—either sleeping or sitting; "alone amongst a crowd," as he once put it. And he never had any problem with being alone, unlike many people. He found that he had more than enough thoughts to occupy himself. Most people seem determined to escape their thoughts one way or another. It was mostly thinking that occupied him during his thru-hikes.

Much of his time on his first Appalachian Trail hike was given over to planning for what he would do after the hike: He would write a book or books and magazine articles; he would develop slide shows to use in making presentations to interested audiences; he would find other ways to generate publicity to save the Trail from becoming lost.

His last hike was something he felt he had no choice about; it was the fiftieth anniversary of the first hike and he simply felt compelled to go out and do it again—one more time. As the miles accumulated during the last hike, he felt more and more disappointed at finding the Trail greatly altered since his last visit—and not in ways that he liked. When the last hike was finished and he thought about it afterward, he was unable to pinpoint a motivation for continuing to the end. He concluded that it must have been pure stubbornness, of which he knew he had plenty.

HIKING DIET

One of the first things many would-be thru-hikers must come to terms with is the need for many more calories per day than they consumed in their previous life. Earl estimated that most thru-hikers wind up eating two or three times as much as they were accustomed to. Among a variety of calorie sources, Earl recommended ice cream, peanut butter (without additives), and hoecakes—what Earl called "pan bread."

Unlike standard hoecakes which are made from corn meal, Earl's pan bread, though simple, was highly flexible. Start with oatmeal, cornmeal, and flour in whatever proportions you prefer—or whatever you happen to have available. Add salt and baking powder, mix with water, and bake in a pan greased with margarine until done on one side. Flip the hoecake over and finish cooking on the other side. "Wonder bread," Earl called it.

HIKING HEADGEAR

On his 1948 hike Earl started with a kind of rain hat which he found to be not much good. Most of the time he walked bareheaded, although with his very abundant head of hair, he rarely needed anything more. By the time of his 1965 hike, his hair had started to thin, and he took to wearing the pith helmet that later became a kind of trademark. To protect himself from mosquitoes he wore a head net.

SAFETY ON THE TRAIL

Violent crime is so rare on the Trail that it is, overall, one of the safest places a person could be. In Earl's experience the only times he felt endangered was when crossing a four-lane highway.

TRAIL MAINTAINERS

Earl had nothing but high praise for the volunteer maintainers who, over the years and against the odds, have kept the Appalachian Trail open and walkable. Of the more recent trend toward the use of paid maintainers, he had mixed feelings. While acknowledging that such crews do work that might not otherwise get done, he noted that the paid crews are generally made up of young people who tend to relish challenges and build trails intended to provide obstacles. The trail that they thus create is likely to be unappreciated by those less vigorous, less healthy, and less young. "And I think that's bad for the Trail," Earl said.

GRANDMA GATEWOOD

During his 1965 hike and again in 1998, Earl heard much about Grandma Gatewood, the charismatic grandmother who had made a name for herself by hiking the Appalachian Trail in a most unorthodox fashion. Emma Rowena Gatewood, older than Earl by thirty-one years, completed her first Appalachian Trail hike in 1955 at the age of sixty-seven, carrying in a homemade shoulder bag an Army blanket, a raincoat, a plastic shower curtain and little else. What food she could not find along the Trail she acquired in stores or homes along the way. She repeated the hike in 1960 and again in 1963 when she was seventy-five. By this time she too had become an Appalachian Trail icon.

Although Earl saw her in person only once, and never conversed with her, the image conveyed by various stories he heard portrayed an opportunistic woman who took advantage of what occasions came her way that might smooth her difficult journey. Among other things he heard reports that Gatewood had accepted rides that enabled her to avoid walking some stretches of Trail.

It was not until the Appalachian Trail Conference general meeting in Plymouth, New Hampshire in 1972 that Earl actually saw Grandma Gatewood. He later described her as being "just a little bitsy woman. And she wore an old fashioned tam, that's what she wore; she was a real character." The two of them never spoke, Earl reported later. "And she was standing over by the wall, only time I ever saw her, never spoke to her and she never spoke to me."

At that 1972 gathering was held the first meeting of "2,000 milers," those who had hiked the entire Trail whether in one trip or in segments. Among its other actions, this elite group formed a committee to recommend procedures for authenticating requests for recognition as a thru-hiker. Earl's suggestion was to require applicants to follow his precedent of keeping a journal in which was recorded, at a minimum, each day's starting and stopping places.

In Earl Shaffer's lexicon a "thru-hike" unalterably referred to a journey on foot along the Appalachian Trail in a single trip, walking always in the same direction. In spite of her iconic status, Earl remained skeptical that any of Grandma Gatewood's three hikes met that minimum standard.

GOVERNMENT ROLE

In some respects, Earl believed the government's role in protecting the Appalachian Trail had been counterproductive. Specifically, when public money became available for acquiring land along the trail's right-of-way, many landowners, who had previously taken a casual, tolerant attitude toward the trail and its users, began putting up "No Trespassing" signs, hoping to induce the government's trail managers to offer money for land that hitherto had been open for hikers gratis.

FOREST MANAGEMENT

When Earl made his first thru-hike in 1948, he encountered many areas where logging activities left him greatly distressed—not to mention inconvenienced. It was clear-cutting that annoyed him most. "Clear-cutting is not logical, no matter where or when. That's a curse on the woodland," he commented. Of course, when the trees were all removed, the trail blazes went with them. The result was that Earl spent many extra miles of walking to find the trail that had been lost because of the clear-cut.

In other places miners of various kinds had come through, probing and digging in search of whatever mineral was on their mind. Left behind would be disturbed land and dilapidated shacks.

In the many decades that have passed since Earl's Long Cruise, forest management practices have certainly improved, as he would likely acknowledge, were he still here. He would probably also point out that we are still a long way from living in a perfect world.

American Chestnut

By 1948, when Earl went through the southern Appalachians, the chestnut blight had done its worst. Introduced in this country by accident in 1904, the blight required only four decades to devastate the nation's majestic chestnut stands. Salvage operations had removed most of the standing trees that were of marketable size. Occasionally, however, Earl encountered a truly huge tree still standing—some as much as five feet in diameter. Chestnut wood is so tough that even fallen ones that have been down for as much as fifty years are often still usable.

THE FUTURE OF THE TRAIL

After returning from the Fiftieth Anniversary Hike in 1998, Earl began mulling over the idea of writing a magazine article (à la Benton MacKaye) in which he could spell out his ideas about the future of the Appalachian Trail. He died, unfortunately, without ever having completely organized his thoughts and committing them to paper. In discussions about this project, however, he did give some clues to where his thoughts were headed. To begin with, his working title for the contemplated essay was "The Appalachian Trail: Its Future." The most urgent issue, in Earl's opinion, is *overuse*. This problem is particularly severe in two areas: the southern Appalachians and New Hampshire. The problem in the south is especially acute in early spring when thousands of hikers are starting their planned thru-hikes. Even though most of those who start at Springer drop out within weeks or even days of beginning their treks, the vast swarm at the beginning simply overwhelms the Trail and its facilities. It is not known what sort of solution to this problem Earl might eventually have offered.

The source of overcrowding in New Hampshire, in Earl's view, resulted from large excursion groups, organized commercially or otherwise, that engulf trail facilities well beyond their design capacity. These groups first fill up and then overflow shelters, leaving no space for "regular hikers." For such organized groups Earl seemed to be leaning toward a requirement for them to make advance reservations for shelters and campsites and to charge them a fee.

THE GREATEST MOUNTAIN
Katahdin, in the language of the Penobscot Indians, means "The Greatest Mountain." For hikers—especially Appalachian Trail hikers—it is a magic place. As such, its summit holds special meaning for those who climb to its peak. Most of those who reach the top do so only once. They may think of it often, and at times yearn to return, but few ever do so. Earl was one of the exceptions. He climbed Katahdin eight or nine times; he wasn't absolutely sure which. "Usually whenever I came within sight of it, I'd climb it."

The first time, which was in 1948 at the end of his historic hike, had special significance and stood out in his memory. Then two days later, as recorded in *Walking With Spring*, he accompanied four others who were climbing to the top. In 1950 (when he returned to retake some pictures that he first took in 1948 but were destroyed in the developing process) he recalled that the aurora borealis was especially brilliant and actually kept him awake much of the night.

In addition to the start of his 1965 hike and the end of his 1998 hike, there were a few other occasions when he repeated the climb. He recalls one occasion in particular when he climbed Katahdin twice in twenty-four hours, getting to the top one day, descending to Chimney Pond, and then going back to the summit the following day.

HEALTH BENEFITS OF HIKING
Of thru-hiking Earl once wrote in his notebook: "I do recommend hiking as a therapeutic practice but do not recommend the end-to-end version. It might only intensify frustration because only about one in twenty succeeds. Shorter hikes definitely are preferable, providing a more leisurely and less hectic experience.

In the course of laying out new trail routes and finding suitable sites for trail shelters, Earl inevitably spent a good amount of time searching for springs. It often happens in the mountains that places without any apparent water are often hiding pure springs only a foot or two below the surface. Once when speaking to a Boy Scout troop, he discussed his technique for uncovering such hidden springs. He began by finding a ravine that dropped off sharply from at or near the crest. Then he would walk carefully and quietly, step by step down the slope. Not infrequently such exploration was rewarded with the sound of flowing water, even where none was visible. Next he walked slowly back up the hillside to the point where the underground water could no longer be heard. Then he would go back downhill again only a couple of feet. At this point he began moving rocks, sticks, and debris, slowly forming a depression in the earth. When he could see the water that he had been hearing, he would continue digging to open a more generous hole. After he stopped digging, he let the water flow for several minutes until it ran clean, clear, and cold. "Then," he said, "you drink deeply. From this you will develop the uncommon ailment known as 'Mountain Fever.' From this disease one never recovers. It may go dormant for a while, but will periodically break out, luring the victim back to the hills where the only known cure is to be found."

It was just such a spring-finding technique that Earl had used in finding the spring that justified the construction of the no longer existing Susquehanna Lean-to that Earl built on Peters Mountain less than a mile east of the Susquehanna River.

PART SIX

THE INDESTRUCTIBLE LEGACY

CHAPTER 29

WRITING

Earl wanted to be remembered primarily for his writing—and above all for his poetry. His love of poetry Earl attributed to his mother who had taught him to read and write by the time he was five and actually had him copying poems when he was only three.

He considered writing to be the most lasting of all the arts because a written work could be republished and reprinted over and over again without losing any of its original quality. Earl believed that "the written word is indestructible." He commented once, "They say a picture is worth a thousand words; well it is for a certain period of time but in the end the words are more important than the pictures."

Moreover, he considered the English language the finest of all writing instruments. Because it is a "conglomeration" of borrowings from many sources, he thought English was the most expressive of all languages.

When he finished his first hike in 1948, Earl was an as yet unpublished author. During his years in the South Pacific he had compiled a manuscript of war poems, including "The Doughboy Odyssey," later to be the featured selection in the anthology *Before I Walked With Spring*, which was not published until after his death. During the years after he left the Army he also wrote dozens of other poems on a variety of topics, mostly relating to the Appalachian Trail and the natural world.

In addition to *Walking With Spring*, Earl's book production plans included a number of smallish books, each no more than about 200 pages: (1) a book about the way he grew up, the people and the customs of the time—but not an autobiography as such, which he felt would be an exercise in vanity; (2) a book about his years in the Army, including much of the poetry written during that time; (3) a book about the Appalachian Trail and the Appalachian Trail Conference; and (4) a book about his life as an auction clerk and general auction buff.

Until near the end of his life, Earl continued to hope that he might live long enough to see at least one of these dreams fulfilled. "A lot of things I'd like to live long enough to get published," he said. "At the rate I'm going now I won't."

One of the last projects Earl worked on was the *Ode to the Appalachian Trail* which was published after his death by the Earl Shaffer Foundation. He had, at best, mixed feelings about *The Appalachian Trail: Calling Me Back to the Hills* which was published the year before his death by Westcliffe Publishers, with photos by Bart Smith. On the one hand, he was surely pleased that a book he wrote had finally achieved commercial publication, even if the text he wrote was not what he would have preferred. Earl's vision had been for the Westcliffe book to contain the text that later appeared in the *Ode*. Westcliffe, however, insisted on a more traditional narrative. Earl was also concerned that the addition of the many Smith photographs had raised the cost of the Westcliffe book to a level which put it beyond the reach of many of those he hoped would read it.

Finally, he felt that Westcliffe had misled him as to their actual plans for the book as regards both text and title. They kept requesting various changes to the text, always with the assurance that the new draft would be published exactly as Earl submitted it. The book was originally to be called *Ode to the Appalachian Trail*, but then they requested some of Earl's shorter lyric poems to include in the volume. After receiving these, they decided to change the title to *The Appalachian Trail: Calling Me Back to the Hills*. When Earl learned this, he became apoplectic, since his poem by that title had been written in 1942 in the South Pacific, and in no way referred to his hiking the Appalachian Trail. He was finally persuaded to accept the publishers wishes rather than lose entirely the opportunity to have the book published.

Ode to the Appalachian Trail, as published by the Earl Shaffer Foundation, contains Earl's original transcript. One suspects that he would have been pleased.

The influences on Earl's writing were limited but varied. Throughout the war he always carried three books with him: a dictionary, a Bible, and a volume of Rudyard Kipling. He had even removed the covers from the Kipling volume to reduce the weight. He also acknowledged the influence of Shakespeare, Pearl Buck, and Sara Teasdale. The voice of Kipling is an echo behind many of Earl's poems. The Shakespeare influence may help account for Earl's fondness for the sonnet form—with a rhyme scheme patterned after Shakespeare's rather than the Petrarchan (Italian) sonnet. In the poems of Sara Teasdale he admired the originality he perceived in her work.

NO RIBBON FOR HIS TYPEWRITER

Late in his life as he continued to try to advance his writing Earl once lamented the inability to use his typewriter. "I don't have a ribbon for it. It's a beautiful little Smith-Corona, made in England. It works perfectly, but I have no ribbon for it." This was typical of the minor nuisances that so often cropped up to impede his work.

CHAPTER 30

POETRY

Poetry is made up of words, which are the poet's basic building blocks. The storehouse in which those words are to be found is the dictionary. For Earl, his poetry was inextricably linked to his dictionary, and both are based on the English language, which he dearly loved. "In the Army," he said, "when I wasn't writing poetry or whatever, I was browsing through the dictionary. This is the way to get a tremendous command of the language and learn new words because you'd be surprised what you find when you start browsing through." Earl preferred the British English dictionary to the American version, chiefly because of the often unfamiliar meanings given to many words.

"The beauty of the English language," he continued, "is that you can express the same thing in half a dozen different ways using different words. Each one has a special slant to it so you try to use the right word for the right place. And in poetry you want to try to rhyme it, and this is even more difficult."

Earl's concept of poetry was very traditional. Not only did he almost always use rhyme, he also made a practice of crafting every line as a complete phrase. Although he much admired Shakespeare, Earl was uninspired to adopt the Bard's frequent use of the run-on line (or in the technical poetic term, enjambment). He believed that his own insistence on end-stopped lines made the writing more difficult, and depended on a close familiarity with the dictionary.

For as long as Earl could remember, he had been composing poetry in his head, although for many years he never wrote anything down on paper. The fragment mentioned earlier about Walter sitting beside a campfire were the first lines of his own he ever committed to paper. Once he started writing them down, he couldn't stop.

Of his war poems Earl commented that they were written in wildly varying circumstances. "They came out of nowhere, unbidden, because they had to." A poet, he believed, writes under compulsion.

His first complete poem, "Wanderer's Quest" was inspired by James Hilton's novel *Lost Horizon,* and was written early in the war:

WANDERER'S QUEST

Somewhere on this earth there's a valley,
A valley that's peaceful and fair;
Where everyone's friendly and all quickly rally
If trouble should ever come there.
A clear flowing stream between high timbered ranges
All covered with maple and pine;
Where all is serene and life never changes
Leisure and peace shall be mine.
Long have I sought that lone hidden valley
But always have sought it in vain;
Yet each disappointment will cause me to rally
And eagerly seek it again.

Fifty-five years after writing "Wanderer's Quest," Earl finally got around to setting it to music.

———————

Once, toward the end of the war, a plane Earl was on made a refueling stop at Guam. This was the base used by the B-29s that had recently been put into service to intensify the bombing raids on the Japanese homeland. Here Earl got his first good look at the newest American bomber. This brief interval led to the writing of the poem "Queen of the Skies." Later Earl stuck this poem in a letter he wrote to his brother Evan and soon forgot about it. Evan had been trained as a B-29 navigator, but the war ended and he was discharged before seeing any action. Years later Evan came upon it while going through his wartime letters from Earl, and had it framed to hang on his wall.

QUEEN OF THE SKIES

Lean grayish shapes touched with silver highlights
Wolfish and grim as they lie at rest
On the fields of Guam as we pass at midnight
Biding the time of the coming quest.
Sprawling and huge and deceptively slender
Coming to life at the break of dawn
Fueled and well loaded with deadly provender
They climb the sky and are swiftly gone.
Flying the way of the war bird's mission
Far to the North where the target lies
Swiftly and surely to wild destruction,
Our B-29, the queen of the skies.

———————————

When Earl got back from the Army in 1945, he put together a collection of his wartime poems and submitted the manuscript to several publishers. The general tenor of the responses was that there was no longer enough interest in the war to make a book about it profitable—especially poetry. Ironically, by the end of his life, interest in World War II had come full circle and there was a surge of publications about it, as the last veterans of that conflict were gradually dying off.

A SPECIAL POEM

When it came to his writing, Earl Shaffer was a perfectionist. He was constantly revising his work in the endless effort to meet a demanding personal standard. And the closer he got to an anticipated publication date, the more likely he was to fiddle with his word choices or adjust the meter of a line. Even during his final illness, as long as he was able, he continued to revise the writings that he still hoped to see published.

An unusually tangled example of this drive for perfection is offered by the poem "Calling Me Back to the Hills." This was a poem that Earl wrote in 1942 while he was serving in the Army in the South Pacific. It comes across as a lyric expression of the classic homesickness that was being experienced at that time by tens of thousands of young men facing mortal danger for their country in strange, faraway lands. In this case the poet recalls the well-watered hills and valleys of his rural home in central Pennsylvania, now on the other side of the world. "Calling Me Back" evokes a generic scene of forested vistas, without mention of any specific place. In any case, it became one of the hundreds of poems that were steadily accumulating in his hoard.

Many decades later, with his three Appalachian Trail hikes behind him, and his life winding down, the time came when, with the help of various family members, the work of sorting and organizing this mass of writing was undertaken. Ultimately the original copies would be entrusted to the Smithsonian Institution. The work involved the typing of many handwritten manuscripts. Although Earl's handwriting was exceptionally clear, the process of transcribing—accomplished by a number of people—resulted in both misreadings and typing errors. Even when Earl himself typed the manuscripts, they were often harder to interpret than the handwritten ones because of his tendency to use worn-out ribbons.

All the while, Earl was busy making more changes. The upshot was that typed and written versions often did not agree. Indeed, in a number of instances we were left with more than one poem with the same title.

This sort of confusion occurred with a great many of Earl's poems. With "Calling Me Back to the Hills," however, a new complicating factor was introduced. Following Earl's Fiftieth Anniversary Hike, arrangements were made with Westcliffe Publishers of Englewood, Colorado, for the production of a coffee-table book about the hike which would include text by Earl and photographs by Bart Smith. Although Earl wanted to do the text in an "ode" form, the publisher insisted on a more accessible modern narrative. Earl unhappily agreed to redo the text. Then Westcliffe requested some of Earl's poems to be interspersed throughout the book. A number of poems were provided, although when Westcliffe asked for still more poems, Earl called a halt. One of the poems that did find its way into Westcliffe's publication was "Calling Me Back to the Hills."

Finally Westcliffe decided that the title of the book would be *The Appalachian Trail: Calling Me Back To The Hills*. As mentioned previously, this decision infuriated the author and it was only with great effort that Earl's brother John finally persuaded him to accept the publisher's preference for a title rather than forgo the opportunity to have it published at all.

By this time there were already numerous variations of the poem. This was compounded when the Westcliffe book was published with more alterations, and no way of knowing with certainty which, if any, Earl had approved. Thus, almost every line offered choices of which reading should be preferred. Most of the variations were minor, but some were more significant. In the end, however, this remains one of Earl's most haunting poems.

Given below is the version favored by this writer (who hopes that Earl would approve):

CALLING ME BACK TO THE HILLS

The whip-poor-will's call and the laughing owl's song
Are calling me back to the hills,
To the best place of all where I know I belong,
Where the waterfall tumbles and spills.

In my innermost dreams is the sigh of the pines
As the soft siren song of the trails,
With the murmuring streams where the laurel entwines
Found out in the wilderness vales.

In the banner that furls at the closing of day,
Returning at break of the dawn,
In the wood smoke that curls to the sky and away
Is the penchant that's luring me on.

Through the mist of the morning that creepingly swirls
Like wraiths through each little ravine
O'er the meadows unshorn where the dewdrops are pearls
I'll gaze on a half-hidden scene.

I'll awake to the song of the thrush in the tree,
Exultant at daylight's return
And I'll know I belong when he's singing to me
That song for which ever I yearn.

Then I'll seek out that most perfect valley of all
That I've pictured so long in my mind
And submit to the ghostlike yet relevant call
Whose lure is to seek and to find.

I never shall mind if the terrain be strange,
My compass is trusty and true.
I'll just travel blind and scout out the range
And trust to my luck to come through.

I'll sit by my campfire alone in the night
And muse of the present and past
And I'll follow the spire of its soul-stirring light
Till I reach that one valley at last.

———————

Earl left a trove of more than 1,300 poems, of which fewer than 200 have been published. *Ode to the Appalachian Trail* is *sui generis*, a form of Earl's own devising that appears to lie somewhere between prose and poetry. Aside from the *Ode*, the longest of his other poems is "Doughboy Odyssey," which consists of some four hundred four-line stanzas with the second and fourth lines rhyming. The number of stresses per line is variable, with all four lines sometimes having four stresses, and at other times the second and fourth lines having three stresses. "Doughboy Odyssey" records Earl's experiences throughout his service in the Army. The influence of Kipling is readily apparent in this work.

The next longest is "Voyage to Angaur," which is about 670 lines of variable length and meter, grouped in stanzas also of variable length. Rhyming is intermittent and may be only inadvertent. This poem records a forty-two-day voyage, near the end of the war, aboard the troopship *Sea Sturgeon*, carrying support troops and their supplies and equipment from Oahu to Angaur, part of the Palau Islands in the western Pacific where a major battle was soon to take place.

Ode to the Appalachian Trail was published in 2007. "Doughboy Odyssey" forms the core of *Before I Walked With Spring*, published in 2008. "Voyage to Angaur" is included in *South of the Sunset*, published in 2011. All three volumes were published by The Earl Shaffer Foundation, Inc.

Of the remaining published poems 23 are included in *The Appalachian Trail: Calling Me Back To The Hills*; 47 are in *Before I Walked With Spring*; and 112 are in *South of the Sunset*.

CHAPTER 31

MUSIC

There was a time, Earl said, when he rather fancied the idea that he might come to be known as the "Singing Trail Hiker." That never happened, but his love for music remained undiminished.

From Earl's earliest childhood, music was always an important part of life in the Shaffer household. In the absence of anything resembling formal lessons, he absorbed his musical ability through a kind of osmosis, first from other family members, and throughout his life afterward from a variety of others with whom he came in contact. In the beginning it was his brother Dan who gave him his first informal music lessons. Dan had served in the Army in Hawaii where he had acquired some skill with a guitar. Earl, however, started out with the ukulele and progressed from that to the guitar. Often in the Shaffer home there would be family music sessions with Dan and Earl playing guitars, Anna the ukulele and occasionally piano, and Evan the banjo. On Saturday nights the whole family would listen to the "Grand Ole Opry" on the radio.

As time passed, Earl picked up skill in a variety of musical styles, both in his singing and in his playing. Hillbilly styles that he acquired ranged from modern versions to ancient singing styles dating back to colonial times, and perhaps even earlier. In addition to hillbilly, Earl enjoyed classical, ballads, and folk. In the latter category he mentioned the songs of Mother Maybelle Carter. Many of the songs that entered his repertoire were picked up from the radio. He was not particularly fond of bluegrass, but "could tolerate it." Initially, he did not much like swing when it first appeared but eventually came to enjoy it.

He even confessed to liking certain nonsense songs, citing as an example "The Walloping Window Blind" by Charles Edward Carryl, first published in 1885 in a children's book called, *Davy and the Goblin*. The flavor of this song is captured in its first verse:

A capital ship for an ocean trip
Was "The Walloping Window-blind;"
No gale that blew dismayed her crew
Or troubled the captain's mind.
The man at the wheel was taught to feel
Contempt for the wildest blow,
And it often appeared, when the weather had cleared,
That he'd been in his bunk below.

In the final analysis, Earl enjoyed almost any type of music except rock and roll, which he never came to accept.

Over the years Earl acquired an extensive collection of books about music, sheet music, and phonograph records (mostly 78 rpm). His personal accumulation was further enhanced by an extensive collection of records belonging originally to his grandfather. Later it passed to Earl's mother along with the phonograph on which the records were played. According to Earl, the record collection ranged "from Caruso to pop." While Earl was in the Army, the records were given to the USO. Although Earl succeeded in replacing many of them, there were some that he could never find.

YODELING

Earl was long frustrated in his efforts to learn to yodel. He had listened to yodeling on records and on the radio and tried over and over again to master that ancient art. Ultimately he succeeded. He compared learning to yodel to the process of learning to ride a bicycle. In both cases he had tried over and over, first to ride a bicycle and later to yodel. His efforts continued to be met with failure. Then, all of a sudden, it happened; he found himself riding a bicycle. Years later, very similarly, he found himself yodeling. In both cases, the skill proved to be one that, "once learned, is never forgot."

CHAPTER 32

SONG

Earl Shaffer was a prolific poet; he was also a talented amateur musician. It was probably inevitable that at some point he would start putting some of his poems to music, thereby turning them into songs. This process began while he was in the Army, serving in the South Pacific, and continued intermittently for the rest of his life. From time to time he taped himself performing some of the songs. Many of these have been made available on two compact discs by the Earl Shaffer Foundation: *Trail of the Tropic Moon* and *Always in April*.

Earl once wrote a song which he called "Keystone Pennsylvania." This song, he thought, would be a suitable candidate for a Pennsylvania state song, but as far as is known he never actively pursued this possibility. He did, however, record the song which is included on the CD *Trail of the Tropic Moon*.

It is interesting to note that in the recorded version Earl changes the wording in one of the verses from an earlier hand-written version. The earlier lyrics for that verse read:

> When our fathers fought for freedom and the last dim hope
> seemed gone,
> It was Keystone Pennsylvania where the faithful carried on;
> In the fight to save the Union when again hope almost died,
> Gettysburg in Pennsylvania was the turning of the tide.

The recorded version, however, alters the second line as follows:

When our fathers fought for freedom and the last dim hope
   seemed gone,
It was Valley Forge, Pennsylvania, where the faithful carried
   on;
In the fight to save the Union when again hope almost died,
Gettysburg in Pennsylvania was the turning of the tide.

The change is generally seen as an improvement.

PART SEVEN

EARL'S
OTHER LIFE

CHAPTER 33

A PLACE
TO CALL HOME

SHILOH

In 1945, when he finally got out of the Army, Earl returned to The Old Place near Shiloh in York County's West Manchester Township where he lived for the next twenty-two years—sometimes with various other family members and sometimes alone. For most of that time Earl's sister Anna and her husband Fred were the householders. In 1952 a verbal agreement was reached whereby John and his wife, Lois, were to buy the property from the estate. At the last moment, however, Anna also expressed an interest in acquiring it, which resulted in the drawing described in chapter 2, and Anna became the new owner.

The Warble

During the 1950s while Earl's sister Anna and her husband Fred were living at The Old Place they kept goats, one of which, named Mazie, was a large, prolific milk producer. One day a lump was noticed on Mazie's udder, prompting the owners to convey the beast to a veterinarian in nearby Dover. After examining the goat, the medical professional announced that the lump was a cancer and the animal should be destroyed.

Very shortly thereafter—but before any action was taken against Mazie's life—Anna and Fred had a load of stones delivered to be used for surfacing the lane to the house. When he came to the door to be paid, the truck driver, an observant teenage boy, asked, "Why don't you do something about that warble on your goat's udder?" When the boy was told about the diagnosis of the veterinarian, he expressed astonishment, commenting with considerable certainty, "My mother keeps goats, and that is a warble." The treatment, the boy assured them was quite simple and required sterilizing a sharp knife and plunging the tip into the warble to allow the contents to escape, after which the wound would heal itself.

A "warble," it turns out, is a swelling caused by the larvae of the warble fly, a large, hairy, beelike insect that preys on farmyard cattle and wild deer. The eggs laid by the fly find their way to a spot just below the surface of the skin where the hatching larva causes the swelling. When mature, this creature punches a hole in the animal's skin and flies away to enjoy its brief life which may last no more than five days.

In any case, Anna and Fred were reluctant to undertake the surgery recommended by a very young delivery truck driver. Earl came to the rescue, however, and before an attentive audience of a half dozen neighborhood boys gathered around the goat's posterior, inserted the point of a sharp sterilized knife. The result of this action was that Earl and all of the watching boys were sprayed with blood and pus when the pressure within the swelling was released.

The wound quickly healed and Mazie continued to produce high-quality milk for many more years.

ALPINE

Except for his time in the Army and various extended hiking trips, Earl had lived at The Old Place for more than forty years when, in 1967, he decided it was time to leave. A suitable property was found about ten miles northwest of Shiloh near the small community of Alpine. Something over an acre in size, and situated across the road that ran along the east side of Pinchot State Park, the property included a house along the road, a barn, and a smaller house in the rear. Perhaps best of all, this package was available for a bargain price of four thousand dollars. Even so, it was beyond Earl's means. By this time, brother Evan had become a minister with a congregation in New Freedom Borough in southern York County, where he was living with his family. Evan saw the Alpine property and was taken with the notion of someday retiring there. Unfortunately, he too lacked sufficient ready cash to supplement the little that Earl had to a level that would permit purchase of the property. Eventually, the problem was resolved by Earl's putting up about seven hundred dollars, with the remainder covered by a loan from Anna to Evan. Title was put in Evan's name, however, with the understanding that Earl could live in the smaller house for as long as he wished.

Earl duly moved into the small, less modern house, and over the first few years did a good bit of renovation work on the structure, including rebuilding the chimney. Apparently in the process of reconstructing the chimney, he failed to leave enough space or insulation between the flue and the outer chimney. One windy day a chimney fire developed and spread to the roof and much of the second floor. The strong wind was blowing the smoke away and it was a while before Earl noticed it. In the meantime, a neighbor had observed the fire and called the fire department which was only a couple of miles away. The firemen quickly arrived and kept the conflagration from totally destroying the building. As it was, Earl lost many of his most treasured possessions which had been stored on the upper floor, including a valuable guitar and some other musical instruments. Fortunately the most valuable guitar was stored in a wooden case which absorbed the fire damage while sparing the guitar itself. Probably the most valuable lost item of all was an antique powder horn which had been on the upper level of the house. Also lost was a painting of Earl's mother that had been done by his father.

The fire inspector who came to do a report on the incident left Earl with some belated good advice: "Fire rises; don't store anything of value on an upper level."

Earl repaired the fire damage and continued to live in the small house.

Evan's wife died in 1976, and in 1977 Evan decided to move to Haiti. The retirement plan was therefore abandoned. Eventually Evan decided to sell the house to his daughter Kay and her husband Bob. Although Earl continued to live there for a time, friction developed between himself and Evan's son-in-law. According to brother John the main reason the two men did not get along was Bob's dissatisfaction with what John describes as Earl's "unkempt ways."

Once again Earl decided it was time to move.

TRENT'S HILL

Much of Earl's life had been spent in a variety of activities relating to the Appalachian Trail. As he grew older, he developed an ever stronger desire to find for himself a place next to his beloved Trail, where he could both live and establish a hostel to provide an overnight facility for thru hikers. In 1980 he purchased a ten-acre tract adjacent to the Appalachian Trail on Trent's Hill, about a mile south of the Trail's Route 94 crossing. Situated on this tract—presumably—was a run-down stone cabin which Earl contemplated restoring and turning into such a hiker facility.

Unfortunately, properties in this area were the victims of a tangled survey history that stretched back perhaps as far as the 18th century. The situation was further complicated by modifications to the highway alignment which had distorted the survey lines. The upshot was that the cabin, on which Earl had his eye, was found to be not on his land, but on the adjoining tract. When Earl sought to buy the neighbor tract, he found that the Park Service was already engaged in negotiations for its acquisition. In time, the Park Service purchased the tract with the coveted cabin—coveted, that is, by Earl; for the Park Service it was a valueless nuisance.

Earl and the Park Service came to an understanding that he would trade a portion of his land for the portion of the Park Service property that included the cabin, and matters seemed headed for a satisfactory resolution. Both Park Service and Trail Conference staff expressed support for Earl's plans. In anticipation of a favorable outcome, Earl set to work on the cabin, repairing the roof and installing a new floor.

Before long, however, things took what seemed to Earl an inexplicable turn. The Trail corridor was enlarged so that the existence of a building at the spot where the cabin stood would not be allowed, and ATC withdrew its earlier support.

Earl felt that he had been double-crossed by the Park Service and betrayed by ATC. He blamed the Park Service reversal on a relative newcomer to the Trail project. What this man's motives might have been, however, remained a mystery. After four and a half years in the Army, Earl had a low opinion of government bureaucracies, and these wartime sentiments were easily transferable to a peacetime agency. More heartbreaking, however, was the betrayal by ATC, the cause for which remains shrouded in shadows.

Perhaps saddest of all (if true) was the rumor that certain members of the ATC staff feared that the image projected by Earl and his hostel might not reflect well on the Trail Conference.

Eventually Earl threw in the towel and sold his entire tract to the Park Service. By the time this point was reached, an amazing five years had passed, absorbing great quantities of Earl's time. In the end this was time that Earl felt had been completely wasted. The cabin itself was bulldozed by the Park Service, and the rubble hauled away.

PEACH GLEN

When it became apparent that no hope remained of living along the Trail on Trent's Hill, Earl began a search for some other residence. What he came up with was the remains of a farm, minus the farmhouse itself, which had been subdivided off and sold separately. The remaining portion consisted of about six acres with three buildings: a barn, a corn barn, and a chicken house, all of which were in poor condition, but fixable with time and effort. The price was an attractive twelve thousand dollars. The reason the package had not yet been sold was the stench that pervaded everything. It seems the buildings had previously been rented to a man who raised hogs and cattle, but who was seriously remiss about cleaning up after his animals. Manure was everywhere, inside and out, along with the occasional dead animal. Most potential buyers could not get close enough to inspect the property, much less buy it. Earl, it seems, was hardier.

This less than idyllic real estate was located in Pennsylvania's Adams County, within about a mile of the northernmost extension of the Blue Ridge. Earl's property was about a mile east of the tiny community of Peach Glen, and a mile west of Idaville, along the aptly named Peach Glen-Idaville Road. It was also about three miles from the Appalachian Trail. The property Earl had decided to buy had some favorable aspects along with the unsavory ones. The land was on a south-facing slope, with two open acres for gardening and four acres of woodland, containing a magnificent pin oak measuring three feet in diameter, and standing about ninety feet tall. There were also some majestic tulip poplars only slightly smaller than the oak. Bermudian Creek flowed through the woods where springs were also found.

Once an agreement was reached with the Park Service regarding their purchase of Earl's Trent's Hill land, Earl placed a one-thousand-dollar down payment on the Peach Glen property and signed a sale contract clearly specifying that the land and buildings were being sold "as is." Unfortunately Earl had not made adequate allowance for the inevitable bureaucratic delays before he actually received the cash that he was expecting. Days and weeks went by and the deadline for making final settlement on the Peach Glen property drew closer and closer. In the end he had to beg and borrow and sell personal effects to have the money available for closing. The final portion was a three-thousand-dollar loan from his sister, negotiated on the morning of the last day. Earl arrived with the needed payment only minutes before he would have forfeited.

Gradually Earl turned his new property into a reasonably livable place. After first clearing away the accumulated animal waste, he set about remodeling the 16-by-36-foot chicken house into an acceptable dwelling. Initially, he said, he was doing little more than camping out there, but gradually he created a single room with a pot-bellied stove and insulation, and the living got somewhat better. A garden was started and a few goats were acquired. Goats were animals of which Earl was especially fond, and he raised several generations of these beasts in a spacious pasture that was a feature of this new home. The dense thickets of burdock, thistle and multiflora rose were gradually cleared, sometimes requiring the use of an axe to cut them down.

Earl's new home was in the midst of Adams County's apple orchards, where another problem was created by the seemingly perpetual spraying of pesticides. The beekeeping which had become one of Earl's hobbies fell victim to the poisons constantly floating in the air. He lost about a dozen colonies before he gave up the effort.

During the time that Earl was living at Peach Glen, his sister Anna and her husband Fred—as the years advanced—were finding it increasingly difficult to maintain The Old Place. Consequently, the urgings of Evan's family that they move to South Carolina were more and more tempting. At this time John was living on a property that adjoined The Old Place, and did whatever he could to assist his sister and Fred. Eventually, however, they decided to make the long-contemplated move.

In the meantime, Earl approached John with a proposal that the two of them jointly purchase The Old Place, with a view to turning the property into a park and museum. John explored this idea with Township officials and was told that such a use would not violate the current Township zoning laws. When this proposal was presented to Anna, she asked for $125,000 for the property. John and Earl both thought the asking price was too high. Anna then proceeded to sell the property to the present owner even though there had been an understanding when Anna first acquired The Old Place that should she ever want to sell the property, every effort would be made to keep it in the family. After the sale was consummated, Earl and John learned that the selling price had been only $100,000.

A few years later, Anna and Fred found themselves dissatisfied with arrangements in South Carolina and returned to Pennsylvania.

Later Earl wrote sorrowfully to a friend:

> I had hoped to return to the "old place" near York when my sister moved but she sold it to a stranger for twice its actual value, more than my youngest brother who was born there, and I could manage. The buyers are proceeding to ruin the old house.

When Earl came back from his Fiftieth Anniversary Hike in 1998, he returned to Peach Glen where he stayed for a little more than three more years, with his goats and Callie, his cat, who slept at the foot of his bed.

Callie was a recent gift from David Donaldson to replace Earl's previous cat who had died. Also in the crowded little house was a steel filing cabinet that contained his poems and a variety of other writing, as well as stacks of cardboard boxes that held a treasured library of books that he had accumulated over a lifetime.

Earl's cat Callie (PHOTO BY SANNE BAGBY)

Even with his health in steady decline, Earl remained active, both physically and mentally. He picked blackberries that grew wild on his property and sold them on the honor system from a table beside the road. He had a barn full of antique furniture which from time to time he worked at refinishing.

Eventually, however, he became too sick to continue living alone. In February 2002 he moved in with his brother John and John's wife Lois, who were at that time living in a house adjacent to The Old Place. This was as close as Earl ever came to returning to his boyhood home. By April, 2002 he required constant professional care and was transferred to a Veterans Administration hospice in Lebanon, Pa., where he died on May 5.

His remains were interred in the Shaffer family plot in Shiloh Union Cemetery, West Manchester Township, York County, Pennsylvania, along with those of his parents and his sister, Anna, and Anna's husband Fred. The grave marker is inscribed, "EARL V SHAFFER, TEC 4 US ARMY, WORLD WAR II, NOV 18,1918 — MAY 5, 2002." It is expected that Earl's brother John and John's wife will eventually be laid to rest in the plot's two remaining grave sites.

At one time Earl expressed a desire to be buried in Hawaii at the National Memorial Cemetery of the Pacific (locally known as Punchbowl), where his friend Walter Winemiller is buried, because the war "was the ultimate period of my life. The Trail thing is secondary actually."

Another time, when asked where he would choose if he could live anywhere in the world, he replied, "I've often thought the Hawaiian Islands. I often regretted I ever came back. When I was there I should have just got a discharge over there and stayed; that's what I think sometimes."

It seems clear that Walter and his death remained powerful influences on Earl throughout his life.

CHAPTER 34

EARNING A LIVING

BEFORE THE WAR

Earl graduated from high school in the midst of the Great Depression. Coming from a family which, like most others in the land at that time, was barely scraping by, he had little choice but to find whatever work he could. Starting in 1935, right out of high school, he worked mostly on farms until 1938 when he switched to carpentry. After a time he moved on to warehouse work. "That's the way it was in the depression," he said, "you worked for whatever you could find."

What money he did earn went to buy clothing and other essentials. "My family was so poor," he recalled later, "it was a struggle all the time; it was for most everybody in the depression days." Eventually he scraped together thirty-five dollars with which, at the age of eighteen, he bought a Model A Ford. By that time he had already done carpentry and stone-mason work, describing himself as a jack of all trades.

Carpentry

After a while he found a job as a carpenter's apprentice, working fifty hours a week—nine hours a day Monday through Friday plus five hours on Saturday—for the grand total of ten dollars a week. "Of course the apprentice got the dirty work," he commented later; "I spent as many as three days in a row pulling nails."

The work site at that time was twelve miles away from home. Without a car Earl was forced to ride a bicycle—twenty-four miles round trip every day. With such a grind it eventually got to the point that he was falling asleep on the bicycle. More than once he woke up when the bike hit a curb or some other obstruction and pitched him to the ground. Finally he was forced to give up the job.

AFTER THE WAR

When Earl came back to Shiloh after the war, he had to struggle not only with the transition to civilian life, but also with a neighborhood that seemed different from the one he had left nearly five years before. Inevitably there were many missing faces inadequately replaced with many new ones. For a while he spent most of his time in the familiar confines of The Old Place which he worked at fixing up.

General Construction

Although Earl became more than merely competent in almost all phases of construction, he particularly enjoyed working with stone. Late in life he reminisced, "I worked on houses in York that now would sell for anywhere from $150,000 to $200,000 and they sold for $8000 then. Imagine, a two-and-a-half-story brick house in an exclusive section of town for $8000. An average house then sold for two or three thousand."

Old Charlie

One of his most valued mentors in the early days of an informal apprenticeship was a man Earl generally referred to as "Old Charlie." This was Charlie Ehrhardt, a self-employed carpenter who had been engaged by a stone quarry company that had acquired some twenty or so farms with rundown buildings. Charlie's assignment was to go from farm to farm and fix up the decrepit buildings. Earl had been hired with the kind of flexible schedule that would allow him to take off, when the mood struck him, for the trail work which was his first love at this time. He was paid by the hour for the time he actually worked.

Although Charlie had no more than a fourth-grade education, during a lifetime in the construction trade he had picked up a substantial storehouse of knowledge—tricks of the trade that he gladly passed on to Earl; for example: how to jack up a building without a jack. When confronted with a building that seemed beyond repair, Charlie would stand and stare at it for a long, long time. Then he would stare at it some more. Eventually he would say to Earl, "Well, let's take a hold and see what happens." They would work on the project for a time until Earl suddenly realized that they were actually fixing the seemingly hopeless structure. The manager came around and said with amazement, "That was a miracle. I don't see how in the world you guys did that."

They never knew ahead of time what kind of building or what kind of material they would find when they headed to a new job. They worked on every type of farm building at one time or another—everything from house to barn to outhouse. Likewise, they worked with every kind of material.

Once another man approached them. He had fired the company that was building his house, leaving the work half done. He wanted Charlie and Earl to finish the job. Without any drawings, with nothing to guide them except the work that had already been done, they finished the job to the owner's satisfaction.

Another time they were working on an old farmhouse when, upon removing some floorboards, they uncovered a cache of moonshine. The illicit activity was well known in the neighborhood although the moonshiners themselves never got caught. Actually, over the years their stills had burned down a number of the farm's outbuildings.

Earl's brother John, who once met old Charlie, remembers him as being thin and wiry like Earl, although shorter and balding, with gray hair. Earl later paid tribute to this admired teacher by writing a short, five-line poem in his honor:

> Anybody who ignores the church,
> Says wise friend Charlie Ehrhardt,
> Is like a person who builds a house without windows,
> And then blames God
> Because he has to live in the dark.

BUYING AND SELLING

Earl later got into various aspects of buying and selling "just by accident." He would go to sales from time to time to look for material he needed for one of the repair jobs at The Old Place. During one of these shopping trips he encountered "some kind of a cousin, a Shaffer," who was working as a sort of middleman, buying and reselling furniture. The cousin eventually encouraged Earl to watch for the kind of items the cousin looked for and then buy them for the cousin's account.

Earl tells of another middleman he met around this time who had a sign in his front window that read: "We buy and sell anything on earth, including part of it." By this was meant that he would even buy land.

Once when there was a parade in York, this man entered his truck on which he had fixed the "buy anything" sign.

During his buying-and-selling days, Earl first met Paris Walters, with whom he would later go hiking on the Pacific Crest Trail. It was Paris who instructed Earl about the ins and outs of the antique business. Gradually, Earl came to specialize in early American antiques, which he found could turn up in some very unexpected places. Paris, who had been selling to the DuPonts and other comparable clients, knew what such people were looking for. He shared his knowledge with Earl.

AUCTION CLERKING

The Dover Auction was one of the places where Earl often went to look for things to buy. "They had anything and everything," he said. A friend who had been trying a clerking job there decided he didn't like it and suggested that Earl give it a try. Earl did and wound up clerking, primarily at the nearby Mt. Royal Auction, on Friday evenings and Saturdays for about twenty years.

Auction clerking is a more important and responsible position than the title might suggest. The clerk is the individual who keeps track of the final bid on each item, receives the money from the successful bidder, and provides an appropriate receipt. In addition, the clerk must be sure that the item delivered is the correct one in each case. A good auctioneer can move a great deal of material in an hour's time, meaning that the clerk was kept moving. Usually there were two auctioneers who alternated that job, but only one clerk handled it all.

Occasionally, Earl filled in himself as auctioneer but decided it was not something he wanted to do permanently.

TRAIL WORK

The job that Earl preferred more than any other was Trail work, which brought him no income at all. In fact, it actually cost him money since he paid for his own gas to get to the work site and often bought needed supplies which were paid from his own pocket. Although he often complained about the lack of physical and financial help from the trail clubs, he was not about to stop doing the work he loved. In any case, one suspects that when it came to trail and shelter activity, Earl would not have been easy to work with.

CHAPTER 35

THE WAY
THE WIND BLOWS
Philosophical Reflections

RELIGION

On the paternal side of Earl's family the religion was solidly Protestant as far back as is known. Although his maternal grandfather, Samuel Francis (Frank) Gallagher, was born into an Irish Catholic family, he and his two siblings were orphaned while still young, and subsequently raised by a neighboring Protestant family. The children themselves later became Protestant, and Francis married a woman of Irish Protestant heritage. The family in which Earl himself was raised was flexibly Protestant. Depending on the family's circumstances and location the specific denomination might be changed for greater convenience. Nonetheless, the family was quite religious and maintained a family altar and conducted prayer and Bible readings every evening.

As Earl grew older, his religious views became more rigidly conservative. When he was a boy, each day in school was begun with a reading from the Bible but there was no prayer. He endorsed this practice as mirroring his own belief that the Bible should be studied in school, although prayer was inappropriate. Prayer, he felt, should always be a private matter. The Bible, he contended, was the source of our moral code, even though "scientists and unbelievers" were trying to keep it out of school. He believed that the Bible is "literally" true, although he acknowledged that there are problems of interpretation.

He also believed that the Bible provides a good indication of what the future holds for humanity. Regarding a biblical prediction concerning the future abandonment of cities, Earl thought that this would come about because of a decline in food production which would lead to mass starvation. He pointed to contemporary environmental disasters as being the beginning of this process.

"Wherever you don't have the Bible you have barbarity," he once said, although another time he called "fanatical religious groups" a major source of cruelty. Earl was in favor of retaining the death penalty. Although he noted the Biblical justification for such punishment, his primary concern seems to have been the cost to society of maintaining the sometimes long lives of individuals whose sentences were life in prison instead of execution.

He flatly rejected evolution, calling it a "religion" rather than a science. Evolution, he said, was a theory based on a fallacy. If evolution is studied in school, then Creationism should be also. In Earl's view it is obvious that there must have been planning in the universe. The great biblical flood, he believed, is fully consistent with ancient fossils that were formed in layers of mud. He complained that young people go to college and wind up being turned into atheists.

RACE RELATIONS

Earl's opinions regarding African-Americans tended to be very mixed. Until he went in the Army, the only black person he had any contact with was a boy in high school. In one class this boy sat at the desk next to Earl's, and tried to strike up conversations and develop a friendship. Earl tried to avoid him but in the circumstances it was impossible. This situation started Earl off with a poor impression of African-Americans, in general. The black boy, in Earl's opinion, was trying to "act white," but "overdid it."

His first extensive contact with African-Americans came during his Army assignments in the South Pacific. Earl's small Signal Corps group often worked with the much larger 810th Engineer Aviation Battalion, which was one of two black Engineer Battalions that had been organized early in the Second World War. Of necessity, the few Signal Corps personnel shared quarters and mess facilities with the engineers. Earl acknowledges that at first he was uneasy, wondering if "the black would rub off," feeling hesitant about eating food prepared by black cooks.

These concerns quickly passed, however, as regular daily contact led to the development of general cordiality and even friendship. He speaks warmly of a number of the engineers, such as "Tate," the man from Baltimore who after his father's death had supported his brothers and sisters through high school and, for some, even college. When Earl first met him,

Tate's face was covered with recently healed scars from a head-on collision with a truck. Earl commented once that "he must have been too tough to die." Tate was a jack of all trades who frequently wound up with the most difficult jobs. The warm relations between the two reached the point where Tate considered Earl a "special friend."

Another of the engineers with whom Earl developed a friendship was Corporal Jackson, the best steeplejack on the island, who apparently had no fear whatsoever as he worked up on poles only flimsily anchored in coral.

After the war Earl returned to a community and to activities which provided very little interaction with African-Americans. Gradually, as the years passed, his views of blacks appeared to revert to those of his youth and of his neighbors. Basically he seemed to favor the "separate but equal" philosophy that the Supreme Court had ruled unconstitutional. At times he seemed to have difficulty in fashioning his own conflicting views into a coherent attitude. He thought that blacks would be better off if they went back to Africa, while at the same time deploring the inability of blacks in Africa to develop the continent's resources and to end the fratricidal wars that were ravaging the land. He criticized the hypocrisy of southern slave owners who treated blacks like animals but then allowed them to raise the owner's children.

He insisted that there was a different cultural level between whites and blacks, and that "The whole thing is a breakdown away from the Bible." It is hard to believe that the man who spoke admiringly of Tate and Corporal Jackson could be the same one who so reversed himself later in life.

Earl's attitude toward race is further confused by his unalloyed admiration for Native Americans, as will be discussed in chapter 37.

ENVIRONMENTAL CONCERNS

Earl Shaffer's environmental concerns were wide-ranging. Spatially they extended from clearcutting in the Amazon rainforest to the melting polar ice caps; temporally, from the ancient problem of species extinction to a newly emerged viral assault on fruit trees in the very county in which he lived. Earl's musings about these issues produced more frustrations than solutions. Still, when it came to environmental matters, his sympathies were nearly always on the side of the angels.

When reflecting on the problem of species extinction, he was reminded of stories he heard as a boy from his father about the sky-darkening flights of great migratory flocks of passenger pigeons. Relentless hunting abetted by habitat destruction drove this once plentiful bird to extinction only four years before Earl was born. This memory would steer his thoughts to the habitat destruction occurring (still) in the Amazon basin as the result of rainforest cutting. This would in turn bring to mind the periodic flooding of the great South American river. From flooding of the Amazon it was but a short mental step to coastal flooding caused by melting polar icecaps.

Next he was reminded of the periodic flooding in the neighborhood where he grew up, flooding which among other problems caused pollution of the springs on which the family depended. He mused too about a fifty-acre meadow below The Old Place which, with every flood, became a small lake.

At one time when John Shaffer was attending a Township Open Meeting, he was approached at the close of the meeting by the Township Engineer who asked John about the flooding history of the meadow. The engineer's initial interest was in connection with a planned bridge over Derry Creek. On the basis of John's information, however, the engineer's thinking about the area in general was changed. The Township's original plan did include development of the meadow and, in fact, a few houses were built at the edge of the high-risk area. Nonetheless, even at that presumably safer location those houses experience some water damage from occasional floods.

The Township immediately closed the area to any further development, and the treacherous meadow has since become a Township Park and Nature Area.

Elsewhere in the floodplain were some hog farms, an enterprise that produces some of the worst agricultural waste imaginable. That waste would be washed to who knew where by the next flood that came along.

Three Mile Island

In 1979 the worst accident in U.S. commercial nuclear power plant history occurred at Three Mile Island in the Susquehanna River, only about five miles from where Earl was living at the time. This event acutely sensitized him to the inherent dangers of nuclear power. Ever afterward Earl remained adamantly opposed to nuclear power, his principal concern being the disposal of the radioactive waste. He could foresee no possible solution to this issue.

Later in an interview he commented, "If Three Mile Island had melted down, it probably would have wiped out the whole area including Lancaster, maybe Philadelphia, and Baltimore. Because that's the way the wind blows. And also the way the water goes. I would never, never agree to nuclear power."

Plum Pox

In 1999, the year after Earl completed his Fiftieth Anniversary Hike, plum pox appeared in the orchards of Adams County, where Earl was living at the time he was being interviewed for this biography. Consequently, this was an issue much on his mind.

Plum pox is a devastating viral disease that afflicts plums, peaches, and other "stone fruit" trees. The pox is transmitted by aphids, and can be spread by the transfer of infected nursery stock to new locations. Plum pox is not a danger to consumers, and it does not kill the trees, although the fruit yield is reduced and the fruit itself is rendered unmarketable. The only control of the disease at present is to destroy all infected trees, which can be a serious financial burden for commercial producers. The disease appears to have arrived from Europe and made its first U.S. appearance in Pennsylvania in 1999.

The outlook at the time was extremely alarming, and Earl feared he might have to destroy all his fruit trees except for the apples. Although plum pox continues to be a matter of great concern, some progress is being made in efforts to develop a plum variety that is resistant to the plum pox virus.

Wilderness

Wilderness is a treasure that is vanishing before our eyes. Earl once said, "Trees are necessary to life. And people, well, they're not." Overpopulation was the key factor, he believed, in the steady erosion of wilderness everywhere. Trees are essential for the production of oxygen needed to replace all that is being consumed by cars and by industry. We cannot keep using up the world's oxygen supply and destroying trees at the same time. This is putting us on a collision course with disaster. The need for oxygen is an immutable law of nature. A person can live five weeks or more without food; maybe five days without water; but only about five minutes without breathing.

GUNS

Earl strongly favored reasonable gun control and had no sympathy with the National Rifle Association. He did not believe that there was a constitutional right to unrestricted gun ownership, especially concealed weapons and automatic assault weapons.

WAR

The only positive value that Earl could find in war was its tendency to reduce the number of people in a world that he considered already too crowded. Otherwise, his view of wars was that they were "horrible," with each one becoming increasingly deadly. He foresaw the eventual destruction of civilization through nuclear war.

CHAPTER 36

LIFESTYLE

MARRIAGE
On Top of Old Smoky
Earl Shaffer's largely solitary lifestyle—whether wandering in the woods or secluded in some remote and primitive residence—was not particularly conducive to establishing sturdy relationships with women. Still, his life was long enough and varied enough for him to cross paths with many. From time to time a spark would flicker, but no flame was ever ignited. Earl himself wondered much about this tendency to avoid any emotional commitment. When asked late in his life about his inability to connect, he offered a litany of what often sounded like excuses for what others might perceive as character failures.

He would generally begin by noting various characteristics in his own emotional makeup that got in the way of romantic relationships. To begin with, he acknowledged that he was "too particular; when you're too darn particular, you do without. I was too particular." Each woman he met turned out to be either just not the right one or already married. He feared that if he should choose the wrong one, marriage would become a "millstone" around his neck. In any case, Earl suspected that he was simply not cut out for marriage. "I always thought I'd be a lousy husband because I've got a streak of wanderlust in me. I'm just a doggone rover. I could have been a Casanova for Pete's sake."

Earl acknowledged his schoolboy romantic interests. "Oh, when I was a kid I had the usual crushes but I wouldn't even tell the girl; you know how that was when you were a kid." He mentioned, in particular, a girl who was in his grade in school even though she was a couple of years older. She got word to Earl through a third party that she was "kind of partial" to him. Earl's failure to follow up he blamed on his own shyness. His theme song, he wistfully commented, was "On Top of Old Smoky," a traditional folk ballad, from which Earl quoted the lines:

> On top of Old Smoky, all covered with snow
> I lost my true lover, for courtin' too slow.

Earl also thought that his years in the Army were partly to blame for his failure to marry. "I went into the Army when I was twenty-two and came out when I was twenty-seven. Those are the years in which a guy usually gets married."

One woman to whom he was initially attracted turned out to be a smoker. As far as Earl was concerned, smoking was a nonnegotiable character flaw in a woman. Another woman started using makeup after she and Earl met, in the mistaken belief that this practice would make her more appealing to him. The actual effect, however, was just the opposite of what was intended.

"That's the way my whole life has been. I don't know why. They were drawn to me but it never came to anything."

There was one instance when Earl believed the possibility of marriage was very real, but the opportunity collapsed because of interference by his sister Anna. Susan, a schoolteacher from Lancaster, Pa., was about ten years younger than Earl, who at the time was thirty-four. Susan went to Earl's sister for counseling, telling Anna that she (Susan) thought she was in love with two men: Earl and her high school sweetheart. Anna's advice was that Susan's first commitment should be to the high school beau. That was the end of any further romantic developments with Earl.

Once, after the Fiftieth Anniversary Hike had brought a flood of nationwide publicity, Earl commented, "And my stupid sister who was always after me to get married goes and tells her there's too much of an age difference. She went off and married the other guy. And I just got a letter from her lately. She said she'd seen my picture and all; she's in California, so she hadn't forgotten me. My sister prevented me from marrying her. She was a real nice young lady."

Earl acknowledged that Susan was "no beauty," but neither was she "homely." Earl considered her "average looking." The two factors that he found most appealing about Susan were her spontaneity and the fact that she was his equal in intelligence. He even got along well with her parents.

Earl became especially annoyed at the way various relatives and friends were constantly asking him when he was getting married. This went on for a number of years, with Anna foremost among the questioners, even though she had (in Earl's view) prevented his one solid chance at a happy marriage.

Earl's sister-in-law Betty (brother Dan's wife) came in for a lesser share of criticism on the marriage front. Once when Earl was visiting them at their home in Philadelphia, a friend of theirs from next door stopped in to visit. Betty later informed Earl that afterward the neighbor (a married woman) proclaimed Earl "the best looking thing I ever saw in my life." This led Betty to make a practice of telling Earl that he could marry some rich woman and be on easy street for the rest of his life. Earl disposed of this suggestion with the retort, "I'm not a gigolo and I never wanted to be."

Earl's trail activities brought him into contact with a different assortment of women. Once when Earl was attending an ATC meeting in Washington, one of the assistant secretaries appeared to be making a play for him. Another secretary, who thought the first one was being too obvious, abruptly called a halt, and the first one backed off. Although Earl had found her somewhat attractive, he made no effort to maintain a relationship. He said that he was just not that interested.

Another woman he met through the York Hiking Club was Frances, to whom at first Earl was attracted. He quickly realized, however, that she had no interest in his trail activities or lifestyle. Frances was a very religious woman, and objected to Earl's doing trail work on Sundays, even though that was the only day of the week regularly available to him for such work. Frances had a job as a typist, but she would never do any typing for Earl even though he desperately needed such help in connection with his writing. She also refused to pick Earl up at the end of a section and take him back to his car. "It would never have worked," Earl said. "She would have just made an ordinary guy out of me, or we'd have fought all the time. It just wouldn't work."

Dorothy Laker

In the spring of 1964 Earl was hiking alone on the southern Appalachian Trail, traveling from south to north. On May 29, a Friday, after hiking all day in a more or less steady rain he stopped for the night at Curley

Maple Gap Shelter along the Tennessee/North Carolina border. He found the shelter already occupied by a woman who was wearing on her head a pair of slacks, one leg over her head and the other cast over her shoulder. Earl tactfully abstained from commenting on the woman's unconventional headgear.

This was Dorothy Laker, four years younger than Earl, who had herself already thru-hiked the Appalachian Trail in 1957. When she and Earl met in these unusual circumstances, Laker was doing her second thru-hike. She had spent the previous rainy night at Curley Maple Gap and after waking up to more steady rain, decided to wait out the weather under shelter. With the rain persisting, she wound up passing the entire day there. Late in the afternoon she decided to go out and gather wood to try to make a fire. In the process her hair got wet and her head got cold, so when she got back to the shelter, she put the pants over her head to try to warm up.

When Earl first introduced himself, his name did not register with her. Later, in conversation, it was mentioned again and she realized that this was *the* Earl Shaffer. For the next six days they hiked together, apparently fully compatible—until the very end. When they camped at night with no spring nearby, Earl would take their canteens and disappear down the mountain, after a time reappearing silently "like an Indian" with full canteens. In the lengthy piece she wrote for Rodale's two-volume *Hiking the Appalachian Trail* Laker enthused, "How the time flew."

Finally, the time came when they were descending to Damascus where Earl would leave the Trail. As they walked along at Earl's usual brisk pace, with him in front and Laker following, he suddenly stopped so abruptly that she nearly ran into him. In the Trail before them was a rattlesnake. Laker began getting out her camera, hoping there would be enough light to get a good picture, when Earl said he would have to kill the creature because it was too close to a community. And kill it he did, removing the rattles and dropping them into his pocket. Laker was horrified. She blamed herself, reasoning that if Earl had not been hiking with her, he would have been on a different timetable that would not have led to his meeting the rattlesnake.

In Damascus Earl left to return to York. Laker got a room for the night, feeling that she would not be welcome in the woods after what had just happened. They had planned on meeting again when Laker got to Pennsylvania, but after what had just happened she seemed to lose all enthusiasm for Earl's company. They never reconnected.

Earl always thought that it was Dorothy Laker who should have been recognized as the first woman thru-hiker. Mildred Norman Ryder (later "Peace Pilgrim") who is usually given that honor had done a flip-flop which Earl steadfastly refused to accept as a thru-hike. As for Grandma Gatewood, Earl simply did not believe that she had hiked the whole trail.

Years later, while doing his 1998 hike, Earl responded to a question about Dorothy Laker by paying her the highest compliment he could pay anyone: "Dot was a *real* hiker!"

My Poems Are My Children

Earl's family and friends often told him that he would make a wonderful father, a suggestion to which he appeared to be somewhat ambivalent. He believed that he ought not to add to the world's population—which he thought already too large—unless he had a truly solid marriage on which to base a family of his own. He questioned his own ability to hold a marriage together because of his temper. This was a weakness that he could usually hold in check, but "once in a great while somebody will cause it to flare up. And when that happens between married people it can wreck a marriage in a hurry."

In the course of a late-life interview, when Earl was asked if he ever regretted not having children, there was a long, silence-filled pause before he answered softly, "The poems, the poems, they are my children." Another time he said, "The poetry is my children. That's what I leave to posterity, and it's more than most people do."

The Shadow of Walter Winemiller

In the course of a long life, Earl's strongest emotional attachment to another human being, beyond his family, was his powerful friendship with Walter Winemiller. It seems entirely possible that the premature loss of this friend in a shell crater on the beach at Iwo Jima may have so scarred Earl's psyche that he became unable ever again to let himself yield to such an intense personal commitment.

DIET AND HEALTH

When he completed his third end-to-end hike of the Appalachian Trail in October of 1998, Earl Shaffer was within two weeks of marking his 80th birthday. This almost-octogenarian, who had just made the last of his several ascents of mile-high Katahdin, had passed his eight decades in vigorous good health. Except for some minor childhood ailments, he had rarely even visited a doctor. In the mid-1990s Earl wrote to a friend "My thatch of hair is mostly gone. What's left is gray. My health has been generally good, no visits to any doctor since Army days, fifty years ago."

Although he would survive for three and a half more years, his health soon began to deteriorate—slowly at first, but then more quickly from various ailments, signs of which had begun to appear even during his historic trek. Arguably, if he had sought medical advice sooner, he might have extended his life for a few more years. Nonetheless, it must be acknowledged that an eighty-year-old man who could maintain a physically active lifestyle without benefit of physician or surgeon must have been doing something right.

In considering Earl's dietary preferences and idiosyncrasies, it should be kept in mind that during his Army years he had little or no choice in terms of what he had to eat. His Army labors worked up a powerful appetite, and he ate what was given to him.

As a child and young man Earl had observed his father's eating preferences and their effect. A typical Pennsylvania Dutchman, Earl's father favored heavy, rich, fatty foods. He raised pigs because he was especially fond of pig meat. More often than coincidence could account for, the meals his father favored brought the man down with what he called "sick headaches." This experience doubtless contributed to Earl's lifelong aversion to meat: pork he avoided totally, and other meat indulged in only sparingly.

When he was only fourteen, Earl read a book by the physical culturist Bernarr Macfadden. This led to Earl's giving up white bread and white sugar, a practice that he followed for the rest of his life. Earl reports that within six months of adopting Macfadden's advice he gained between thirty and forty pounds and added four inches to his height. This growth occurred, however, at an age when boys often experience dramatic growth spurts. Macfadden may or may not have helped the growth along.

Later in life Earl came upon some of the folk medicine writings of DeForest Clinton Jarvis of Vermont. Jarvis advocated the consumption of a "health tonic" consisting of a mixture of honey and apple cider vinegar. Like Macfadden, Jarvis also rejected white flour and white sugar, to which list he added processed foods in general. He especially recommended eating fish, corn, and apples. Seaweed, especially kelp, was also given his seal of approval. Although Earl was fond of fish, corn and apples, he says nothing about kelp, an item to which he would probably not have had ready access.

Earl enthusiastically embraced both honey and vinegar, although his preference was to take them separately rather than mixed. Cider vinegar he often promoted as a cure-all, recommending a daily dose of up to a tablespoonful in a glass of water. Whenever the symptoms of a cold or flu began to appear, he advised additional doses until the symptoms disappeared. He was adamant in condemning white vinegar, which he described as "whiskey without the alcohol; it's made out of grain, the same as whiskey. That is a big deception, and it's as bad for you as white sugar."

Honey he believed to be a far better sweetener than any type of sugar. For a time he kept his own beehives and collected his own honey. Even after he gave up raising bees, he bought honey rather than sugar for sweetening.

Favorite Foods
Earl's preferred diet relied heavily on vegetables and fruit. For much of his life he kept a garden and grew most of his own food. When called upon for some examples of food preferences, he would cite tomatoes, watermelon, cantaloupe, carrots, and onions—noting that "I eat a lot of onions."

As for protein, he said, "Maybe once a month I might eat a hamburger (but no red meat as a rule). I'll eat fish but not red meat. Once in a while I'll eat some turkey." Earl much preferred turkey to chicken, which he rarely ate, believing it to be more fatty than turkey. He enjoyed many kinds of fish, especially salmon. Tuna he found too bland for his taste. In advocating the consumption of fish, Earl would often cite "an old friend of mine that had cancer so bad they opened him up and sewed him right back together and sent him home to die, and he lived ten years after that by living almost entirely on fish." Seasoning for his various meals was most likely to come from sea salt which he believed to contain most of the same nutrients as those found in fish.

When hiking, he expected to consume two or three times as many calories as he normally would. Many novice hikers, he noted, plan on eating the same number of calories as usual, and then find themselves debilitated. He considered ice cream an acceptable source of additional calories. Peanut butter, too, he found to be a good calorie source, provided it was not the "creamy" type, which he thought to be chemically treated. He despised freeze-dried foods and the noodles which many of them contain.

Earl followed no fixed meal schedule. Some days he ate the traditional three meals; other days he would have a late but hearty breakfast, after which he would not eat again until evening.

Doctors

Earl did not have a high regard for the medical profession in general. Most modern doctors he described as "chemical doctors," and believed them to be part of an extensive conspiracy to turn natural remedies into chemicals that could be put in bottles and sold for a profit. Although he acknowledged some modern efforts to return to natural treatments, he thought that most doctors still opposed it. "The Medical Association doesn't want cures that will eliminate their medicines because it's a big business."

Always the Sunday Paper

After he returned from the Fiftieth Anniversary Hike, however, it was not long before his health began deteriorating. In an interview at that time he said: "Since I'm back, I'm handicapped by poor health, medications and visiting doctors at the Veterans Administration." Medications were costing Earl about three hundred dollars a month until the V.A. finally started sending him pills directly.

One day he reported having pains in his chest: "Most people would have ended up in the hospital thinking they were having a heart attack, but I just wait until it goes away. Some day it won't; then there'll be a funeral. Ha ha!"

He even began considering the possibility of selling everything and going into a retirement home where he could walk for exercise and get on with his writing. This would have been a dramatic change in Earl's lifestyle. "I'm changeable," he said, "but I always buy the Sunday paper because that keeps me up on current events."

CHAPTER 37

KINZUA DAM

A treaty forever George Washington signed.
He did dear lady, he did dear man,
And the treaty's being broken by Kinzua Dam
And what will you do for these ones?

—Buffy Sainte-Marie
"Now that the Buffalo's Gone"

Probably influenced by the Shaffer family's general belief that some Native American blood flowed in their veins, Earl throughout his life was very sympathetic to the plight of those earliest Americans. He was passionate in their defense and, on at least one occasion, an activist in their support. Earl's great-grandfather on his mother's side, Daniel Gallagher, came to this country during the potato famine of 1845–52. Eventually—according to family tradition—he married a woman named Mary Ellsworth who was half Native American, and is known to have lived at one time in LaPorte, Iowa. If true, this would make Earl more than six percent Native American—not much obviously, but enough to be proud of.

At one time Earl's brother John and his sister Anna interviewed a neighbor of their maternal grandfather Samuel Francis Gallagher, who was the son of Daniel and Mary. Samuel Francis, also known as Frank, would therefore have been one fourth Indian. In family photos of Frank there can be seen the high cheekbones that are typical of Native Ameri-

Kinzua Dam (PHOTO: U.S. ARMY CORPS OF ENGINEERS)

cans. Frank's neighbor told John and Anna that their grandfather had a complete Indian Chief's headdress as well as other artifacts. At times he would wear the headdress and perform some of the Indian dances. These Indian relics were unfortunately disposed of in a public sale held after the death of Frank's second wife.

At that time the Irish and Native Americans were both near the bottom of the social ladder. One problem the two groups shared, in Earl's view, was that when they were not fighting outsiders, they were fighting among themselves. This is what prevented the formation of a broad alliance among all the Native American tribes to resist the Caucasian invasion.

In Pennsylvania, the Native Americans initially received better treatment than elsewhere. William Penn and his family at least paid for the land they took, although the amounts were quite modest. Later, Benjamin Franklin tended to be sympathetic to the natives. This attitude did not last long, however. First there was the infamous Walking Purchase of 1737. In what the *Encyclopedia Britannica* described as a "land swindle," officials of the Pennsylvania colony claimed to have found a lost treaty of 1686 whereby the Delaware tribe had agreed to give to Pennsylvania a tract of land extending from the junction of the Delaware and Lehigh Rivers as far as a man could walk in a day and a half. The Indians understood this distance to be about forty miles. Thomas Penn, however, hired three men who specialized in rapid walking and offered rewards to whoever went the farthest. The winner covered a distance about twice as much as the Delaware tribe expected. Their protests were to no avail, however, and all the good will previously established between the Penn family and the Delawares was dissipated.

Still later, the Treaty of Canandaigua became another source of bad feeling. Signed in 1794 by representatives of the Six Nations of the Iroquois Confederacy and by Thomas Pickering as the official representative of George Washington, the President of the United States, the treaty purported to affirm peace and friendship between the United States and the Six Nations. The treaty also extended to the Six Nations in perpetuity extensive land rights in New York and Pennsylvania.

As long ago as the 1920s, a proposal surfaced to construct a giant multi-purpose dam in Warren County, Pennsylvania. The Kinzua Dam— named for a small town that would shortly cease to exist—to be built along the Allegheny River, would provide flood control for Pittsburgh and other downstream areas, it would generate electric power, and it would offer extensive outdoor recreation opportunities. It would also flood some ten thousand acres of tribal lands that had presumably been given to the Senecas in perpetuity by the Treaty of Canandaigua. The flooded area would include the last Seneca land left in Pennsylvania, and require the relocation of 130 Seneca families

From the very beginning the proposal was bitterly protested by the Senecas and by many others who sympathized with their plight. Nonetheless, the Kinzua Dam was authorized by the Flood Control Acts of 1936 and 1938. Actual construction did not begin until 1960, and was completed in 1965. Protests continued throughout this time.

Among the many groups and organizations working to have the plans for the dam revised so as to flood less of the Seneca lands was the *Treaty of 1794 Committee*. This largely Quaker group adopted as its motto: "Great nations like great men should keep their word." The Quaker interest in the Kinzua Dam issue grew out of their historical involvement in the negotiation of the 1794 treaty and their subsequent designation of themselves as guarantors of the terms of the treaty.

Earl's interest in the Kinzua Dam was sparked by his own long-standing concern for American Indians and their historical mistreatment. In time, he became involved with the *Treaty of 1794 Committee* and participated in many of their activities. On August 11, 1961, President Kennedy announced that he could not (or would not) halt the construction of the dam which was already in its early stages. The following day, August 12, the Committee began a twenty-four-day "vigil," during which participants lined the highway at the dam site and spoke to thousands of motorists about the government's breaking a solemn 167-year old treaty. On weekends during the vigil, Earl drove to northwestern Pennsylvania to lend his support.

The August 29, 1961, issue of *Kinzua Vigil Newsletter* concludes with a poem by Earl expressing the sadness laced with outrage felt by all the Vigil participants at the shameful violation of a solemn treaty.

THE QUESTION OF KINZUA

In the valley called Kinzua, where the Allegheny flows
Through the fertile fields and meadows and between the
    mountains high
Dwell the Seneca forever—so the treaty wording goes—
But forever is no longer and that promise is a lie.
Lo, the fathers of our country struck a bargain, signed and
    sealed,
That the tribe should have this remnant of their once far-flung
    domain,
That the enmity and rancor of the bloody past be healed
And the Seneca should never be harassed and shorn again.
As the Cherokee was driven from the land of Wala-Si,
As the Delaware was hounded from the valley Minisink—
Is the outrage never over? Must avenging angels cry
To deter the rank maneuver and the politician's wink?
Let the judgment be impartial. Isn't there a better way?
Must we take the reservation? There is still a chance to choose.
Has America a conscience? Does injustice rule today?
Will the people of Cornplanter be the only ones to lose?

                                    —*Earl V. Shaffer*

CHAPTER 38

TOMORROW'S WORLD

ON CLOTHES AND BIG KNEES

As Earl grew older he found himself increasingly at odds with the world around him. In his hiking life, he had on occasion taken a wrong turn and followed the path for a time into strange places where he did not want to be. Now more and more in his everyday life he would stray from the trail he had set out on, and getting back became ever harder. His estrangement from the world he had wandered into began with the very clothes he wore.

When shopping for clothes he found it increasingly difficult to obtain items that he could wear comfortably. This was especially true of pants. The chief problem was Earl's knees, which he described as big and knobby. Most American pants were tight around his knees and flopped awkwardly below. Foreign-made garments often fit him better than those made domestically. The best shopping strategy of all, however, proved to be secondhand shops where he could usually find something that suited both his fancy and his build.

On the bright side of this problem, however, was the fact that Earl had never had any knee trouble. Working on farms as he grew up had given him big strong knees, knobs and all.

COMPUTERS

Earl was willing to acknowledge the usefulness of computers, up to a point. Unfortunately, in his view, many of the uses to which they were put were either nonsense or criminal. There was a time when the theft of a million dollars was a major undertaking requiring the skills of a master criminal. Now a bright teenager might pull off such a stunt with a few keystrokes. As with most modern technological advances, the good done by computers is often outweighed by their potential for evil. On the other hand, the computer in a certain sense plays a role comparable to that of the Colt 45 which earned that legendary firearm the nickname of the "great equalizer." As the old saying goes, "God made men, but Sam Colt made them equal." A modern home computer gives ordinary people the ability to compete with great institutions.

METAL DETECTORS
At the end of the Fiftieth Anniversary Hike in 1998, Earl and his brother John flew from Portland, Maine, to New York City for Earl's appearance on "The Today Show." This was Earl's first flight since his World War II days. As he walked through the metal detector, he set the device off and started some commotion. The culprit, it turned out was the metal-toed hiking boots he was wearing.

He had a similar experience at the York County Courthouse where in the past he had been accustomed to wander freely as he searched titles or for other reasons. Things had changed by the last time he visited there. Not knowing what the metal detector was, he started to walk around it, rousing the ire of the suspicious attendant.

THE FUTURE
Earl's expectations for the future were darkened by a pervasive pessimism as he neared the end of his life. Despite the abundances of technological advances he had observed during his many years, he failed to find any corresponding improvement in the human condition. Indeed, as technological miracles proliferated, the quality of life in general experienced a proportionate decline. World War II marked for Earl Shaffer the turning point after which humanity gradually began a slow but accelerating slide downward which continues into the present. It required little prompting for Earl to launch into a litany of human failings ending with the flat assertion that he would not want to live fifty more years. All of the troubles that he cited he saw as a clear sign that we were entering the "end time."

MORAL STANDARDS
The gradual erosion of the traditional moral codes, Earl believed would "be the downfall of this country eventually." This was the pattern

followed in the collapse of many past civilizations, ancient Rome being a perfect example. A popular addiction to sports was part of the pattern. In Rome it was watching the gladiator battles in the Colosseum, an amphitheater that would hold fifty thousand bloodthirsty citizens. In the U.S. spectator sports are generally less violent, but often no more uplifting. Earl blamed Dr. Benjamin Spock whose teachings about child-rearing, in Earl's view, unwisely turned parents away from the traditional disciplines.

LEGAL SYSTEM
Earl believed that the courts—and especially the Supreme Court—have seized more power than the Constitution intended them to have. "It's become more difficult to have true justice," Earl said. He did not think that plea bargaining should be allowed. Also undesirable, in his view, is the seemingly endless number of appeals that can be made. It just encourages people to shop around until they get a favorable ruling. The large number of lawyers in this country is also an obstacle to speedy and fair justice. He claimed that "there are more lawyers in all the United States than the rest of the world combined."

"Our justice system in this country," Earl said, "is supposed to be based on the laws of Moses." He then went on to itemize what he claimed were included in those laws: "The death penalty was used in the case of gay people or perverts, and also in cases of adultery. If they were caught in adultery they were stoned, same with gays. And if a man raped a virgin he had to marry her even if he already had a wife, and he could never divorce her. Wouldn't that change things if they had it now!" He avoided, however, stating specifically whether he would favor the modern application of such punishments.

PART EIGHT

THE FINAL CLIMB AND DESCENT

CHAPTER 39

REPRISE

THE PRELIMINARIES

As the years slipped by, one by one, drawing steadily closer to the fiftieth anniversary of his first thru-hike, Earl grew more and more restless. He decided that he would simply be unable to stay home on such an occasion. His brother Dan said that Earl had developed "itching feet," recalling perhaps the time many years ago when their maternal grandfather had left The Old Place, never to be seen again, after telling their mother that he had to move on because his feet were itching.

It may have been itching feet that provided the primary impetus for Earl's wanting to return to the Trail, but that was not the only driving force. One of the reasons for the first thru-hike had been the hope that it would generate enough publicity to facilitate the publication of his poems—especially the war poems. Although he dreamed of becoming known as "the poet of World War II," that hope failed to materialize. What publicity he did receive was neither as abundant nor as enduring as he had wished. In the years since then, he felt that he had been marginalized. His reputation and recognition had dwindled. He failed to find a publisher for his poems, and only barely succeeded in getting *Walking With Spring* published—and that more than thirty years after the event. He reasoned that if he were to repeat the hike now, in his eightieth year, he might get more notice and perhaps find the publisher that had managed to elude him all these years.

Once he had made up his own mind, there came the challenge of presenting the project to the rest of his family. Earl, by this point in his life, was enough of a realist to accept that at his age he would need more support from his family than had been needed in 1948. The initial reactions of his sister and brothers were all colored by apprehension, and tempered by awareness that if Earl had made up his mind, they were unlikely to dissuade him.

Earl appears to have presented the planned hike not as a thru-hike but merely an Appalachian Trail hike that would take him as far as he could comfortably walk, at which point he would return home. Brother Dan accepted this version of Earl's plans, commenting, "I knew that he wasn't crazy enough to kill himself and it's what he enjoyed doing . . . so I thought, 'there he goes, he's happy.'"

Anna was probably the most resigned of Earl's siblings. "By that time I knew it was no use to fuss to my brothers about anything," she later said. She did confess, however, that this time she worried that her brother's lifeless body would at some point be discovered along the Trail.

Evan was the least worried of them all. He was concerned naturally, but he described Earl as being tough as nails. "I had some apprehension; I knew what he was facing. And I knew his age."

It was John who worried most. A year or so before announcing his Fiftieth Anniversary hiking plans, Earl had experienced a few fainting spells. He finally agreed to go into the hospital for a battery of tests to try to determine the cause of the fainting. This was his first time in a hospital since his Army days, fifty years before. John dismissed the physical examination Earl was given prior to his discharge by saying that the Army doctor "didn't really care other than if he was breathing; they didn't do much of a physical then."

The hospital tests found nothing wrong, and it was concluded that the cause was probably dehydration. The hospital discharged him, and a few days later he passed out at a sale. On that occasion he was taken directly to a hospital from which he called John to say, "Come and get me."

Not surprisingly, when Earl informed John of his new hiking plans, John at first dug in his heels. He asked Earl if he was really in condition to undertake a long hike. Earl's response was, "Yeah, I'm all right now." John continued to worry, however, and insisted that he and Earl take a three-day hike together to assess Earl's fitness.

When Daniel learned about the fainting episodes, he told John that they should not let Earl go. "Make him stay home," Dan said. John scoffed at this proposal, noting that it would be impossible to stop Earl if he was determined to go. "The best we can do," John said, "is go out and hike with him and see if he's up to it. Maybe after three days he'll decide he can't do it."

It was decided that Dan would drive his two brothers to Caledonia State Park where they would start hiking toward Pine Grove Furnace State Park, a distance of about twenty miles. They finished the distance in only two days. Earl did well, John remembers, with no signs of passing out, or any other problems for that matter. "We were both slow going uphill," John reported. "I was overweight and Earl was out of shape. And older!" After this test there were no more objections, and planning moved ahead.

BACK ON THE TRAIL

Earl had decided that he would start the hike no earlier than May 1 and no later than May 20. The reason for selecting this window was twofold. First, he anticipated that starting during this period would minimize the risk of dangerous weather in the Southern mountains, while still bringing him to Katahdin before the winter shutdown. Second, he knew that the great annual flood of hopeful thru-hikers would have started at Springer in March or April. He wanted that crowd out of his way when he set off. The drop-outs would by then be gone, and the remaining aspirants would be well on their way toward Maine. As it happened, this plan meshed nicely with a major Shaffer family event scheduled for the first of May in Greenville, South Carolina, where Earl's brother Evan was planning his second marriage. Most of the family, of course, would be there for the occasion, thereby facilitating Earl's travel needs to the start of the hike.

As boys, Evan and Earl had hiked many a mile together, some on the Appalachian Trail, some elsewhere. Although Evan might have liked to accompany Earl to Springer Mountain, and perhaps even walk with him for a ways on the trail, this was not possible since Evan had contracted polio at the age of twenty-seven, leaving him with impaired use of one leg. (Of course, Evan's new wife might have taken a dim view of her new husband's embarking on such a trip the day after their wedding.)

In any case, on the second of May, Earl was transported to the southern terminus of the Appalachian Trail on Springer Mountain, accompanied by so many relatives that two cars were needed to accommodate everyone. One of the family members in the entourage was Evan's oldest son, Bobby who, at the age of sixteen, had been introduced to hiking by his uncle Earl when the two of them took a weeklong trek on the A.T.

from Groseclose to Catawba in southern Virginia. Bobby's role in 1998, however, appears to have been to monitor Earl's hiking performance for a few days to be sure the older man seemed fit enough for the major challenge he was undertaking. By the time they reached Neels Gap, after hiking thirty miles, Bobby was reassured and left the Trail to fly back to his job in Seattle.

For most of the '98 hike, one way or another, Earl was kept track of by various family, friends, other hikers and assorted trail people. In addition to the human watchers, John had sought to make use of modern technology by convincing Earl to take with him a cell phone for communication with the home folks, and a small plastic radio to provide himself with weather reports. It was not long before both gadgets came back to John in the mail. Of the cell phone Earl commented that it didn't always work in the mountains, and anyway it was too heavy. As for the radio Earl noted that it was not really much help since even if he knew it was going to rain, there was nothing he could do about it in any case.

During the early part of the hike much assistance was provided by Gail and Dan Johnston, whom John describes as Earl Shaffer groupies. The Johnstons, friends of the Greenville Shaffers, were both A.T. hikers themselves—Gail a thru-hiker and Dan a section hiker. They had become ardent admirers of Earl, to the extent that upon completion of his hike, Gail requested a souvenir—specifically a shirt that Bobby had given to Earl, and which Earl had worn during much of the hike. She was somewhat disappointed, however, because the shirt when she received it had been laundered and no longer had the "trail smell" that she had hoped for.

Until Earl reached the area of Damascus, Virginia, the Johnstons periodically drove to where they believed him to be and, after finding him, delivered food and other supplies—not to mention such delicacies as applesauce cake. They also provided email reports on Earl's progress to John and others.

Beyond Damascus the drive became too much for the Johnstons to undertake on a regular basis. From here on, the task fell chiefly to John and his family. As often as possible one or more would drive, usually on a weekend, to where they thought Earl probably was. Sometimes he was easier to find than others.

On one occasion John and his daughter Robin drove down to the Roanoke area, as did John's son David with the latter's daughter Maggie. They all spent the weekend prowling around in an unsuccessful search

David, Earl, and Maggie Shaffer in Virginia

for Earl. Eventually, because of other obligations, John and Robin had to return home, while David and Maggie stayed behind to continue the search one more day. This turned out to be a possibly lifesaving decision for Earl. The following morning they encountered a hiker who informed them that Earl was in urgent need of water. From his own dwindling supply the hiker had given Earl a pint, but without more—and soon—Earl would be in grave danger. David and Maggie loaded up with a generous quantity of water and headed up the Trail. Within a couple of miles they caught up with Earl who, as he later wrote in the *Ode*, "drank two quarts without stopping." When Earl finished drinking, they exchanged information and learned that the previous day the searchers had missed Earl at Boy Scout Shelter by a matter of minutes.

When Earl reached the Appalachian Trail Conference headquarters in Harpers Ferry, West Virginia, in the middle of July, there was a modest celebration with a special cake that featured a picture of Earl in the icing. This was all arranged by Laurie Potteiger of the Conference staff. Laurie hiked along with Earl and Bill Bowden, a reporter from the *York Daily Record* for the 18 miles from Harpers Ferry to Turners Gap in Maryland where they were met by Laurie's husband, Dick, who then shuttled them back to Harpers Ferry. It was during this walk that Laurie began to seriously worry about Earl's ability to successfully complete his trek, even as

The cake that awaited Earl
at Harpers Ferry

she acknowledged Earl's excellent physical condition. Weighing in the balance the weather he would likely encounter in New England because of his steadily slipping timetable; the increased length and degree of difficulty of the Trail since his previous two hikes, and his age; she concluded that the odds were heavily against him. Such thinking led her to believe that Earl's best strategy would be to do a flip-flop hike.

A "flip-flop hike" is one in which the hiker starts at one end of the Appalachian Trail (usually the southern end), walks to some point near the middle of the trail, then travels to the other end to walk back to the point at which he made the flip-flop. There has not been much controversy about this hiking strategy, as such. It's main advantage is that it minimizes the opportunity for bad weather to prevent completion of a planned hike. Even Earl acknowledged that a flip-flop could be a godsend for many people. His objection was to calling such a hike a "thru-hike."

Fortunately, we have in Earl's own words his definition of a thru-hike. The following statement was recorded by David Donaldson in the course of one of his interviews with Earl following the 1998 hike:

> A thru-hike is when you start at one end and go through to the other end without skipping and without any unnecessary delays. In other words, do it in one season from one end to the other in a continuous journey. That is a thru-hike. A lot of people do the flip-flop and claim that they did a thru-hike which can't be done because you can't go through a tunnel halfway and then go through the other half the other way. It just doesn't work that way; you don't go through. Some do part of it and they won't make it, maybe they do half or better one year then come back the next year and finish it out. That's two trips. That's not a thru-hike. But some try to claim that, even though they're incapable of doing the thru-hike. And the thru-hike is the hard part; therefore it should be recognized as such.

Laurie did not immediately broach her suggestion to Earl, but rather to his brother John. When John mentioned the idea to Earl, along with all of the arguments in its favor, Earl's reaction was predictable. Once he had established a principle for himself, however misguided it may have been, he stubbornly adhered to it. He dismissed with scorn any thought of his doing a flip-flop. He would do a genuine thru-hike or he would fail. There could be no compromise.

As it happened, the following day was to be the Gallagher family reunion in Harrisburg. The Gallaghers were Earl's mother's family, and he wanted to attend the reunion. Bill Bowden offered to take Earl with him back to York. (This was a rare instance of the media providing a service to Earl, rather than the other way around.) The offer was accepted, and Earl arrived in York around midnight. The next morning he and John drove up to Harrisburg for the family festivities. They left early, however, because Earl wanted to stop at his house to see if he could find a better pack since he thought the one he had been carrying was somewhat big. The only alternative possibility he found at home was a little too small, so he wound up retaining the same pack. John then took him back to the point where he had left the Trail, and Earl walked five more miles before stopping for the night.

Another seventy miles brought him to Hunters Run in Pennsylvania, very near his Adams County home. At this point Earl decided to hitch-hike home for the night and return the next morning. Not surprisingly, while in Pennsylvania family contacts became more frequent. Brothers John and Dan and their wives met him at Route 501 and drove him to a store for supplies. John met him once again at Port Clinton, the last of their meetings in Pennsylvania.

Earl's passage through Massachusetts brought an unusual change of pace. Mary Margaret Kellogg, a generous benefactor of the Appalachian Trail, having heard about Earl's extraordinary effort in his eightieth year to hike the whole trail a third time, expressed an interest in meeting him. The Conference, of course, was eager to please such a valuable resource. Reflecting perhaps the prickly relationship with Earl at that time, Conference officials elected to solicit the help of brother John in setting up the requested meeting. It was finally decided that Earl would go first to the residence of the Vinings, neighbors of Mrs. Kellogg, who lived across the road in South Egremont. Joined by John and Dan and their wives, Earl had supper with the Vinings and discussed plans for the meeting with Mrs. Kellogg that was scheduled for the next day. When the meal and talking was finished, the Vinings offered Earl a bed for the night. The celebrity hiker, however, in his typically idiosyncratic style expressed a preference for sleeping in the barn that he had earlier noticed on the property. The record does not show how the Vinings reacted to this unexpected request, but it was duly honored and the following morning's meeting proceeded to everyone's satisfaction.

THE KINDNESS OF STRANGERS
The assistance of relatives and friends in accomplishing a project as ambitious as Earl's 1998 hike is certainly a precious resource. But there are a limited number of such people, and they tend to be clustered in one area, whereas the Trail itself extends over more than two thousand miles. If the slack is to be taken up, some reliance must be placed on strangers. And such there were aplenty, although perhaps not all strangers in the truest sense of the word. They may never have known Earl personally, but they certainly knew of him and admired him and wanted to touch him in some symbolic way. Add to these a number of total strangers who offered assistance and encouragement to an aged man carrying a heavy pack along a difficult way, and you end up with a sufficiency of support to see him through.

As Earl neared Damascus, Virginia, having covered more than 400 miles, he stopped one day to rest at a shelter where a forestry worker came by to talk. At the conclusion of their conversation, the workman said, "More than half the hikers drop out before Damascus, but you'll make it. You have the look." Such encouragement is spiritually as nourishing as even a soggy cinnamon bun to a hungry man.

Having taken a side trail to Mt. Rogers, which at an elevation of 5,729 feet is the highest peak in Virginia, Earl was approached by a day hiker who had brought along his copy of *Walking With Spring* in hopes of encountering Earl, who provided the requested autograph. In exchange, the stranger gave Earl a Swiss Army knife.

Near Pearisburg, Virginia, there was a sign on a tree that commanded, "Earl, go down to Woods Hole, Tillie's breakfast is famous, Tim and Gary." Earl did go down, and the breakfast lived up to its billing.

At Glencliff, New Hampshire, he met a couple who invited him to spend the night, before returning him to the Trail the next morning. Upon departing, they gave him a stocking cap which the steadily dropping temperature made more than welcome.

In the White Mountains at Lonesome Lake Hut where he made a brief stop, the caretaker on duty gave him the soggy cinnamon bun mentioned earlier. He reached Galehead Hut in cold, foggy weather and asked to stay for the night. The crew said he should have gotten a reservation, but after some discussion decided to let the old man stay anyway.

PUBLICITY

The Appalachian Trail is a footway more than two thousand miles long that meanders across the highlands of the eastern United States from Georgia to Maine. It is certainly not a straight line, but it is still a relatively narrow two-directional path. During the hiking season it can become crowded, not only with the smallish number of aspiring thru-hikers, but also with the considerably larger number of section hikers, as well as the weekend and holiday swarms of day hikers. Even so, it would not seem at first glance to be conducive to the easy transmittal of word-of-mouth communication from one end to the other. Contrary to such an apparently logical assumption, the Trail has proven itself a surprisingly efficient medium of communication. Although the thru-hikers are mostly headed in one direction—south to north—the other hikers are as likely to be headed in one direction as the other. And hikers are constantly passing one another; those going in opposite directions obviously, but also those traveling in the same direction as they intermittently overtake and fall behind each other. The result of all this intermingling has been the creation of a startlingly efficient communication network. From that day in May 1998 when Earl set off from Springer Mountain, the A.T. Communication Network was activated, and it was not long before the news had raced all along the length of the great pathway: *Earl Shaffer's back on the Trail.*

The publicity that Earl hoped to generate was slow enough in getting started. The first media contact did not come until he had completed more than four hundred miles. At the Kincora Hostel in Tennessee where Earl had stopped for the night, a friend of Bob Peoples, the proprietor, who worked for the local newspaper visited to get an interview. Another fifty miles brought Earl to Damascus, Virginia, where a local reporter interviewed him as well as some other hikers. In this instance the story was picked up by the Associated Press and given wider distribution.

By the time Earl reached central Virginia, the level of media attention was approaching a crescendo. Since the hiker himself was largely unreachable, it was brother John who had to field the mounting inquiries. He kept a list: ABC "Nightline," CBS, NBC, NPR, and even the Canadian Broadcasting Corporation. After conferring with Earl and some other advisors, it was decided to agree to a meeting with the NBC "Weekend Today" show in the Shenandoah National Park. This took place shortly after the Fourth of July and delayed Earl for most of three days. In the midst of all this, a reporter and photographer from the *Philadelphia Inquirer* appeared and accompanied Earl for several miles when he resumed his walk. Later at the Lesser Shelter just before leaving Virginia, Ernie Imhoff of the *Baltimore Sun* turned up and walked with Earl for a time.

In John's words, "The news media was just hounding us; they wanted to meet up with Earl." John began by giving them vague responses that he hoped were unspecific enough to keep them from actually finding his brother. When some succeeded in slipping through John's web of obfuscation, he resorted to providing downright misleading directions. In spite of the most devious of efforts, some would occasionally locate Earl. When he reached the Birch Run Shelter in Pennsylvania, awaiting him there were two reporters from the Associated Press who "tagged along" for ten miles to Pine Grove Furnace State Park where they watched to see if he would eat the traditional half gallon of ice cream. (He did.)

At ATC Headquarters in Harpers Ferry, along with the cake and other festivities, there was an informal news conference including, as previously noted, Bill Bowden of the *York Daily Record*. Farther along, at the ATC Regional Office in Boiling Springs, Pennsylvania, there was another small news conference. In New Jersey, reporters were waiting at the High Point State Park Headquarters. Again, in Massachusetts there were reporters in South Egremont following the meeting with Mrs. Kellogg.

AND SO IT GOES
In the middle of August, on a mountain near the Connecticut/Massachusetts line, Earl encountered Linda Ellerbee, a prominent journalist whose career began in the print medium, moved to radio, and then to television. She became an important personality on NBC, and later a mainstay of the Nickelodeon Channel. Unlike the other journalists who bedeviled Earl's hike, Ellerbee was not out there looking for him. Their meeting was purely fortuitous. She had made a practice of celebrating her birthday (August 15) by taking a solitary hike, making it each year somewhat longer than the previous one. In 1998 she was marking her fifty-fourth birthday with a forty-mile hike which was in its third day when she saw Earl coming along the Trail. Her first thought, she tells us, when she saw this bedraggled old man carrying an ancient pack and wearing notably unstylish clothing was that he was "either the world's most determined panhandler or an unshaven elderly gentleman out for a hard day's hike."

She knew about Earl's groundbreaking first hike in 1948 and was vaguely aware that he had embarked earlier in the year on a repeat.

Knowing his age, however, she dismissed this as a quixotic venture with little likelihood of success. She was suitably stunned when subsequent conversation determined the identity of the rather taciturn man in a pith helmet with mosquito netting who stood before her. Even though Ellerbee had not been seeking Earl, she could not resist the journalist's inherent propensity for asking questions. When she finally let him go and Earl had started again down the Trail, she called one last inquiry: "What's been the worst part of the hike this time?"

Earl may or may not have been aware of the celebrity of the woman calling to him when, without turning around, he gave his reply: "Reporters and their questions."

Ellerbee later wrote a moving article about this encounter, "The Best Birthday Present of Them All," which first appeared in the November 1998 issue of *New Choices*, and was later included as an Afterword in *Calling Me Back to the Hills*.

———————

Shortly after entering New Hampshire, Earl began finding notes from a reporter who wanted to meet him. Earl was initially put off by this approach and hoped to be able to avoid the newsman. Within a few miles, however, the reporter materialized and hiked along. Earl mentioned in passing that he needed to get a warm jacket. When they got to town, the reporter drove Earl around until he found one that he bought for Earl. Then the reporter bought him lunch, all in all another rare example of favors from a reporter.

And so on and on it went until the climax in Maine.

RACING THE WINTER WEATHER
Earl had planned on reaching Katahdin by the end of September. As things turned out, September was already winding down before he left New Hampshire. Various factors contributed to this delay, including relocations that had made the Trail both longer and more difficult; delays resulting from the dozens of people who had heard he was back on the Trail and wanted to talk to the famous man (and perhaps get his autograph); the swarms of media, especially near the end, whose demands verged on the absurd; and—not least—his own advancing age and deteriorating health.

It remains an amazing fact that when he finished this trek, Earl was less than a month from his 80th birthday. And those years were weighing heavy. He had not even left New Hampshire when his brother John had heard from Bruce Pettingill of Hiker's Paradise, a hostel catering to hikers in Gorham, that when Earl was there he seemed depressed and even mentioned the possibility of quitting the trail. Bruce thought that John should come and get him. Still Earl plodded on.

By the time he got to the Maine line on September 21, Earl knew that he was in a race with winter to reach Katahdin before it was closed for the season. October 15 was the official closing date, but the unpredictability of the weather in Maine at this latitude and elevation made an earlier closing more than just remotely possible. And he knew that this would be his final chance for a last hurrah. Although reluctantly, he also admitted to himself that his pace was slowing down. Before him stretched slightly more than 280 miles of mostly harsh—though beautiful—terrain. So be on your way, Ridge Runner.

His first two days in Maine were not auspicious. After camping the first night near Carlo Col, only about a mile inside the state line, the highlight of his second day was the crossing of Mahoosuc Notch, considered by many thru-hikers to be the most difficult single mile on the entire Appalachian Trail. It took Earl three hours to cover this distance. That night he slept in the Speck Pond Shelter where the weather turned fiercely cold. With his food supply exhausted and his fingers frostbitten despite his having tucked them inside a pair of woolen socks, he continued his walk. Earl progressed less than five miles when at Maine Route 26 he got a ride with a state park ranger who took him to a store where he replenished his empty stock of food. It was here that he was invited to spend the night at "The Cabin," a hostel near the town of Andover, an offer that he happily accepted. Operated by Margie and Earle Towne (known to their familiars as Honey & Bear), The Cabin was a legendary benefactor of hikers who were struggling along the Appalachian Trail and had been more or less overcome by Maine's hazards. This turned out to be the first of several nights Earl spent at The Cabin, and had his flagging spirits revived.

It was during one of the evenings at The Cabin that Earl had a significant conversation with David Donaldson (a co-author of this biography) who was also doing an end-to-end hike, his first. Earl and David had encountered each other at times on the way from Georgia to Maine, but it was at The Cabin on September 28 that they made the decision to finish their hikes together. (As Earl put it in *Calling Me Back to the Hills*, "Maine in late autumn is not a place to hike alone.") David had been an admirer of Earl even before embarking on his trek, and had taken the trail name

"Spirit of '48" in honor of the fiftieth anniversary of Earl's first historic end-to-end hike.

Three days of hiking together brought the two to Spaulding Mountain Lean-to in cold, rainy, windy weather. Sharing the shelter with them that night were a young couple from Michigan, the female half of which was a girl of 18, less than a fourth of Earl's age. During the night the temperature turned bitterly cold. The preparation for departure in the morning is described by Earl in his *Ode to the Appalachian Trail*:

> We stayed at Spaulding Mountain Lean-to
> Where it rained all night, and in the morning I looked
> Out and said "I can't, I can't. I'll wait here today
> Until the weather gets better, then head for home."
> Meanwhile I was pulling my cold wet boots
> Over shivering feet and packing my gear for
> The trail ahead, and telling myself as I faced
> The cold rain, "You've known all along
> That this would be your last hiking trip.
> Make the most of it. Isn't that why you
> Couldn't stay home? The cracked rib is
> Healed, the twisted knee is better.
> The black eye and bruises, the stresses and
> Strains, the rocks and roots and deep mud
> Holes, logs over swampland, sheer rock
> Climbs and cold rushing rivers to wade
> Are all part of the package, so carry on."
> Dave looked a little puzzled but said nothing.

So they set out into the forbidding weather, and after walking only a bit more than five miles they were met at a road crossing by Bear, who shuttled them back to The Cabin where they passed a better night than the previous one.

Three more days of hiking brought them, on October 4, to the Avery Memorial Campsite where after a night of sub-zero wind chill and high wind gusts that persisted into the next morning, they decided to get off the Trail early. When they came to a fire warden path, they took it down to a road where they managed to get a ride into Stratton. From a market in that village they first tried calling The Cabin, but learned that neither Marge nor Earle was there. Next, they called a number that had been posted beside the pay phone they were using. This succeeded in getting them a twenty-five-dollar ride to the other side of Bigelow Mountain where they were scheduled to meet Harry Smith and his CBS TV crew for an interview and filming the next day. Eventually, everyone who was expected, including Earl's brother John, got to the meeting point. The CBS people hosted dinner that evening at a local restaurant, and after what had been a long frustrating day, they spent the night in a motel in Bingham.

The next morning, October 6, a three-vehicle convoy took the group to a section of Trail near Pierce Pond. Earle and Marge Townes, who were assisting the CBS TV crew, led the way; following them was a van that carried the crew itself along with all their equipment; and bringing up the rear were John, Earl, and David in John's van. After filming Earl hiking and talking, the action moved to the official Appalachian Trail canoe carrying Harry Smith and Earl across the Kennebec, with everything being captured by a CBS cameraman.

It was at this stage of their journey that they were confronted with a serious problem. While Earl and Harry Smith were crossing the Kennebec, John had been in touch with Buzz Caverly, the superintendent of Baxter State Park and learned, to everyone's dismay, that Katahdin had already been closed for a week because of icy conditions. However, the weather seemed to be improving, and it was possible that the mountain could be opened again the next day. Faced with the heartbreaking prospect of hiking another 150 miles only to find Katahdin closed and their ultimate objective thwarted, they held a hurried conference at which it was decided to take the ascent of Katahdin "out of sequence." They would immediately drive to Baxter State Park, spend the night in the Park and, with a little luck, climb the mountain the next day. After the drive in John's van, Earl, John and David were greeted at park headquarters by Park superintendent Caverly who treated them to dinner

In the meantime, hurried phone calls had been made to Earl's nephew Bobby in Seattle, and to Dan and Gail Johnston in South Carolina, all of whom were hoping to join Earl for his climb up Katahdin. Dan and Gail drove non-stop to Maine and Bobby hastily found a flight to the East, and all were on hand in time for the long-awaited ascent. John, whose assistance through the "Hundred Mile Wilderness" would later prove invaluable, was unable to participate in the climactic climb because of an injured knee.

The following morning, the seventh of October, in clear, crisp, picture-perfect weather Earl's final climb of Katahdin took place. As the party went up the challenging Hunt Trail, David commented to another hiker that climbing Katahdin was a major achievement in itself, but to be doing it in such weather and doing it with Earl Shaffer was like winning the trifecta. As he scrambled and clawed his way up the mountain, using fingers, elbows, knees—whatever was necessary—Earl appeared to the troop of observers to be the very image of a determination that would not be denied. By the time the goal was reached, the group had grown to more than twenty thru-hikers, all of whom were making the ascent before the advancing season foreclosed the possibility. When they neared the summit, David fell back, allowing Earl to reach the official

Earl atop Katahdin, 1998

sign first, whereupon cheering and clapping erupted. The old man had done it once again.

Earl initially experienced some remorse that he had resorted to a mini-flip-flop; "a botched thru-hike" he once called it. After reflection, however, he became reconciled to this "operational necessity" that was imposed upon him by the weather. In any case, he did not hike any portion of the trail in the opposite direction. He merely hiked one piece of it out of sequence.

The next day Earl and David Donaldson hiked the stretch of trail from Abol Bridge to Katahdin stream before spending the night at Shaw's Boarding House in Monson. Like The Cabin in Andover, some 140 miles to the south, Shaw's is a legendary institution among Appalachian Trail hikers in Maine. It is reported that prior to 1977 Shaw's was operated as a boarding home for the mentally ill. In that year a hiker stopped at the door and asked if he could spend the night. Permission was granted and the next day as the grateful hiker headed north, he told a passing southbounder about Shaw's, and from there the efficient trail information network took over. It was not long before Shaw's gave up the specialty license and replaced it with a more general lodging-and-meals license, catering primarily to Appalachian Trail hikers. Some cynics might contend that the evolution from caring for the mentally ill to feeding and lodging long distance hikers is really quite a natural one.

Monson sits at the southern edge of the Hundred Mile Wilderness which, as has been sardonically noted by many, is neither a full hundred miles long nor technically a true wilderness. It is, however, quite wild enough for most hikers, of whom few would wish it longer.

After a night spent in John's van, the following evening found them back at Shaw's, where they were saddened to learn that a thru-hiker David had first met on Springer Mountain in Georgia the day after starting out, had met with a heartbreaking mishap. "Caterpillar" had just entered the Hundred Mile Wilderness when he fell and broke his leg. This is the nightmare that haunts the dreams of nearly every aspiring thru-hiker: to get almost within sight of Katahdin only to have success snatched away by the merest chance. "But," David later commented, "that's the reality of the Trail." David understood quite well; he had himself fallen six times on the long walk; Earl even more. Fortunately, neither ever experienced a hike-threatening injury.

After three more days of hiking in mostly steady rain, they were more than ready for another night at Shaw's. Their feet had not been dry in four days, and the effects were being felt, with blisters and "hot spots" appearing at various places on their feet and toes. Back on the Trail, the rainy weather continued, making Earl and David downright miserable.

At Chairback Gap Lean-to where they spent the night three days later, they had to crowd seven bodies into a six-person shelter, but somehow they managed. The following morning, with rain still falling, everyone in the crowded shelter was gloomily preparing for another day of wet hiking. Suddenly, coming up the Trail appeared "Allison Wonderland," shaking from the cold, crying, and to all appearances half dead from exposure. A young woman, apparently in her twenties, she had been overtaken by darkness about a mile short of the shelter, where she spent what must have been the most miserable of nights, sitting with her back to a tree with nothing but the cold, the wind, and the rain for company. David had just finished fixing his breakfast, which he unhesitatingly handed to the woman. With no possible way to get her dry at the shelter, there was no alternative but to walk to the first road crossing where, by great good fortune, John was waiting with a new batch of supplies for Earl and David. Allison was packed into the van and driven by John to Millinocket where all could thoroughly dry out and spend a warm comfortable night before returning to the unwelcoming Maine woods.

The following day, now well into the Hundred Mile Wilderness, the rain finally stopped and they hiked in near perfect weather,. Miraculously, the good weather persisted through the end of the hike at Abol Bridge. Although the fact that the hike ended fifteen miles short of Katahdin had been dictated by weather concerns, this had the unintended effect of providing the media with a more accessible place where they could greet the weary walkers. It must be reported, however, that the media, being as they are, avid practitioners of one-upmanship, were not all content with waiting patiently at Abol Bridge. A number of reporters and photographers walked an additional three and a half miles to the Hurd Brook Lean-to to welcome the hikers there and accompany them the rest of the way. One exceptionally intrepid reporter from a Portland paper got up before breakfast, hiked to the Hurd Brook Lean-to, and then a couple of miles beyond that, so that he could get exclusive time with Earl. As John commented later, "That poor guy hiked well over ten miles that day to get an interview."

At 4:15 P.M. on Wednesday, October 21, 1998, Earl and David walked across the Abol Bridge, and their long hikes were finally finished. The drama would surely have been somewhat greater if the hike had actually ended atop Katahdin, but this was to some extent balanced by the greater

Earl and David Donaldson after arriving at Abol Bridge

accessibility of the Abol ending. There was a crowd of reporters, photographers, TV crews, hikers, park rangers, and general onlookers. There were family and friends, and there was much applause. And one must suspect that Earl himself was quietly delighted at the warm reception he received.

An arrangement had been negotiated with NBC for the network to fly Earl and John to New York immediately after the hike was finished so that Earl could appear on "The Today Show." Upon receiving word that the hike had been successfully completed, NBC wanted Earl and John to fly down the same day, a Wednesday, so that Earl could appear on the Thursday morning show. John flatly refused, saying that Earl needed a good night's rest first. They would spend Wednesday night in Maine, and fly to New York on Thursday to appear on the Friday morning show. In the meantime, CBS was planning to show on Friday evening the interview with Earl crossing the Kennebec River in the company of Harry Smith.

This was Earl's first time on a plane since his World War II days, more than fifty years before, and his metal-toed hiking boots activated the Portland airport's metal detector to Earl's consternation and bemusement.

NBC had also agreed to fly Earl and John to Harrisburg following his "Today Show" appearance. There remained, however, one important logistical detail: John's van was in Maine. The matter was resolved by convincing David Donaldson to accompany the Shaffer brothers to the

Press conference at Hurd Brook lean-to

Portland airport, and then to
drive John's van back to Pennsylvania's York County. For David it
was a long, lonely, tiring drive.
During the War, Earl was forever scribbling poems—when
they came to him if he could,
otherwise, at the first opportunity. There were times when this
would be at night in a foxhole
by the light of periodic flares
intended to prevent the conceal-
ment of lurking snipers. One of
his last nighttime poems was
written in more comfortable circumstances. After his final climb
of Katahdin, when they were

*Earl presenting the original handwritten
copy of the poem "Katahdin"
to Buzz Caverly*

staying in the Baxter State Park guest house, he awoke in the middle of
the night with a poem going through his head. He promptly wrote it
down on a scrap of paper which in the morning he presented to Buzz
Caverly, the Park Superintendent.

Caverly commented that Governor Baxter would be pleased at this
description of Katahdin. He later arranged to have the poem included in
the 1999 edition of the history of Baxter State Park.

KATAHDIN

You love it and you fear it
It is big and harsh and high
A mass of ancient granite
Towering into the sky
From the Indians who revered it
To the climber of today
A symbol of a spirit
That can never pass away.

CHAPTER 40

REFLECTIONS

AGING HIKER, CHANGING TRAIL

Earl Shaffer is credited with thru-hiking the Appalachian Trail three times over a span of fifty years. In reality, however, he hiked three different Trails. From each hike to the following one there were so many changes in the Trail that, although there remained significant overlap, the general character of the Trail was quite different. Even the end points of the Trail did not remain fixed. By the time of the 1965 hike, the southern terminus had shifted from Mount Oglethorpe to Springer Mountain.

In 1948, when the Trail was often described as a "mountain footpath," several hundred miles were still along roads where the hiker shared space with vehicular traffic. Admittedly, such traffic was often very light; nonetheless, its mere existence would seem to make the designation "footpath" inappropriate by most standards. At that time the total length of the Appalachian Trail was reckoned to be 2,028 miles; Earl completed his hike in 124 days for an average of 16 miles per day.

Seventeen years later, in 1965, when Earl made his north-to-south hike, long Trail relocations in North Carolina, Virginia, Pennsylvania, and elsewhere had eliminated much of the road walking. The Trail, however, remained (in Earl's words) hiker-friendly. He assumed that by then the route of the Trail was essentially permanent. This was a major factor in prompting him to set off on another thru-hike. At this time the total length of the Trail was 1,999 miles and Earl completed his hike in 99 days, averaging 20 miles per day

By 1998 the official Trail length was 2,160 miles which he covered in 173 days. That's an average of only 12 miles per day.

In 1968, with passage of the National Trails System Act, the Appalachian Trail became a National Scenic Trail with administrative responsibility vested in the National Park Service. This development was generally greeted with pleasure by the Trail community since it would allow the establishment of a protected route, not subject to the frequent relocations that had previously made efficient Trail management so difficult. This shift in general oversight was accompanied naturally by the usual bureaucratic complexity associated with governmental agencies.

Earl came to believe, however, that the saddest shortcoming of the new organizational arrangement was its decision to turn away from Benton MacKaye's original vision for the Appalachian Trail as a series of linked shorter trails. As the Park Service embarked on the task of securing a permanent right-of-way, the Trail planners seemed more and more to seek out the most difficult and dangerous routes, often with no obvious benefit over the previous route or other less difficult possibilities.

This policy was often defended as presenting the hiker with a challenge. Earl considered that this claim was inaccurate. He believed that if these challenges are offered to the hiker, they should be as alternates to less demanding routes. A challenge, he felt, implies a choice. If the difficult route is the only one available, it is not a challenge; it is a "take it or leave it." The result of all of the post–Park Service changes is that what used to take four months for the average thru-hiker now takes six months. This tends to present most hikers with serious weather difficulties, especially in the northern mountains.

TARNISHED SILVER

The new Trail policies had their most dramatic effect in Maine, where the Trail today is described by Earl as "a series of obstacle courses." The hiker regularly encounters rock climbing, boulder hopping, root dodging, and stream wading. "Maine," he said, "is now an ordeal instead of an adventure."

In 1937, Myron Avery published a guide to the Maine Appalachian Trail that he called *The Silver Aisle*. This poetic title derived from the nature of the Trail in Maine as it wound through "the spruce and fir forest, with cathedral like stillness." The way is marked by the silvery gleam of white blazes shining in the darkness of the forest background. Avery wrote: "By reason of the terrain, the Appalachian Trail route across Maine necessarily cannot adhere to its ideal of following a continuous mountain ridge crest. Instead, it presents an alternating pattern of mountain, forests, stream, and lake. It is even further varied by two canoe crossings."

This was no longer true, Earl lamented. "It is my emphatic opinion that the present A.T. through Maine bears scant resemblance to the Trail route in Myron Avery's *The Silver Aisle.*"

An apparently unanticipated, although wholly predictable side effect of this change in the Trail's nature has been an increase in what Earl considered cheating. Faced with the uncertainty of Maine's early winter, hikers get shuttled to Katahdin so they can climb the mountain before it is shut down for the season. Indeed, Earl himself did this. Unlike Earl, however, many hikers do not return to hike the sections they have bypassed. It is not hard to understand the psychology here. The lodestar of the great mountain has been reached; the summit has been climbed. To go back and hike those preliminary miles would be anti-climactic. Some shuttle and hostel providers often refer derisively to those hikers who insist on walking the entire trail as "purists."

A related problem, in Earl's view, was that the Appalachian Trail Conference required no documentation of a purported thru-hiker's success. He believed that every request for thru-hiker status should be accompanied with a daily log. Of course, a daily log can be falsified, but apparently Earl believed that the requirement to submit one would discourage fabrication.

REMEDIES
Earl was a deep as well as a broad thinker. When he identified a problem, he went on to try to offer a solution. So this propensity was applied to the Trail problems that he saw, and he came up with some actions that he thought would help. He realized that we could never turn back the clock fully and return to the conditions of 1965, but he thought that there were things that could be done to make the current situation better.

- Wherever the Trail and a road intersect, there should be a Trail sign showing the name and/or number of the road. Guidebooks generally tell the hiker what a road leads to, but without knowing what a specific road is, it is easy to go astray. Earl himself sometimes walked a considerable distance on a road before realizing that it was not the one he thought.

- Why should the Trail bypass all small towns? Most hikers will have to visit them at least occasionally for food and other needs. If the Trail avoids them all, hikers generally resort to hitchhiking which can be dangerous, especially for women, and is actually illegal in some jurisdictions.
- Stream wading has become the bane of the Appalachian Trail in Maine. This is another problem that leads to bypassing. Except for committed thru-hikers, some sections with much stream wading get very little use. When it is necessary to retain a stream crossing, but without the construction of a bridge, it ought to be possible to install cables within reach of the struggling hikers. One end of the cable could be permanently anchored while the other could be removable during the non-hiking season.
- Thru-hiking should be downplayed. It tends to be over-glamorized and presented with little or no reference to the difficulties and dangers involved. This results in a large number of hikers setting off on what is expected to be a thru-hike with little or no understanding of what really awaits them. Earl often quoted approvingly an entry he found in a Trail register: "The only way to get in shape for backpacking is by backpacking."
- Steep, gullied climbs, which are encountered mostly in the South should be replaced with switchbacks.
- Existing long switchbacks, which invite shortcutting, should be shortened and steepened. Earl reports that in conversations with Trail maintainers he found that many of them recommended an incline of one in eight to being ideal. (This means that for every eight feet of horizontal distance the Trail elevation would change by one foot.) The same ratio should be applied to slanted Trails, which could replace "straight up the mountain" climbs.
- In many places where land ownership and other factors permit, the trail should be returned to earlier, more hiker-friendly locations.
- Long, rocky, ridgetop sections should be interrupted periodically to drop down to lower elevations where water, wildlife, and varied vegetation are more likely to be encountered.
- New shelters should be placed within sight of the Trail whenever possible. Each shelter should have a sign showing the name of the next shelter in each direction along with the intervening mileage.
- Intersections with other trails should be clearly identified. The Appalachian Trail blazes at the intersection should be accompanied

with some indication of the direction. Earl's suggestion was a V (pointing downward) to indicate south and an inverted V (pointing upward) to indicate north. Side trails to water or a trailhead should be clearly identified in some manner.

It is hard to know how much of Earl's dissatisfaction with the Trail as he found it in 1998 reflects his advanced age. Probably less than one would normally expect. After all, few hikers on the brink of becoming an octogenarian would even embark on a 2,000-mile backpack through the mountains of the eastern United States, let alone successfully complete such a quest. Still, his physical stamina was surely eroding, however slowly. But it would be wrong to casually dismiss him as an aging crank. Certainly on some topics he had views that were eccentric, but when it came to the Appalachian Trail, Earl Shaffer, of all people, can surely be said to know whereof he speaks.

CHAPTER 41

THE END
OF THE TRAIL

THE DECLINING YEARS

Even before he completed his Fiftieth Anniversary Hike as he was approaching his eightieth birthday, Earl's health began showing the burden of all those years. Or perhaps it was merely rebelling against the torture to which it was being subjected. In any case, he complained that this longer and tougher version of the Appalachian Trail was putting an unexpected strain on his heart. If he had not been pausing briefly on the most rigorous stretches, he was convinced that more than once he would have just collapsed. But he kept on walking.

After he had returned home following the hike, a medical diagnosis confirmed that his heart was failing. Once while hiking in Virginia a pain developed in his chest. The incident is described in the *Ode*:

> About a week ago I began feeling
> A dull ache in my left lung, which moved
> To the side. Suddenly I began to breathe
> Freely. The shortness of breath I had blamed
> On old age must have been a collapsed lung.
> It must have miraculously revitalized itself.
> The human body certainly is a remarkable
> Creation.

This self-diagnosis may or may not have been accurate, or the pain may have been another manifestation of the incipient heart failure. Whatever was the cause, the fact is that Earl had a pain but he kept on walking and the pain went away.

After returning home, it was not long before brother John noticed that Earl's health was perceptibly declining. When it became apparent that Earl was retaining fluid, John became more forceful in his efforts to convince his brother to seek medical assistance. Earl continued to resist taking this step until John threatened to break off all contact between the two. At this point Earl agreed, and John took him to Gettysburg Hospital where the heart problem was confirmed, and his prostate was found to be enlarged to the point that the examining doctor pronounced it the largest he had ever encountered. A diuretic was prescribed to deal with the fluid retention, and treatment for the prostate cancer was begun.

On a happier note, it was in 1999 at York County's annual "Sports Night" that Earl was inducted into the York Sports Hall of Fame, a York County tradition that extended back to 1973. Of the more than sisty inductees at that time, the number of votes cast for Earl was second only to those cast in 1973 for Bob Hoffman, the "Father of World Weight-lifting" and founder of the York Barbell Company. With this honor Earl joined, among others, Vic Wertz, with whom he had once played baseball in the Palau Islands in the South Pacific during World War II.

DAMASCUS TRAIL DAYS

Damascus is a small town in southern Virginia close to the Tennessee border. The U.S. Census for 2010 listed a population for Damascus of 814. The Appalachian Trail goes down the main street, and there has always been a close relationship between the town and the Trail. The northbound hiker reaches Damascus after walking about 460 miles from Springer Mountain.

In 1987 to mark the fiftieth anniversary of the completion of the Appalachian Trail the Town Council decided to sponsor a trail festival. Although a modest event in its early years, "Trail Days," as it came to be called, quickly turned into an annual event with an enthusiastic and steadily growing following among the hiking community. Held the weekend following Mother's Day each spring, Trail Days brings a crowd of tens of thousands to this tiny community. It is estimated that Trail Days pumps more than one million dollars into the local economy.

For the 1999 event Earl was invited to serve as Grand Marshall for the traditional hikers' parade. Since Earl's brother John had other commitments that weekend, he asked David Donaldson to accompany Earl to

Damascus. They planned on driving down on Thursday, May 13, the day before the start of the weekend's festivities. Because of a series of misunderstandings, miscommunications, and forgetfulness the start for Damascus was seriously delayed. It was not until about 1:00 A.M. Friday morning that they finally reached Damascus. With a long, tiring weekend ahead of them they went promptly to bed, but even so, it was not much after 6:00 A.M. when they were roused for breakfast. About 10:00 A.M. Earl and David decided to walk into town. It took them a good hour to go two blocks because of the swarms of hikers on the street who recognized Earl and wanted to shake his hand, take his picture, get his autograph, congratulate him and just converse.

Finally, they went into an outfitter's shop to thank the proprietor for arranging for their lodging during the weekend. This promptly attracted a crowd in the store, where Earl and David became separated. After a time David went looking for Earl but could not find him anywhere on the premises. When it became obvious that Earl was not inside, the proprietor drove David around town for twenty minutes or so, checking in all the likely places, including the bed and breakfast where they were staying. At length David decided to walk back to the B&B and wait there. As it happened, however, as soon as he stepped outside he spotted Earl walking along in conversation with some other men.

At this point David decided that he needed to get Earl back to the B&B for some rest in preparation for a presentation he was scheduled to give later in the afternoon. Earl's health was a concern all weekend; he was taking a strong diuretic related to his heart problem and he was feeling generally run-down. Nonetheless, with characteristic determination Earl drove himself to fulfill the commitments he had made for the weekend—and more besides.

The presentation later was a summary of Earl's hike of the previous year accompanied by a video that John had put together of interviews and news reports, as well as a number of pictures. The program was well received, and the audience gave Earl a standing ovation at the end, as was the conclusion at every other weekend event in which Earl participated. Earl's brother Evan arrived with his wife just as Earl was finishing his presentation. Evan and Jeannie had driven up from Greenville, South Carolina, and were planning on staying at a nearby motel Friday night.

Following the presentation, Earl and David sold copies of *Walking With Spring* outside the auditorium. As Earl's health had steadily deteriorated—and aggravated by the diuretics he was now taking—he had started experiencing occasional episodes of incontinence. One such event occurred during the bookselling. It was, however, dealt with expeditiously and tactfully by Evan and David.

That evening they had dinner at a restaurant in downtown Damascus where their meal was frequently interrupted by people who wanted to speak to Earl. One man asked Earl to autograph his T-shirt. Earl complied and, in fact, never refused a single request during that weekend.

The following morning Earl participated in a panel discussion about the future of the Trail. Both Earl and his message were well received. He talked about his great disappointment at what had been done to the trail in Maine, as well as about the now common practice of running the trail up one hill after another, whether or not there is any view to be gained. "What's the point?" he asked, to general applause.

In his role as Grand Marshall for the afternoon Hikers Parade, Earl rode in a yellow Jeep, standing in the back waving happily at the cheering crowd.

For an early evening dinner, Earl and David went with Evan and Jeannie to a restaurant some way out of town to avoid the crowd of well-wishers. During the meal Earl and Evan, seated side by side, laughed as they reminisced about their younger years and childhood adventures. After eating, Evan and Jeannie left for home and Earl and David returned to the B&B for some rest before the slide show about his 1948 hike that Earl was scheduled to present that evening. They arrived at the auditorium a half hour early to find it already packed. The show went well and was enthusiastically received.

The Town Council presented Earl with an award, and the Appalachian Long Distance Hikers Association (ALDHA) gave him a large trail map signed by members of the Association. Then he returned home to face more doctors and medical tests.

———————————

During one of his hospital visits, a cancer was discovered on Earl's liver, although it was at that time not very far advanced. At this point John embarked on a career as Earl's chauffeur, driving him to various doctors and specialists for treatment. In a conversation with one of the doctors, John asked about Earl's probable survival time. The doctor estimated between a year and a half and two years, which ultimately proved to be very accurate. On the drive home, Earl asked John what he had learned from the doctor. Knowing that his brother would want to hear the truth, John told him. Earl seemed resigned to the timetable.

In January 2002, barely three months before his death, Earl attended a hiker gathering in nearby Pine Grove Furnace State Park along with his guitar. Although clearly thin and worn, he played and sang for the group to their manifest delight.

Eventually Earl became too sick to continue living alone in his home in Idaville. An effort was made to find an apartment for him near John, but nothing suitable seemed available. Finally it was agreed that Earl would move in with John and Lois where he could have the ground floor recreation room, with his own bathroom and entrance.

It was February 2002, when Earl moved in. Within two months, however, he had failed so much that it was beyond the abilities of John and Lois to continue to care for him. John then approached the VA hospital in Lebanon, Pa., where Earl had been receiving outpatient treatment. This facility had a hospice program to which Earl was accepted. While he was there, the hospital staff was puzzled by his rapid deterioration, since the liver cancer was not far enough advanced to be causing the problem, and the prostate cancer was more or less under control. Whenever John visited, the staff questioned him in an effort to uncover whatever might be the cause for Earl's rapid decline. It finally emerged that Earl's drinking water came from an untreated mountain spring. John was asked to bring

Earl's grave marker, Shiloh Cemetery, York, Pa.

in a sample of the water, which he did. Testing revealed three different parasites in the water, which the hospital people decided were the source of Earl's problems.

The cause of his death was listed as prostate cancer because it was the most advanced of Earl's various ailments.

York's William Penn Senior High School, from which Earl had graduated, has a "Hall of Fame" group composed of students with a faculty counselor. Each year the group honors various graduates and prominent local residents. On one occasion, in conversation with his brother, Earl wondered why the group had never honored him. John quietly assembled a scrap book that included reports and news releases concerning Earl's various achievements. The scrap book was then delivered to the high school. As a result Earl was awarded the honor in 2002. By then he was in the VA hospice and was unable to attend the assembly at which the awards for that year were being given, where he would also, following tradition, have addressed the gathered students and faculty. Instead, the award was presented in the hospital room where it reached him barely before his death.

JUST EARL
At one time, early in his writing days, Earl was impressed by the fact that many writers he admired always used their middle names along with the first and last. Examples of this practice included Henry David Thoreau and James Fenimore Cooper. When it was suggested that perhaps Earl ought to do the same, he toyed with the idea for a time, but never acted on it. Following the celebrity that accompanied his final hike, he reflected back on this, and commented: "But now I've reached the point the middle name is superfluous, just like Elvis. They don't even say Presley; they just say Elvis. And everybody knows who it is. It's gotten to the point that it's almost that way with me among hikers. I'm just Earl."

"Just Earl" he may have been, but Earl Victor Shaffer was also a very complex man whose pursuit of elusive dreams and aspirations generally seemed to fall short—until near the very end when public acclaim finally arrived, along with a physical decline that kept him from fully enjoying it. "Better late than never" is bittersweet consolation for an octogenarian who no longer has full control of his bodily functions.

He was proud of his military service and its accomplishments, even though, because of being on detached service and away from his home base whenever promotions were handed out, he never was given the rank he thought he had earned.

The War also deprived him of a friend who had been a close part of his life from the time they were both five years old; a friend with whom he first experienced the joy of wandering in the woods and following remote pathways. Combined with the earlier loss of his mother, this second jolt to his emotions left him for the rest of his life unwilling to expose himself to the potential devastation of another assault on his already scarred sensibilities.

Having turned away from any human object for his affection, it was his poems that became his first love. He wanted, first, to see his poems published and, second, to be known as the Poet of World War II. Neither goal was reached in his lifetime. After his death, three volumes of his poetry were published by the Earl Shaffer Foundation, but this still accounts for only a small fraction of a total of more than 1,300 poems by Earl Shaffer that are known to exist.

Earl believed that his Trail achievements, both as a hiker and as a trail planner and builder, deserved better than the betrayal he blamed on both the Appalachian Trail Conference and the National Park Service when he was denied the opportunity to live and establish a hostel adjacent to the Trail on Trent's Hill.

Finally, it was his own determination that drove his aging body one last time over the length of an Appalachian Trail that seemed to have intentionally been made more difficult in order to thwart him. He succeeded, however, and public recognition for at least this much of his life arrived in abundance. The applause of those thousands of hikers in Damascus must have been pure balm for his battered spirit.

Appendix

THE EARL SHAFFER FOUNDATION

As Earl's life wore on towards its end, he continued to be haunted by the obsessive dream that had accompanied him for most of his years. He wanted desperately to see his poetry published. Those few poems that had appeared in *Walking With Spring* and *Calling Me Back to the Hills* represented only a tiny percentage of the 1,300 known poems by Earl Shaffer. The vast majority were still waiting to see the light of publishing day. Another worry of his later years was that his income might increase to a level that would affect his veteran's pension.

He discussed these concerns with his brother John, who suggested that it might be possible to establish a Foundation that could solve both problems at once. The Foundation, over time, could facilitate the publication of Earl's poems and other writings. Income from these publications or other sources could be channeled to the Foundation to be used to benefit causes important to Earl without affecting the level of his personal income.

The first constitution and bylaws of the Earl Shaffer Foundation were signed March 28, 2002, with Earl Shaffer as President, Evan Shaffer Vice President, and John Shaffer Secretary/Treasurer. In April, 2002, with Earl in failing health, David Donaldson replaced him as President. In addition Dan Bruce, Daniel Shaffer IV, David Shaffer, and Robert (Bobby) Shaffer were added as directors. When an application for non-profit status was submitted to the Internal Revenue Service, however, it was rejected because the Board of Directors was too heavily weighted with Shaffers. In response to this concern, a number of non-family members were added, and the application was approved.

As of April 2014, the Board of Directors consisted of the following:

Officers and Directors
Sanne Bagby, President
Nancy Shaffer Nafziger, Vice President
David Shaffer, Secretary/Treasurer
David Donaldson, Assistant Secretary/Treasurer
Daniel Shaffer IV, Assistant Secretary/Treasurer
Chris Bagby, Member
Kimberly Shaffer, Member
Larry Luxenberg, Member
Mack Thorpe, Member

BOOKS AND RECORDINGS BY EARL SHAFFER

Books and recordings are available from the Earl Shaffer Foundation www.earlshaffer.org. Books are also available from various commercial booksellers.

Books
Walking With Spring, 1983 (4th Edition, 2004), ISBN 0-917953-84-3.

The Appalachian Trail: Calling Me Back To The Hills, 2001,
ISBN 1-565579-382-X. (Originally published by Westcliffe Publishers.)

Ode To The Appalachian Trail, 2007, ISBN 978-0-9795659-1-5.

Before I Walked With Spring: The Doughboy Odyssey and Other Poems of World War II, 2008, ISBN 978-0-9795659-2-2

South of the Sunset: More Poems of World War II, 2011,
ISBN 978-0-9795659-3-9

Recordings
Walking With Spring: Earl Shaffer's 1948 Appalachian Trail Slideshow, (DVD).

Always in April, Music CD written and performed by Earl Shaffer.

Trail of the Tropic Moon, Music CD written and performed by Earl Shaffer.

Earl Victor Shaffer: Pictorial Biography 1918–2002 (DVD).

APPALACHIAN TRAIL MUSEUM
Under the leadership of Larry Luxenberg, the Appalachian Trail Museum Society was formed in 2002 for the purpose of establishing a Museum to preserve as much as possible of the history and artifacts of the Appalachian Trail. Assisted in its fragile early days with support from the Earl Shaffer Foundation, the Museum finally opened in 2010 in a modified historic grist mill located in Pennsylvania's Pine Grove Furnace State Park. The Museum's inaugural displays gave pride of place to a shelter that Earl himself had originally built on Peters Mountain in Pennsylvania.

APPALACHIAN TRAIL HALL OF FAME
In 2011 the Appalachian Trail Museum inaugurated an Appalachian Trail Hall of Fame to honor individuals who have "made an exceptional and positive contribution to the Appalachian Trail or Appalachian Trail community." Appropriately—and perhaps inevitably—Earl Shaffer was included in the "charter class," along with such other Trail icons as Benton MacKaye and Myron Avery.

WARRIOR HIKE PROGRAM
When Earl Shaffer set off on his 1948 thru-hike of the Appalachian Trail, part of his motivation was a hope that he could thereby "walk off" the still lingering stresses of the war. Taking its inspiration from Earl's experience, the Warrior Hike project is cooperating with the Appalachian Trail Conservancy to sponsor a "Walk Off The War" program for wounded veterans trying to adjust to civilian life. Participating veterans are provided with support as they embark on their own journeys along all or part of the Appalachian Trail.

The Earl Shaffer Foundation is supporting this effort by donating 100 copies of *Walking With Spring* to be disstributed to participating veterans.

A Tribute
to John Shaffer

ohn Shaffer died this spring as this biography was going through its final stages prior to publication. No one looked forward to it more eagerly or had more to do with it than John. While a younger brother to Earl, in life and after Earl's death, John looked out for Earl and tirelessly guarded his legacy. When Earl did his third Appalachian Trail thru-hike in 1998, John was his support crew, handled logistics, frequently met him along the A.T., and handled the swarms of reporters who wanted to chronicle the story.

Earl was a renaissance man, a creative thinker, who lived on the margins of society. John, too, was multi-talented. While at home in the woods, John fitted comfortably into modern society. When Earl became seriously ill, he and John made plans to form the Earl Shaffer Foundation. The foundation supports Earl's causes and works to get his many unpublished writings, poems and songs into print. Both of the authors and myself have been active with the foundation (www.earlshaffer.com).

One of John's early efforts was to get Earl's most precious artifacts accepted in the Smithsonian Institution. In 2009, the Smithsonian's National Museum of American History had a major exhibit on Earl's 1948 thru-hike and put on display his boots from that hike and his journal, among other things. John was involved with that exhibit at every stage and attended the opening. For years John labored to scan Earl's photographs, to sort through his writings, to work with the Foundation's upcoming publications and CD's and DVD's.

I got to know John around the time of the 1998 thru-hike. At the time, I was just beginning to work on forming an Appalachian Trail Museum and John was supportive from the beginning. He attended many of our early meetings. I remember one in January 1999 when four of us gathered in a hallway at Ironmasters Hostel in Pine Grove Furnace State Park. We were about as far from the Smithsonian as it is possible to get but John never wavered in his support of the Museum. The foundation contributed money and artifacts to the A.T. Museum and much needed moral support.

After years of difficulty in finding a location for the Museum, I mentioned to John our dilemma. We'd found a building in a nearby state park that would do nicely but the park manager wasn't supportive. John mentioned that he had a friend in the state parks and he'd look into it. Soon he told me that we couldn't have that building, but we could have one near the Ironmasters Hostel, the historic Old Mill. It turned out to the be a perfect location for the Museum. John helped the Museum to preserve the Earl Shaffer Shelter (a multi-year process) and that became the key artifact when the Museum opened in 2010. John was in the front row that June, when the Museum held its grand opening on National Trails Day before a crowd of 750.

The following year, the Museum started an A.T. Hall of Fame and Earl Shaffer was one of the first members of that class of six inducted into the Hall. Even as John's health deteriorated, John was supportive of this biography and helped ease us through some difficult spots. John was a quiet man and not one to shine the spotlight on himself. When there was work to be done, he didn't look over his shoulder but set to the task at hand. But for one who wasn't a long distance hiker nor had any of the usual roles in the hiking world, John left a significant mark on the Appalachian Trail community and his legacy, like Earl's, is one that we and his many friends will treasure for years.

—Larry Luxenberg
April 19, 2014

Acknowledgments

DAVID DONALDSON

The following helped greatly towards the completion of this work in a variety of ways; it is as much their work as mine.

To Larry Luxenberg and the Appalachian Trail Museum, for publishing this book. Thank you for all you have done and continue to do to preserve the history and the heritage of the great Appalachian Trail.

The Appalachian Trail Conference Archives, Harpers Ferry, West Virginia, which provided a wealth of information on trail history, including several articles written by Earl.

Chris Bagby, whose leadership of The Earl Shaffer Foundation allowed me a bit more free time to work on the biography.

To Sanne Bagby and ArtoftheTrail.com, for producing the cover artwork and several of the illustrations used throughout this book.

Buzz Caverly, Director, Baxter State Park, who shared with me his thoughts on Earl, and of that most magnificent mountain along the trail, Katahdin.

Bruce Dunlavy, a close friend of Earl's for his support and stories.

Eb Eberhart, the Nimblewill Nomad, from whom I gained inspiration and insight on how to get published.

The late Ed Garvey, a true gentleman of the trail, who I met while Earl and I were staying at The Maples Bed and Breakfast in Damascus, Virginia. He allowed me the privilege of interviewing him a month before his passing in 1999, sharing stories of the trail and his thoughts on Earl.

Jane Greber, past president of the Susquehanna Appalachian Trail Club, who kindly provided me a history of the club, written by Ralph Kinter, which detailed Earl's role in founding the club, as well as Earl's eleemosynary work during the 1950s relocation of the trail through the St. Anthony's Wilderness.

Thurston Griggs, former ATC board member and longtime acquaintance who urged Earl to seek publication of *Walking With Spring*.

Ellen Roney Hughes, curator at the Smithsonian Museum of American History, who was primarily responsible for overseeing the inclusion of Earl's original hiking gear to the Smithsonian.

Cathy Keen, archivist, Smithsonian Museum of American History, for her help in assembling and providing access to Earl's papers, and to the staff of the Archives Center in Washington, D.C for their assistance.

Millinocket Memorial Library, where I spent many a cold day during the winter of 2000 doing research.

Laurie Pottieger, information specialist at the Appalachian Trail Conference, who ably assisted my research efforts at Conference headquarters, as she has so many countless others.

Bob and Pat Peoples, Kincora Hostel who shared stories of Earl's stay there during his hike in 1998.

Bruce Pettingill, who has shuttled thousands of hikers in the New Hampshire area, including Earl in 1998, for sharing his thoughts of Earl and the trail.

Virginia Marksteiner and Jacqueline Donaldson-Pippins, my sisters, who provided me with the recording equipment I spent so many hours frustrating Earl with.

Mrs. Earlyn R. Repman, who first met Earl at an auction over fifty years ago, for sharing her thoughts with me.

Anna Shaffer-Miller, Daniel and Betty Shaffer, Evan and Jeannie Shaffer, John and Lois Shaffer; in particular, John's help to both Earl and myself during our hike in the Hundred Mile Wilderness was indispensable; and the entire Shaffer family, who let me into their homes and made me feel like a member of the family.

The Earl Shaffer Foundation

Our guest readers

Marge and Earle Towne, a.k.a. Honey & Bear, of The Cabin, Andover, Maine, without whom this book would never have been written, a very special thank you.

To Margaret Nelling Schmidt, for publication design, layout, typesetting, keen eye and kindly suggestions. Thank you.

Finally, to Maurice Forrester, I am indebted to you for your time, energy, and passion in giving life to what was a scattering of boxes, documents, and handwritten notes. You are truly a gentleman and scholar of the highest order.

MAURICE J. FORRESTER

I am indebted to several people who provided assistance in connection with the writing of this biography.

Foremost is John Shaffer, Earl's youngest brother, who answered numerous questions that arose in the course of drafting the manuscript. John also dredged up from his hoard many useful documents and photographs. As a witness to many of the events described herein, John willingly shared his memories. Regrettably, John did not live long enough to be able to actually hold in his hands a finished copy of this book to which he contributed so much.

Members of my immediate family also contributed—more or less willingly. My wife, Mildred, put up with my irritability and distractedness. Other family members read portions of the manuscript and offered suggestions. These included my two sons, Maurice III and Mark, who never hesitated to criticize their aging father's prose. Likewise, daughter-in-law Susan and granddaughter Charity also read parts and made suggestions. (Susan proved to have a special knack for spotting typos.)

Laurie Potteiger of the Appalachian Trail Conservancy staff, who hiked with Earl for a while during his 1998 hike, provided much information.

Nancy Nafziger offered encouragement and advice, along with memories of her Uncle Earl.

Larry Luxenberg, author of *Walking the Appalachian Trail*, shared his impressions of Earl. Larry also was the prime mover in arranging for the publication of this book by the Appalachian Trail Museum

Bruce Dunlavy, Cathy Keen, Larry Luxenberg and Nancy Nafziger all reviewed the final manuscript before publication.

Chris and Sanne Bagby offered many helpful suggestions. In addition, Sanne designed the cover for the book and offered valuable comments concerning the text.

Finally I must acknowledge the overarching importance of David Donaldson to this project. Writers are a dime a dozen, but only one person could have done the groundwork that made this book possible. Without David, this could not have happened.

About the Authors

DAVID DONALDSON was born and raised on the East Coast. Shortly after graduation from college he moved to the West Coast. After a dozen years and nearly as many jobs, including working for the University of California, San Diego, in 1998 he decided to take a hike on the grand-daddy of all hiking trails, the Appalachian Trail. Choosing as his trail name "Spirit of '48" in honor of the fiftieth anniversary of Earl Shaffer's first hike along the A.T., Donaldson was initially awestruck when meeting the legendary hiker who had embarked upon his third and final thru-hike that same year. Bumping up and down the trail since that first meeting in North Carolina, Donaldson could hardly believe his great good luck by finishing his hike in Maine alongside Shaffer. Shortly thereafter, Earl agreed to let Donaldson write his biography.

In 2004 after moving to York, Pennsylvania and buying the property owned by Earl's brother John, Donaldson began working in York County as a special education teacher. He received his master's degree and is currently enrolled as an education doctoral candidate. He is married and is the father of twins.

MAURICE J. FORRESTER has served as Treasurer and Board member of the organization that later became the Appalachian Trail Conservancy (ATC). He is also a past president of Pennsylvania's Keystone Trails Association, and a former member of the Board of Directors of the Appalachian Trail Museum .

He first met Earl Shaffer at a Trail gathering in Plymouth, New Hampshire, in 1972. Thereafter the two would run into each other periodically at one event or another. Eventually, Forrester wrote the foreword for the ATC-published edition of Shaffer's classic Trail memoir, *Walking With Spring*.

In 1994 Forrester also wrote the foreword for Larry Luxenberg's *Walking the Appalachian Trail*, which has become another Appalachian Trail standard.

Forrester has served in a volunteer capacity as a governor's appointee on the following Pennsylvania government advisory bodies:

- The Pennsylvania Appalachian Trail Committee;
- The Pennsylvania Citizens Advisory Council (CAC) to the Department of Environmental Protection, and later to the CAC to the Department of Conservation and Natural Resources;
- The Pennsylvania Hardwoods Development Council.

In 1988 he was named by Governor Robert Casey as one of three Pennsylvania representatives on a multi-state panel commissioned to study population and development pressures on the Chesapeake Bay.

Since 1968 Forrester has lived in Pennsylvania, where he currently resides in the Borough of DuBoistown.

CPSIA information can be obtained at www.ICGtesting.com
Printed in the USA
BVOW07s1058280714

360567BV00001B/1/P

9 780991 221523